STUDIES IN LIFE
FROM JEWISH PROVERBS

STUDIES IN LIFE

FROM

JEWISH PROVERBS

BY

W. A. L. ELMSLIE, M.A.,

Fellow of Christ's College, Cambridge

WIPF & STOCK · Eugene, Oregon

Wipf and Stock Publishers
199 W 8th Ave, Suite 3
Eugene, OR 97401

Studies in Life From Jewish Proverbs
By Elmslie, W. A. L.
Softcover ISBN-13: 978-1-7252-9783-8
Hardcover ISBN-13: 978-1-7252-9785-2
eBook ISBN-13: 978-1-7252-9784-5
Publication date 1/20/2021
Previously published by
James Clarke & Co., Limited, 1917

This edition is a scanned facsimile of
the original edition published in 1917.

To

MY WIFE

"Forsan et hæc olim meminisse juvabit"

PREFACE

A WRITER of many books once said to me that he regretted every preface he had written. Seeing that I have the highest respect for his talents, I am constrained to take to heart the moral, which (particularly in a book on proverbs) would seem to be "least said, soonest mended." But whatever else he may choose to leave unsaid, an author is expected to give away his secret in the preface, making known his intentions as discreetly as he can but still explicitly. That duty accomplished, he is at liberty to give thanks, and so conclude.

The greater part of this volume (Chapters V. to XII.) is occupied with a study of the teaching of "Wisdom" among the Jews in Palestine during the Hellenistic Age, so far as the subject is represented in the two great collections of Jewish sayings, the *Book of Proverbs* and *Ecclesiasticus*. It would be too much to claim that in these chapters the book breaks new ground, for the importance of the Hellenistic period is recognised by students of history, and there have been many commentaries on the *Book of Proverbs*, nor has *Ecclesiasticus* been without its expositors. But the historian devotes himself to the relation of events, and the commentator is busy with the thoughts of the several proverbs or with the textual difficulties they present, rather than with their precise historical setting. Here an endeavour has been made to bring the proverbs into

Preface

close connection with the history, and it is hoped that not only do the proverbs thereby acquire fresh interest, but also that there emerges a picture of the men who made them and used them in the furtherance of morality and faith. Even to professed students of Jewish history the makers of the " Wisdom " proverbs are apt to remain distant and shadowy figures ; but we cannot afford to neglect any of the makers of the Bible, and I venture to think that the method followed in this volume makes it possible to appreciate the outlook of these men, to realise their difficulties, and if not to sympathise wholly with their views, at least to feel that they were very human. Whether this brief sketch is successful in attaining its object or not, it is certain that the subject deserves more attention than it has hitherto received.

Besides the numerous maxims in *Proverbs* and *Ecclesiasticus*, there are some interesting popular proverbs in the historical and prophetical books of the Old Testament. To these a part of Chapter IV. will be devoted. Occasional references will also be made, especially in the second half of the book, to proverbial sayings taken from the Rabbinical literature of the Jews. The titles of Chapters XIII. to XX. sufficiently indicate the nature of their contents, and require no further comment here.

In translating the proverbs the Revised Version has been used as a basis, but liberty has been exercised in making any alterations that seemed desirable on textual or literary grounds. Most of the changes thus introduced will readily explain themselves to those who are acquainted with the original texts or may care to consult modern commentaries, such as that of Professor Toy on *Proverbs* (International

Preface

Critical Commentary) and of Dr. Oesterley on *Ecclesiasticus* (Cambridge Bible Series).

Any volume, such as this, that touches a wide range of subjects must have correspondingly many obligations. I welcome this opportunity of recording my gratitude to the authors whose writings are referred to in the following pages, and in particular I desire to acknowledge my indebtedness to the Right Rev. E. L. Bevan's illuminating work on the Hellenistic period, to the writings of Professor Toy and Dr. Oesterley mentioned above, and to Professor C. F. Kent's short study and analysis of *Proverbs* in his book *The Wise Men of Ancient Israel*.

W. A. L. E.

Christ's College, Cambridge.

CONTENTS

CHAPTER		PAGE
I	THE CHARACTERISTICS OF PROVERBS	13
II	THE PROVERBS OF THE JEWS	28
III	FORGOTTEN YEARS	43
IV	THE DAY OF SMALL THINGS	60
V	IRON SHARPENETH IRON	75
VI	A SOWER WENT FORTH TO SOW	100
VII	MEN AND MANNERS	108
VIII	THE IDEAL	136
IX	THE EXALTATION OF WISDOM	166
X	THE HILL "DIFFICULTY"	178
XI	HARVEST	194
XII	VALUES	214
XIII	NATURE IN THE PROVERBS	229
XIV	HUMOUR IN THE PROVERBS	237
XV	FROM WISDOM'S TREASURY	245
XVI	THE BODY POLITIC	248
XVII	A CHAPTER OF GOOD ADVICE	261
XVIII	CONDUCT	265
XIX	FAITH	273
XX	THE GIFT OF GOD	280

CHAPTER I

The Characteristics of Proverbs

MOST writers on proverbs have thought it necessary to attempt a definition of their subject, but the task is difficult, and the phrase that will silence criticism has yet to be produced. Lord Russell's epigram describing a proverb as " The wisdom of many and the wit of one " is as good as any, but it leaves so much unsaid that as a definition it is certainly inadequate. On the other hand, it is a true remark, and the facts it emphasises may conveniently be taken as the point from which to begin this study.

No saying is a proverb until it has commended itself to a number of men ; the wisdom of one is not a proverb, but the wisdom of many. Countless fine expressions well suited to become proverbial have perished in the speaking, or lie forgotten in our books. To win wide acceptance and then to keep pace with the jealous years and remain a living word on the lips of the people is an achievement few human thoughts have compassed ; for thousands that pass unheeded only one here or there, helped by some happy quality, or perhaps some freak of fortune, is caught from mouth to mouth, approved, repeated and transmitted. Every accepted proverb has therefore survived a searching test, all the more severe because judgment is not always passed upon the merits of the case. Popular favour is at the best capricious, and often an admirable saying has died out of use and a

Studies in Life from Jewish Proverbs

worse become famous. But of one thing we can be certain: general recognition is never won except by that which expresses the beliefs, or appeals to the conscience, or touches the affections of average men. However many the defects of any given proverb may happen to be, it is sure to possess some quality of human interest.

In the second place, it is generally true that, although proverbs have a sovereign right to utter commonplace, there is no such thing as a dull proverb. No matter how pedestrian may be its doctrine, somewhere in its expression will be manifest the " wit of one "—a flash of insight or imagination, a note of pathos or power. Of course, many sayings through age and the changes of fashion have lost their savour for us, but—the point is important— even these are not inevitably dull. *All* were once piquant. If we could but recapture the attitude of the men who made the phrase proverbial, its interest would be felt again. But although it thus appears that proverbs are essentially human and generally witty, the study of them is attended by certain difficulties. It is wise, therefore, to acknowledge at the outset the obstacles that will beset our path; to be forewarned is to be forearmed.

Many proverbs have achieved popularity, not on account of what they say, but of the way they say it; the secret of their success has been some spice of originality or of humour in their composition. Originality, however, is a tender plant, and nothing fades more quickly than humour. A graphic or unexpected metaphor will delight the imagination for a little while, but how swiftly and inexorably " familiarity breeds contempt "; a phrase which is itself a case in point. Whenever therefore, in studying the Jewish proverbs, we come upon famous and familiar words, we must endeavour to let the saying for a moment renew its youth, by deliberately quickening our sympathy and attention, by counting it certain that words which have not

The Characteristics of Proverbs

failed through so many centuries to touch the hearts and minds of men deserve from us more than a passing glance of recognition.

Many proverbs speak truth, but a true word can be spoken too often. Every preacher in Christendom knows how little, through much iteration, the words "Hope" and "Love" may convey to his hearers, although most men are conscious that of the realities of Hope and Love they cannot possess too much. So also with the truths expressed in proverbs. For example, many excellent men have lacked only promptitude to win success, and we have need to be warned thereby ; but when the fact is put before us in the words "Procrastination is the thief of time," what copybook boredom rises in our indignant soul ! We will not learn the lesson from so stale a teacher. Every effort to indicate the genius of proverbs is attended by this disadvantage of verbal familiarity ; and, of course, it is the finest sayings that suffer most. But just here the tragedy of the great European War lends unwelcome aid. The intensity of human experience has been raised to a degree not known for centuries ; and, as a recent writer in the *Spectator* admirably puts it, " In all times of distress dead truisms come to life. They confront the mind at every turn. We are amazed at the vividness of our thoughts, and confounded at the banality of their expression. We imagined that only fools helped themselves out with the musty wisdom of copybooks, but now it seems that even a fool may speak to the purpose. There is nothing so new as trouble, nothing so threadbare as its expression. ' All is fair in love and war ' . . . How vividly that falsehood has been impressed upon us by our enemies. Yet how dull and indisputable it seemed such a little while ago. Even those of us who have least personal stake in the war grow terribly impatient at its slow movement. Almost every man who buys an afternoon paper thinks of the ' watched pot.'

Studies in Life from Jewish Proverbs

How many people have lately known the heart-sickness of 'hope deferred'? 'Dying is as natural as living': that is a dull enough expression of fact, when death is far off: but, when it is near, it cuts like a two-edged sword."[1] Life for the present generation has verily been transformed; it is both more terrible and more inspiring, more poignant in its sorrows, more thrilling in its achievements and its joys: all things are become new. Once we could say glibly, "The heart knoweth its own bitterness," using the phrase to point a trivial trouble, but not now; and perhaps never again in our life-time. Thank God, it is not only the sorrowful sayings which rise in our heart with new meaning, but also those which speak of courage and strength, of loyalty and faith.

There is a third danger against which we require to be on guard Proverbs cannot be absorbed in quantity. Like pictures in a gallery, they stand on their rights, each demanding a measure of individual attention and a due period for reflection. Many chapters in the *Book of Proverbs* are unpalatable reading, not because they are prosy, but because they are composed of independent maxims connected by no link of logical sequence or even of kindred meaning. To read consecutively through a series of these self-contained units is to impose an intolerable strain on the mind. The imagination becomes jaded, the memory dazed by the march of too swiftly changing images. The disconnected thoughts efface one another, leaving behind them only a blurred confusion. This will appear the more inevitable the more clearly we realise what a proverb is. For consider: not one nor two but countless observations of men and things have gone to the making of a single proverb; it is the conclusion to which a thousand premisses pointed the way; it is compressed experience. And further, a proverb usually gives not just the bare inference from

[1] *The Spectator*, Sept 11, 1915.

The Characteristics of Proverbs

experience, but the inference made memorable by some touch of fancy in the phrasing. Hence the meaning of a proverb is not always obvious, that it may seem the sharper when perceived. Some curious comparison, some pleasing illustration, is put forward to catch and hold attention until, from the train of thought thus raised, a truth leaps out upon us or a fact of life confronts us, familiar perhaps but now invested with fresh dignity. A proverb is not, as it were, a single sentence out of the book of human life, but is rather the epitome of a page or chapter; or, if you please, call it a summary, now of some drama of life, now of an epic or lyric poem, now again of a moral treatise. From a literary point of view proverbs are rich, over-rich feeding. They cloy. There is in the *Book of Proverbs* a remark that adroitly puts the point:

> *Hast thou found honey?*
> *Eat so much as is convenient for thee* (Pr. 25[16]).

It follows that frequent quotation of proverbs will be apt to fatigue the reader, yet the danger is one which cannot wholly be avoided in this volume. Something, however, can be done by setting limitations on the scope of our subject, and in the following pages no attempt will be made to present any systematic survey of the whole immense field of Jewish proverbs, ancient, mediæval, and modern. Attention will be given chiefly to two pre-Christian collections—the *Book of Proverbs* and *Ecclesiasticus*—and, even so, many good sayings in those books will be left unnoticed. Moreover, proverbs are not quite chaotic, for all their natural independence. They are like a forest through which many paths conduct; by following now one, now another topic it is possible to penetrate in various directions, as inclination prompts. But, even so, the peril of wearying the reader by over-many proverbs will only be lessened not removed; wherefore again—'tis a

Studies in Life from Jewish Proverbs

word of high wisdom—*Hast thou found honey? Eat so much as is convenient for thee.*

Enough of difficulties and dangers! Woe to him who goes "supping sorrows with a long spoon"! A happier task, however, does remain, before we set sail upon our quest: we have still to count our blessings. What are the virtues of proverbs? What the interests we may hope to find in our subject?

The proverb does for human life something that science does for the world of Nature: it rouses the unseeing eye and the unheeding ear to the marvel of what seems ordinary. As for Nature, most of us who are not scientists are still deplorably blind to her perfections, but popular text-books have so far succeeded that we confess our ignorance with shame, and some are even penitent enough to desire that they might grow wiser. We are at least aware that there is nothing in the world not wonderful. We used to pass the spider's web in our gardens with never a thought, but now—is not Le Fabre whispering to us of "rays equidistant and forming a beautifully regular orb," of "polygonal lines drawn in a curve as geometry understands it." "Which of us," says he, pricking our human vanity, "would undertake, off-hand, without much preliminary experiment and without measuring instruments to divide a circle into a given quantity of sectors of equal width. The spider, though weighted with a wallet and tottering on threads shaken by the wind, effects the delicate division without stopping to think."[1] The astronomer does not guard his secrets like the jealous astrologer of old; so that now-a-days many a man who possesses neither the higher mathematics nor a telescope knows more than his eyes can show him of the marvels of the stars and the mystery of space. Professor J. A. Thompson writes of *The Wonder of Life*, and behold!

[1] Le Fabre, *Life of the Spider*, Ch. ix. (Eng. trans. by Teixeira de Mattos, 1912).

The Characteristics of Proverbs

even he that hath no skill in biology may learn that the barren seashore is a teeming world, more strange than fairyland. Science does not make Nature marvellous; she lifts the veil of ignorance from our mind. Proverbs perform the same service for the life of man. Taking the common incidents of experience, they point out their meaning. Perceiving the principles in the recurrent facts of life, they discover and declare that the commonplace is more than merely common. That is a task greater and more difficult than at first sight may appear: as has been well said, "There is no literary function higher than that of giving point to what is ordinary and rescuing a truth from the obscurity of obviousness."[1] Most men are slow, desperately slow, to perceive the significance of the experiences they encounter daily; yet from the iron discipline of these things none of us can escape. They are our life-long schoolmaster, and woe betide the man who from that stern teacher learns nothing or learns amiss. Nor is it sufficient that the facts should be brought before us. As a rule, the truth requires to be pushed home. Ask us not to observe that the reasoning faculties of the human being are seriously and sometimes disastrously perturbed by the impulses of affection; but tell us "Love is blind," and—perhaps—we shall not forget.

Proverbs are superlatively human. Suffer the point to have a curious introduction. In certain ancient colleges it is the custom on one Sunday in each year to hold in the chapel a service of Commemoration, when the names of all those who were benefactors of the college are read aloud. Few ceremonies can convey more impressively the continuity of the generations, the actual unity between the shadowy past and the vivid present which seems to us the only *real* world. The roll may begin far back in the fourteenth or fifteenth

[1] R. J. Moulton, *Modern Reader's Bible*, p. 1456.

Studies in Life from Jewish Proverbs

centuries, commencing with the names of the Founder and a few mediæval Benefactors (some of them famous men), but steadily and swiftly the years move onwards as the roll is read, until, listening, we realise that in another moment what is called the past will merge into the present. Somehow the magical change takes place; the past is finished, and the record is telling now " the things whereof we too were part," ending perhaps with the name of one whom we called " friend," who sat beside us in the chapel—was it only a year ago to-day? On these occasions the lesson is usually taken from a chapter in *Ecclesiasticus* known as *The Praise of Famous Men* :—
Let us now praise famous men and our fathers that begat us. The Lord manifested in them great glory, even his mighty power from the beginning. Such as did bear rule in their kingdoms and were men renowned for their power, giving counsel by their understanding ; such as have brought tidings in prophecies ; leaders of the people by their counsels, and by their understanding men of learning for the people—wise were their words in their instruction ; such as sought out musical tunes, and set forth verses in writing ; rich men furnished with ability, living peaceably in their habitations : all these were honoured in their generations, and were a glory in their days. There be of them that have left a name behind them, to declare their praises. And some there be which have no memorial ; who are perished as though they had not been and are become as though they had not been born. What! even of those who were *famous* men? . . . *perished as though they had not been and become as though they had not been born.* The verdict is too hard. Granting that they missed genius, did they not live nobly, speak wisely, make many beautiful things, do generous deeds, giving of themselves the best they had to give? But . . . *as though they had not been.* Surely they merited some kinder fate than that? And what of the multi-

The Characteristics of Proverbs

tudes of the unrenowned ? If the famous are nothing, then the rest of men are less than nothing and vanity, and, dying, they certainly can leave no trace behind them, no word to carry the tale of how once they laboured, loved, hoped, endured. All their exquisite human longings, all their pleasant thinking, must be for ever lost ? No ! for proverbs are the memorial of ordinary men ; their very accents ; record of their intimate thoughts and judgments, their jests and sorrowings, their aspirations, their philosophy. And this even from distant ages ! There are proverbs old as the Iliad. Men of genius have not a monopoly of immortal words. Perhaps at the start one man of keen wit was needed to invent the happy phrase or the smart saying, but before it became a proverb countless ordinary folk had to give it their approval. We know that every popular proverb has seemed good to a multitude of men. Essentially therefore it has become their utterance, and is filled with their personality. And, of course, proverbs are not only a memorial of the unknown dead ; they are equally a language of the unknown and unlearned living. The humblest of men experience deep emotions which, however, they cannot articulate for themselves. Proverbs, we repeat, come to the rescue of the unlettered, supplying words to fit their thoughts, unstopping the tongue of the dumb. Just what effects this simple treasury of speech has had in history who can calculate, but that it has not been slight is dexterously suggested by these words of anger and chagrin which Shakespeare makes Coriolanus speak :

" Hang 'em,
They said they were an hungry, sighed forth proverbs ;
That *hunger broke stone walls*, that *dogs must eat*,
That *meat was made for mouths*, that *the gods sent not
Corn for the rich men only ;* with these shreds
They vented their complainings."

Studies in Life from Jewish Proverbs

Poor wretches! with their "meat was made for mouths." Doubtless they should have prepared for the most noble Coriolanus a treatise setting forth their preposterous economics, and humbly praying that in due course their petition might be brought before the Senate. But—"dogs must eat." Faugh! "No gentleman," said Lord Chesterfield, "ever uses a proverb." Perhaps not, in an age of false gentility. But men of genius in many a century have taken note of their rich humanism and their value as a real, though undeveloped, science of life. Aristotle, Bacon, Shakespeare, Montaigne, Cervantes, Hazlitt, Goethe, thought fit to use them. Despite my Lord Chesterfield, let us continue the subject.

In the third place, proverbs are like a mirror in which the facts and ideals of society may be discerned. This is so obvious a truth that its importance may be under-estimated until it is realised how clear and detailed the reflection is. Proverbs prefer the concrete to the abstract. They contain many allusions[1] that are like windows opening on to the land of their birth and offering glimpses of its life and scenery—the rain and the sunshine ripening its fields and vineyards; the valleys and mountains, the open country, the villages, and towns. The activities and interests of the inhabitants are still more clearly disclosed. Manners and morals are laid bare, all the more faithfully because the witness is often unintentional. "Proverbs," said Bacon, "reveal the genius, wit, and character of a nation." In them Humanity, all reticence forgotten, seems to to have cried its thoughts from the housetops and proclaimed its hidden motives in the market-place. Suppose that almost all other evidence for the history of Italy or

---

[1] Cf. such sayings as "Coals to Newcastle"—a proverb that has a parallel in many countries, for example, the Greek phrase, "Owls to Athens."

The Characteristics of Proverbs

Spain were blotted out but the national sayings were left us, there would still be rich material for reconstructing an outline of the characteristics and not a little of the fortunes of those peoples. In respect of national disposition how terribly would the lust for vengeance appear as the besetting sin of Italy: *Revenge is a morsel fit for God—Revenge being an hundred years old has still its sucking teeth*. From the copious store of Spanish proverbs could be substantiated such facts as the Moorish occupation of Spain, the power and pride of her mediæval chivalry, and the immense influence for good and evil which the Church of Rome has wielded in the length and breadth of the country.

Archbishop Trench lays stress upon this quality of proverbs. Speaking of Burchardt's *Arabic Proverbs of the Modern Egyptians*, he remarks,[1] " In other books others describe the modern Egyptians, but here they unconsciously describe themselves. The selfishness, the utter extinction of all public spirit, the servility, which no longer as with an inward shame creeps into men's lives but utters itself as the avowed law of their lives, the sense of the oppression of the strong, of the insecurity of the weak, and generally the whole character of life, alike outward and inward, as poor, mean, sordid, and ignoble . . . all this, as we study these documents, rises up before us in truest, though in painfullest, outline. Thus, only in a land where rulers, being evil themselves, feel all goodness to be their instinctive foe, where they punish but never reward, could a proverb like the following, *Do no good and thou shalt find no evil*, ever have come to the birth ": altogether a black picture of Mohammedan society. It is a healthier, happier scene that the Jewish proverbs will unfold to us.

[1] Trench, *Proverbs and their Lessons*, first published in 1857: a learned and brilliant little volume to which the present chapter is indebted for several suggestions.

Studies in Life from Jewish Proverbs

The last general characteristic of proverbs, to which we need pay attention, is their inexhaustible variety. The world is their province. Religion and ethics, politics, commerce, agriculture, handicrafts, riches and poverty, diligence and idleness, hope and contentment, unrest and despair, laughter and tears, pride and humility, love and hatred: what is there you can name that we cannot set you a proverb to match it? Proverbs enter the palace unsummoned, take stock of his Majesty, and then inform the world what they think of his doings. They sit with my Lord Justice on the bench, and he shall hear further of the matter if he judge with respect of persons. But lo and behold! they also keep company with highwaymen and thieves, and the tricks of most trades are to them no secret. Proverbs are at home with men of every degree: they dine at the rich man's table, they beg with Lazarus by the gate; and shrewdly do they analyse the world from both points of view. Chiefly, however, they have dwelt in a myriad normal homes, where neither riches nor poverty is given, but where a hard day's work, a sufficient meal, and a warm fire in the evening have loosened tongues and opened hearts. Whereupon these unconscionable guests proceed to criticise the family. They interfere between husband and wife, parents and children, and teach all of them manners with an unsparing frankness. They play with the children, counsel their parents, and dream dreams with the old. Again, proverbs are both country-dwellers and town-dwellers. Have they not observed the ways of wind and water, sunshine and silvery starlight, seen the trees grow green and the seeds spring into life, the flowers bloom and the harvest ingathered? Yet also they have spent the whole year in the city, walking its streets early and late, strolling through the markets and bargaining in the shops. Ubiquitous proverbs! There is nothing beyond their reach, nothing hid from their eyes.

The Characteristics of Proverbs

The advantages of this abundant variety are clear. Almost any topic of human interest will find sufficient illustration in proverbs. Frequently a saying will be found useful from more than one standpoint : vary the topic and the same material may appear in new and unexpected guise. On the other hand, whatever subject be chosen, a serious difficulty will be encountered. As soon as the proverbs bearing upon it have been gathered together, an extreme confusion of opinion will be apparent. The trumpet gives a most uncertain sound ! Thus, let ethics be our starting-point. Many, no doubt, will be the maxims that breathe an easy, practical morality, and these, being careful not to be righteous overmuch, may seem tolerably compatible one with another ; but then in violent contrast will be some that soar to the very heavens, and some also that surely emanate from hell. These will suffice from the devil's forge : *Dead men tell no tales—Every man has his price—* or this Italian proverb, *Wait time and place for thy revenge, for swift revenge is poor revenge.* For the heavenly, here are two from ancient Greece, *The best is always arduous*[1]— *Friends have their all in common*[2] : or this tender English one, *The way to heaven is by Weeping-Cross,* or this strong Scottish phrase, *The grace of God is gear enough*[3]. Verily, proverbs do battle one against another. Trench quotes the following : *The noblest vengeance is to forgive* compared with the infamous *He who cannot avenge himself is weak, he who will not is vile.* *Penny wise pound foolish* is cried in our one ear ; *Take care of the pence, and the pounds will take care of themselves* in the other. Could anything be more disconcerting to our hope of investigating the ethical system of proverbs ? But in like manner their social teaching at first

[1] χαλεπὰ τὰ καλά.

[2] κοινὰ τὰ τῶν φίλων.

[3] A version, doubtless, of *Proverbs* 10²².

Studies in Life from Jewish Proverbs

sight seems a wilderness of contradiction, their theology a babel of conflicting tongues. The natural perplexity thus occasioned can, however, be resolved very simply. Two points must be kept in mind. First, that when with rough and ready justice men are classified as pious or wicked, clever or stupid, generous or miserly, hopeful or despondent, rich or poor, young or old, wise or ignorant, and so forth, these terms do represent real distinctions between persons, although perhaps no one category suffices fully to describe any given individual ; and second, that a proverb necessarily expresses a sentiment shared by a number of people. It follows that what we ought to seek in proverbs is not one point of view but many. We shall find the attitude of various classes and types of men. We shall see life as it appears now in the eyes of the just and the merciful, now of the evil and the cunning. Here in one group of sayings will be the way the world looks to a lazy man, here again are the convictions of the unscrupulously shrewd. Here is some complacent merchant's view of social questions, here the exhortations of an idealistic soul. When once this fact about proverbs is recognised, the difficulty of their contradictoriness instantly is removed. Instead of feeling that they speak in hesitating accents, we discover that they are answering our questions, not with *one*, but with many voices, far from uncertain in their tone. The confusion vanishes. We find ourselves listening to the speech of men who, differing sometimes profoundly one from another, have sharply defined ideas, and can utter their thoughts with brevity, force, and wit.

It will be seen that our object is wide and deep, and that there are many avenues of approach to it. One road, however, would seem to be impossible—proverbs as literature. That an occasional popular saying would have some touch of literary value, is, of course, to be expected. But a winged word now and then, a lovely image flitting once in a

The Characteristics of Proverbs

while across the plains, will not justify the topic, "Proverbs as literature." The individual proverb failing, what hope is there that a collection of them will come nearer the mark ? Suppose the very best of our English proverbs were gathered together, there might be much to interest, amuse, or edify our minds, but literature such an assemblage would assuredly not be. The vital element of unity would be lacking. As well string the interjections and conjunctions of our language into verse, and call the result a poem ! And yet the incredible has happened. Once a collection of proverbs was so made as to be literature—but where and when must be left for the next chapter to relate.

CHAPTER II

The Proverbs of the Jews

OF the facts we have been considering one is specially relevant to the subject, not only of this volume but of the series in which it forms a part—namely, the intimately human quality of proverbs. Mr. Morley has called them " The guiding oracles which man has found out for himself in that great business of ours, of learning how to be, to do, to do without and to depart.[1]" The Humanism of the Bible ought therefore to be visible nowhere more clearly than in Israel's proverbs, *if* these are to be found within its pages. But stay! What right have we to expect their presence? Surely little or none, if the Bible is what many persons conceive it to be—only a book of religious teachings. For consider the reasonable expectation, and contrast the extraordinary facts. In such a book we might reasonably expect to find a few proverbs: that a king should quote a saying to suit his purpose, a counsellor press home his wisdom with some well-known maxim, or a prophet edge his appeal by the use of a popular phrase—that would be quite natural, and indeed occurs. But actually (and here is the astonishing matter) there are proverbs by tens and by hundreds, gathered together in one Book of the Bible, following verse by verse, chapter by chapter, till they choke one another through sheer profusion, like flowers in an

[1] John Morley, *Aphorisms · An Address to the Edinburgh Philosophical Institution* (1887) p. 7.

The Proverbs of the Jews

unkept garden. Thus in five chapters of the *Book of Proverbs* (13-17) there are 154 separate adages. So strange a phenomenon challenges attention. It might be supposed that the Hebrew language had been ransacked for proverbs, but that suggestion will not stand scrutiny. On investigation, the Book proves to be no deliberate, systematic, attempt to collect the Hebrew proverbs. Thus, when we look for the few, but famous, popular sayings that occur in the historical and prophetic writings of the Old Testament, we find that *not one* of them is included. As for system, a casual glance will demonstrate its absence. In most chapters of *Proverbs* not even an effort is made to classify the material. The Book cannot be explained as an anthology of Hebrew sayings—the most witty or worldly-wise, the most moral or religious. Whatever the explanation, here assuredly is something less artificial than an anthology. Good, bad, and indifferent proverbs alike are present. Many of the sayings unmistakably reflect a conception of morality more practical than exalted, and some appear grossly utilitarian. Time and again the consequences of sin are naïvely presented as the reasons for avoiding it, whilst the rewards of virtue are emphasised unduly. Later on we shall find reasons for holding that the utilitarian attitude is not fundamental, and therefore not so destructive of the ethical value of these proverbs as it might seem. But until both the circumstances which gave rise to the proverbs and the ends they were meant to serve are understood, until (as it were) we have seen the men who spoke the maxims and the people who repeated them, that more generous judgment is scarcely possible ; and meantime, be it freely admitted, there are many things in the Book not agreeable to modern ethical taste. Religiously, too, the *Book of Proverbs* is on the surface disappointing. Neither the fire of the Prophets' faith is visible, nor the deep passion of the Psalmists' longing after God. Who amongst us, seeking spiritual

Studies in Life from Jewish Proverbs

help, would choose a chapter in *Proverbs* when the Gospels or the Letters of St. Paul are open to him ? So then on literary, ethical, and religious grounds there are plain reasons why this Book has lost something of its former favour. Contrast the estimation in which it was held only two generations ago. Ruskin records that four chapters of *Proverbs*, the third, fourth, eighth and twelfth, were amongst those portions of the Bible which his mother made him learn by heart and " so established my soul in life "; they were, he declares, " the most precious and on the whole essential part of all my education." Not so long ago, *Proverbs* was a text-book in many schools ; probably it is nowhere so used to-day.[1]

Even if neglect of this part of the Scripture is partly chargeable to heightened standards of ethics or theology, the loss incurred is great. As a matter of fact, depreciation of its ethical temper is often based on inaccurate notions, often is exaggerated. In comparison with our fathers, who without commentaries read through their Bibles from cover to cover, we have not gained as we should ; for, whilst we pride ourselves (with what measure of justice is uncertain) on being more sensitive to religious values, they were far better acquainted with the religious facts. They at least knew the contents of Scripture; we, who have at our disposal abundance of interpretative help whereby to learn the nature of the Bible and with instructed minds consider its spiritual worth, too often are ignorant both of text and commentary. Doubtless the fault is due to certain characteristics of our time. This is a feverish impatient age ; if our mental fare is not served us like our daily

---

[1] As a text-book it was at least memorable. A distinguished man of letters tells me that one of its injunctions, taught him in his first school, he might claim never to have forgotten : *Let thy foot be seldom in thy neighbour's house, lest he be weary of thee and hate thee* (Pr. 25[17]) His friends bear regretful and emphatic witness that the facts completely justify his claim.

The Proverbs of the Jews

information, put up into easy paragraphs, so that he who runs may read, we will not stay to seek it; and the Old Testament is not an easy book, though it answers patience with astonishing rewards. Candidly, how does it stand with knowledge of the Bible at the present time? In charity let the question be addressed only to those who have a genuine interest in the Christian religion, desiring to rule their lives by its ideals and cherishing its promises. Even to such persons what is the Bible? A few there are who have found or made opportunity for serious consideration of its Books, and these have certainly felt the fascination of the vast and varied interests that have won and retained for biblical study the life-long service of many brilliant scholars. But to the others, and obviously they are thousands of thousands, the Bible is essentially the book of religion. As such, the New Testament means the Gospel narratives, some immortal chapters from St. Paul, a few verses in *Hebrews*, and St. John's vision of that City where *death shall be no more*. And what—religiously— in similar fashion is the Old Testament, except a few, comforting, beautiful Psalms; some childhood memories of Abraham, Joseph, Moses, generous David and brave Daniel; a tale or two of Elijah; a procession of Kings, and an uncharted sea of grand but most perplexing Prophets? Asked for a more general account, some would describe the Old Testament as a record of the laws, history, and religious ideas of the Hebrew people; others would answer that it is " part of the Word of God," but they might all be at a loss to say what is the religious value of *Leviticus*, what the spiritual relation between *Genesis* and the *Gospel*, between *Kings* and *Chronicles*, between *Job* and *Revelation*. Probably the great majority of men at the present time would be quite willing to confess that their knowledge of the Bible is vague and insufficient, but few, we believe, would suspect that there is anything

Studies in Life from Jewish Proverbs

wrong with the basis from which their thinking proceeds: so firmly is it fixed in men's minds that the Bible is merely the book of religion. The Bible is that, but more also, more and yet again more. And how easily we might have realised the fact! Ought not the presence of these surprisingly heterogeneous proverbs alone to have stirred our curiosity, and so compelled the enlargement of our thoughts about the Old Testament? Without needing to be urged, men should, of their own accord, have perceived the astonishing range of interest and the wealth of literature the Bible contains, and should have seen in this variety a clue that would lead them by pleasant paths to treasures artistic and intellectual as well as religious. Thereby no loss could ensue religiously, but on the contrary gain. The greater our recognition of the artistic qualities of the sacred literature, the more exact and full our understanding of the history of the Jews and of their beliefs and interpretation of life, so much the more wonderful will the actual development of religion in Israel be seen to be. This is the point to which the above remarks are meant to lead. If the Biblical proverbs compel as a first conclusion the recognition of how much more the Old Testament is than a text-book for theology, that is a minimum and an initial discovery; our appreciation of its meaning will assuredly not end there. The growth, in Israel, of the knowledge of God into a high and holy faith is an indisputable fact. Increase your comprehension of the circumstances attending this development, and your faith in the reality of a self-revealing God should increase also.

So much for the presence of these proverbs in the Bible. Now consider the affirmation with which the first chapter concluded: that proverbs have once been literature. That claim may be advanced on behalf of the sayings of the *Book of Proverbs* and *Ecclesiasticus*. It is of course obvious that the difficulty which has to be overcome is the

The Proverbs of the Jews

essential independence of proverbial sayings: each is so relentlessly complete in itself. How can they be so related to each other as to acquire the higher unity indispensable for literature? The lack of system in the *Book of Proverbs* has already been admitted frankly; but the point must again be emphasised. So far from the five chapters with the 154 maxims, referred to above, being exceptional they are typical of the greater portion of the Book. Continually we encounter the same astonishing disregard for consecutive, or even cognate, thought in the grouping of the proverbs. And yet, despite this fact, the attentive reader will become conscious of a subtle unity pervading the Book. The impression will grow that the confusion is not absolute; somehow it is being held within bounds, whilst here and there chaos has evidently yielded to the command of a directing purpose. Obstinate independents as proverbs are, one discovers that here their masses, unruly though they still may be, have nevertheless become an army, a host sufficiently disciplined to serve a common end. As with a complicated piece of music through the intricacies of the notes runs ever an underlying theme, so here through the medley of disparate sayings can be heard the preaching of one great thought—"Wisdom." Behind the proverbs, behind the Book, we discover men, preachers and teachers of an Idea, enthusiasts for a Cause—"Wisdom." Just what that phrase implied, just what manner of men those advocates of Wisdom were, we shall see in due course. The point for the moment is that these Jewish proverbs were not gathered haphazard, nor simply as *a* collection of Jewish proverbs; but for the express purpose of illustrating, developing, and enforcing the conception of Wisdom. Thus, through the influence of this specific intention, they received in sufficient measure the unity of literature. This fact is of the utmost importance for our subject, for it means that these proverbs may

Studies in Life from Jewish Proverbs

be considered not merely one by one but in their totality; that is, in their combination as text-books inculcating Wisdom. So regarded, they afford a glimpse of a remarkable class of men in the intensely interesting century or two when the intellectual foundations of Western civilisation were being laid down. No doubt each proverb bears the impress of reality and has its individual interest, is (as it were) a coin struck out of active experience; but the same may be said of the collected proverbs *as a whole*, and because the whole has its own significance, the parts acquire a meaning and value they would not otherwise possess. The Jews are an astonishing people. St. Paul perceived that they had a genius for religion, but they have had genius for many other things besides, as their strange fortunes testify. Their hand prospers, whithersoever it is turned. Who but the Jews can claim to have had a Golden Age in proverbs? In utilising their popular sayings for a definite purpose, and in thus making them literature, the Jews succeeded in a feat that other nations have scarcely emulated, far less equalled. Moreover in the process the Jews made their proverbs superlatively good. Some think that for wit and acuteness the ancient sayings of the Chinese are unsurpassed; for multitude and variety those of the Arabs and the Spaniards. But the Jewish proverbs of this " Wisdom " period excel all others in the supreme quality of being a possession of all men for all time. They are marvellously free from provincial and temporary elements; and this is the more remarkable in that the Jews were intensely nationalistic, and their literature, as a rule, is steeped in racial sentiment. Of these proverbs, however, very few must be considered Hebraic in an exclusive sense, or indeed Oriental. The mass of them have been at home in many lands and many centuries, because they speak to the elemental needs of men. Again and again they touch the very heart of Humanity. They are universal.

The Proverbs of the Jews

But that is the characteristic of genius. If therefore proverbs be our study, we could ask no better subject than these proverbs of the Jews.

Even so our theme is far from easy. Life, when visible before us, can with difficulty be portrayed. Harder by far is it to recall life from literature, translating the symbols of letters into the sound of speech and looking through words into the colour and movement of the scenes that by the magic of human language are there preserved, accurately enough, yet only like pale shadows of the reality. Hardest of all is it, when the documents to be studied are records of a far-past age and the life that of an alien people. But how well worth every effort is the task! " Many of us," writes Mark Rutherford, " have felt that we would give all our books if we could but see with our own eyes how a single day was passed by a single ancient Jewish, Greek, or Roman family; how the house was opened in the morning; how the meals were prepared; what was said; how the husband, wife, and children went about their work; what clothes they wore, and what were their amusements."[1] Information so detailed as Mark Rutherford desired will not be afforded by the Jewish proverbs. Nevertheless they are full of frank, intimate, comment on the ways of men and women, and of reflection on the experiences we all suffer or enjoy, and certainly should learn how best to encounter. If they yield less than might be wished for, still what they show is shown in the naïve and homely fashion that is so illuminating. Such being the difficulty of our task, and such the encouragement to pursue it, the reader will perhaps permit at the outset a short statement mentioning the writings where Jewish proverbs are to be found, and giving somewhat fuller information regarding the dates and composition of the two works from which the material of the following chapters will chiefly be derived.

[1] Mark Rutherford, *The Revolution in Tanner's Lane*, p. 238.

Studies in Life from Jewish Proverbs

THE SOURCES OF JEWISH PROVERBS

I. OCCASIONAL PROVERBS. In the historical and prophetical Books of the Old Testament there are to be found some popular sayings current in early Israel. Though few in number, they possess considerable interest, and will therefore be discussed in Chapter IV.

II. THE BOOK OF PROVERBS. This Book is the principal " source " of the proverbs considered in this volume. Unlike modern writings, which are usually the work of one author and will rarely require a longer period than five or ten years for their composition, many of the Books of the Bible have reached their *present form* as the outcome of a protracted process of compilation and revision perhaps extending over many generations and involving the work of numerous writers. The words of earlier authors were utilised again and again in later times by others who, having somewhat similar ideas and purposes in view, exercised complete liberty in reproducing, or modifying, or adding to the material they found to hand.[1] Such a book is *Proverbs*. The consequence is that the question of date and authorship cannot be answered in a sentence. The problem of the *structure* of the Book rises as a preliminary subject.[2]

[1] In the final form of the Book thus gradually evolved it is sometimes very easy, sometimes difficult or impossible, to distinguish with exactitude the earlier from the later ' sources ' out of which it has been composed; but the main stages of the compilation can generally be determined with a high degree of accuracy, just as in an old cathedral through the varying modes of architecture employed the general history of the building is clearly visible to the trained perception.

[2] Evidence for the statements here given is omitted, partly because they are matters of general agreement among modern students of the Bible, but still more because the full evidence has been repeatedly set forth in works accessible to any who may have inclination to consider the subject in detail. Reference may conveniently be made to C H. Toy, *Proverbs*, or to the same writer's article *Book of Proverbs*, in the *Encyclopædia Britannica* (11th edition); or to G F Moore, *Literature of the Old Testament*, ch. xxii. (Home University Library).

The Proverbs of the Jews

(a) *Structure*. The *Book of Proverbs* in its present form represents the combination of five originally independent collections of the single proverbs which are of course the ultimate material of the Book. There is some evidence that these five collections were themselves built out of still smaller groups of proverbs, but such subdivisions cannot be traced with certainty, and for our purpose may be neglected. The five main sections are as follows:—(a) In chs. 1-9, a number of epigrams, sonnets, and discourses in praise of wisdom. (b) In chs. 10^1-22^{16}, a collection of two-line ("unit") proverbs. (c) In chs. 22^{17}-24^{22} and $24^{23\text{-}34}$, two very similar collections of four-line ("quatrain") proverbs. (d) In chs. 25-29, a collection of two-line proverbs. (e) In chs. 30, 31, epigrams, sonnets, and an acrostic poem.

(b) *Date and Authorship*. Both in its component parts and as a composite whole the *Book of Proverbs* is an anonymous work. It is true that titles, such as "The proverbs of Solomon, the son of David, king of Israel" (Pr. 1^1), are prefixed to several portions of the Book[1], but they do not imply authorship, although to those unacquainted with the nature of ancient books that may seems the necessary meaning. Their significance will be considered later, on p. 71.

The date of origin and the authorship of single proverbs are seldom discoverable: a tantalising circumstance for those who would write about them. And yet, perhaps, their reticence is wise. It may be that some of the noblest sayings have sprung from the lips of a poor man in a peasant home; and there are fools who would thenceforth despise them for their birth. Of the individual sayings in the *Book of*

---

[1] Cp also 10^1 *The proverbs of Solomon*; 22^{17} *Words of the Wise*, 24^{23}, *These are also words of the Wise*; 25^1 *These are also proverbs of Solomon which the men of Hezekiah, king of Judah, copied out*; 30^1, *Sayings of Agur, son of Jakeh*, 31^1, *Sayings of Lemuel, king of Massa* The last two of these titles rest on an uncertain Hebrew text. For the allusion to Solomon see pp 71, 72.

Studies in Life from Jewish Proverbs

Proverbs a few, in matter if not in exact phrase, may go back to ancient days; some may be due to Solomon himself or date from his period; but the vast majority[1], for cogent reasons of style, language, tone, ethical and social customs and so forth, are post-exilic—that is, not earlier than about 450 B.C.; nor on the other hand are they later than about 200 B.C., by which time the several sections had been combined to form substantially the present Book.[2]

Something may be said concerning the relative priority of the five sections of the Book. Internal evidence points to sections *b* and *d* as the oldest portions, then section *c*; sections *a* and *e* (*i.e.*, chs. 1-9, 30, 31) being probably the latest groups. But of the precise date when these collections were severally formed and combined, and of the names of the men by whom the work was done, we are unaware. Fortunately our ignorance of detail is but a negligible trifle compared with our firm knowledge of the general fact that *in their present form these proverbs belong to the period, 350-200 B.C., and their authors and compilers were men who styled themselves " The Wise," and were known in the Jewish community by that term.* A hundred and fifty years may

---

[1] Perhaps almost all, in their present polished form Thus Toy (*Proverbs*, p xi) declares that "none of the aphorisms are popular proverbs or folk-sayings They are all reflective and academic in tone, and must be regarded as the productions of schools of moralists in a period of high moral culture" This observation is generally true, and of great importance; but it is not to be understood as meaning that the Book, or even the several sections, sprang out of nothing. In and behind the finished product there may well be a great deal of earlier material.

[2] *i.e*, any subsequent changes were of a minor character, introduced occasionally by some scribe or copyist. The year 200 B C. may reasonably be taken as the lower limit of date, partly because *Proverbs* has features (notably its attitude to the Mosaic Law) which suggest that it was finished earlier than *Ecclesiasticus*, a work composed about 190 B.C. This argument, though strong, is not conclusive; but in any case the peaceful, comfortable, tone which pervades *Proverbs* indicates that it is not later than the years of persecution preceding the Maccabean revolt in 167 B.C.

The Proverbs of the Jews

seem a wide margin, but it is a mistake to wish it less ; if anything, it ought to be increased. For the point to be grasped is that *Proverbs* represents the thoughts and ideals of the Wise throughout that whole period (350-200 B.C.) and even longer. The exact dates of the combination and final revision of the component collections of sayings are therefore questions of minor importance. The Book is not to be treated as a fixed literary product of any one particular year, but as representative of the teachings of the Wise during very many years.

To the same class of men we owe, besides *Proverbs*, other famous writings, of which two, *Job* and *Ecclesiastes*, were also included in the Old Testament Canon, and two are to be found in the Apocrypha, namely, *Ecclesiasticus* (or, as it is often called, *The Wisdom of Ben Sirach*) and the *Wisdom of Solomon*. Of these four writings the two first, *Job* and *Ecclesiastes*, are considered in other volumes of this series,[1] and therefore, except for one or two quotations, will not be utilised here, although they both contain a number of proverbial sayings. The *Wisdom of Solomon* also will seldom be noticed in this book : it is much later in date than *Proverbs*, and is not a collection of proverbs, but a set of discourses in praise of Wisdom.

III. ECCLESIASTICUS. On the other hand, the book of *Ecclesiasticus* or *The Wisdom of Ben Sirach*, is—next to *Proverbs* — the source from which we shall derive most material. Like *Proverbs* it is a storehouse of sayings about Wisdom, but fortunately, unlike *Proverbs*, it is not anonymous, and can be dated with some exactitude. The author or compiler of the book was one, Jesus ben (*i.e.*, Son of) Sirach, who lived in Jerusalem about 250-180 B.C., his volume being finished about 190 B.C. Some fifty years later his grandson, then living in Egypt, translated it into Greek,

[1] See for *Ecclesiastes* the volume *Pessimism and Love* by D Russell Scott, and for *Job*, *The Problem of Pain*, by J. E McFadyen.

Studies in Life from Jewish Proverbs

and until recently the book was known to us only in its Greek form. Now, however, a large part of the original Hebrew text has been recovered, with the happy result that the Greek version can frequently be checked and obscurities be removed by means of the Hebrew.

Besides the single, "unit," proverbs, there are in *Ecclesiasticus*, and in *Proverbs* also though to a less extent, a number of short sonnets and essays. These longer passages will be freely referred to, but perhaps a word in justification will here be in place. It has been said with truth, that " often a parable is an elaborate proverb, and a proverb is a parable in germ." That comment excellently indicates the nature of the passages in question; most of them are expansions of some brief gnomic phrase[1]. When, for example, in E. 20^{14f} we read, " **The gift of a fool shall not profit thee, for his eyes are many instead of one**; *he will give little and upbraid much and he will open his mouth like a crier; to-day he will lend and to-morrow he will ask it again: such an one is a hateful man.* . . " it is obvious that the verse is only an elaboration and explanation of the enigmatic proverb printed in heavy type.

IV. THE NEW TESTAMENT. Scattered through the pages of the New Testament are more allusions to popular sayings than one would readily expect. Almost all offer interesting comment on the life and manner of the times; but, unfortunately, they will fall outside the scope of this book, except for occasional references.

V. Finally, a great number of Jewish proverbs are mentioned in the post-Biblical RABBINICAL writings—the tractates of the *Mishna*, the *Midrashim*, and *Talmuds*. Embedded in a vast and difficult literature (how difficult only those know who have attempted seriously to study it), these later Jewish sayings have been somewhat inaccess-

[1] *N B* Hereafter the abbreviation "E," will constantly be used for Ecclesiasticus, and "Pr." for Proverbs.

The Proverbs of the Jews

ible to Gentile students. They are interesting in many ways, but the development of our subject in this volume will give opportunity for the mention only of a few. Should any reader desire to know more of these Rabbinic sayings, he can now be referred to a small but trustworthy collection recently made by A. Cohen and published under the title *Ancient Jewish Proverbs.*

The question is, What can the Jewish proverbs tell us about human life ? The conclusion of the first chapter left us perplexed by indicating too many paths that might be followed. This chapter solves the difficulty by suggesting that these proverbs will have a great deal to say to us, if we choose to treat them in their historical aspect. To do so is to follow the king's highway ; but when the plain road promises an interesting journey, it is folly to search for bypaths. The human story seems naturally to divide into past and present ; and, because the present immediately concerns us, we are all tempted to ignore the past and count it negligible. To the uneducated man the past is dead ; and he fails to perceive that, if the facts of history are unknown, the present, though it may fascinate, will prove bewildering. The truth is that history is one and continuous, the present is organically related to the past, and the division between them in our thought is artificial and perilously misleading. Nothing is of greater practical value than to learn and ponder the narrative of the past, provided heart and mind are kept alert to discern the guidance it continually offers to ourselves. To neglect its lessons is to starve the power of judgment in the present. Much that by our own unaided trials can only be learnt slowly, painfully, and at great hazard, may be discovered swiftly and securely by observation of the experience of other men. In this spirit let our studies of the Jewish proverbs be first of the *past:* what glimpses of former days are discernible in their homely words ?

Studies in Life from Jewish Proverbs

Let us commence as if we had some leisure at our disposal, and let us use it by following up occasional traces of very ancient times. Then we shall proceed to the more strenuous and more rewarding task of recovering a picture of the stirring years when Wisdom was moulding the Jewish proverbs to her urgent needs. Always, however, as the records yield up these tales of byegone days we are to keep in mind ourselves and our own generation, striving so to interpret the fortunes of men of old that we in our turn may learn from them how to avoid folly, endure trials, use success, and discover the secret of content. Finally we shall gather such of the proverbs as may please our fancy, and briefly consider them in themselves for their perennial, as opposed to their original or historical, interest.

CHAPTER III

Forgotten Years

THE past of human life offers an unimaginably long vista for our contemplation. Vastly many more are the years that have been forgotten than those that are remembered. Mr. Stephen Graham is therefore quite right when, in his book *The Way of Martha and the Way of Mary*, he insists that Christianity after nineteen hundred years is still a young religion, its doctrines imperfectly understood, its possibilities not yet unfolded. But for that matter history itself is young, since history knows at the most some six or seven thousand years of human history, and Man has been on earth hundreds of thousands of years. Glimpses of human life in those dim and distant ages are occasionally possible (as we are about to observe in the Jewish proverbs) and have a certain fascination; but their interest is apt to be overwhelmed by the disquieting ideas which the thought of so vast a stretch of time naturally raises in our mind. In comparison, our personal hopes seemed dwarfed into utter insignificance, and it is no comfort when a Psalmist (more than twenty centuries ago) suggests that to the Deity time may be a very little thing: *Thou turnest man to destruction, and sayest, Return, ye children of men. For a thousand years in Thy sight are but as yesterday when it is past, and as a watch in the night.* God may expend so many myriad years as seemeth good to Him in the making of sun, moon, and stars, earth and sea—what matter? But when the living bodies of men are racked with pain,

Studies in Life from Jewish Proverbs

when tyranny endures and love and liberty are delayed, then what is the millenial patience of God but terrifying? *We* cannot wait for its slow maturing. Does He not know that we who would see the salvation of the Lord in the land of the living are ready to faint?

Perhaps, however, our distress arises from the adoption of a mistaken standpoint. For, first, let the question be considered not from the point of view of God's patience but of His greatness, and the infinitely long development will seem less dreadful. The immensity of time may then be regarded, not as a token of God's indifference to man, but as a measure of His eternal majesty, and as evidence of an intention sublime beyond our present power to apprehend, yet not antagonistic to the value of the individual being—as indeed the author of *Isaiah* 40 perceived: *Why sayest thou, O Jacob, and speakest, O Israel, My way is hid from my God and my glory is forgotten by my God? Hast thou not known? hast thou not heard? the everlasting God, the Lord, the Creator of the ends of the earth, fainteth not, neither is weary; there is no searching of His understanding.* And, secondly, there is something to be said regarding the brevity of our bodily existence, to which an analogy will furnish the best introduction. Suppose that men were able to perceive the world of Nature only in its immensities, seeing the oceans but not the tumbling waves, seeing the plains but not each green or golden field, would they not fail to perceive an incalculably great portion of earth's beauty? How unutterably more wonderful are all natural objects when the microscope reveals the marvel of every particle. The tree is loveliest to him who has an eye to see the perfection of each leaf or knows the miracle of its growth from a single seed or shoot. Is it not possible that something similar is true of the human spirit in its apprehension of reality? Suppose that our personality was unable to taste life except on the grand scale, so that for man a

Forgotten Years

thousand years were only a passing moment, experienced only " as a watch in the night," would not the half of life's glory then be hidden from those who were ignorant of what *one* year can be ? May not participation in reality on a small scale—time felt as a day, an hour a minute—be indispensable if the human spirit is to grasp the amazing fulness of conscious life ? Apparently circumscribed by the limit of our three score years and ten, are we here to learn that consciousness, even when measured in days and minutes, is of eternal worth and pure delight ? For we do learn that lesson. We do discover that an instant of perfect and unselfish tenderness may be of immeasurable value. Perchance Man can never love God till he has loved his brother, never know with the Divine knowledge, until in faith, hope, and charity he has desired to win the knowledge which is in part. The cup of cold water must first be given lovingly unto the least of His brethren, or we shall never comprehend to give it into the hand of Christ Himself. "He that is faithful over a few things," said Jesus, "shall be set over many." Perhaps only to those who have sought to find Heaven in life *sub specie temporis* can life *sub specie eternitatis* be imparted ; for to know life fully must be to know not only its infinite extension and its Divine splendour, but also the exquisite perfection of its fleeting moments.

I

Proverbs are one of the most ancient inventions of Man, far older than history. Four centuries before the birth of Christ, Aristotle, gazing as far into the past as his glance could reach, saw proverbs still beckoning him back. He spoke of them as "fragments of an older wisdom which on account of their brevity or aptness had been preserved from the general wreck and ruin." Even the *Book of Proverbs*, late as it is in date, has features which, if we follow out their

Studies in Life from Jewish Proverbs

significance, will lead us back to the life of men in long forgotten years. The signs, of course, are slight, but they are none the less real; and even a faint trace may be a sure thread of guidance. Only some grooves upon the surface of the rock, but the lines were indubitably made by the movement of ice in the glacial age. Only a piece of jagged flint, but the edge we finger was chipped by human hands for an object conceived in a human brain. See how the conical marks where each stroke of the hammer fell are still as clear and purposeful as on the day when they were made. Flaking a flint is skilled work: the blows must be cunningly aimed and exactly struck, or the stone will be shattered instead of sharpened. This one, being well wrought, is doubtless a Neolithic weapon. But here is a specimen more rude and primitive. It is probably a thousand years older than the one we have just examined. Nevertheless, we know that it also was worked by man, and that human eyes chose it and human hands held it, and fashioned it, in days when man shared Europe with the mammoth.

What faint but real traces of a far antiquity can be seen in the Jewish proverbs?

(1) The first trace is to be found in the Numerical Sayings, a curious type of aphorism, half proverb and half riddle. Four of these occur in *Proverbs* 30.

Four Things Unsatisfied.

Three things there be unsatisfied,
Yea! four that say not " Enough "—
The land of death; the barren womb;
Earth unsated with water;
And fire that says not " Enough " (Pr. $30^{15b, 16}$).

Four Small Wise Things

There be four things upon the earth small but exceeding wise:
The ANTS—*a people little of strength, but in summer they store up food:*

Forgotten Years

The CONIES—*these be a feeble folk, but they make their homes
 in the rock:*
The LOCUSTS—*are they that have no king, but they march
 in an ordered host:*
The LIZARDS—*on which thou canst lay thine hand, though they
 dwell in his majesty's court* (Pr. 30$^{24\text{-}28}$).

FOUR THINGS UNBEARABLE.

Beneath three things the earth doth tremble,
Yea beneath four it cannot bear up—
Beneath a slave become a monarch;
Beneath a fool that is filled with meat;
Beneath an old-maid that hath found a husband;
Beneath a handmaid heir to her mistress (Pr. 30$^{21\text{-}23}$).

FOUR STATELY THINGS.

There be three things of stately step,
Yea, four of stately gait—
The LION, *that is the strongest beast,*
And flees before no foe;
The . . . ; the HE-GOAT *too;*
And the KING, *when . . .* [1](Pr. 30$^{29\,31}$).

Simple as these riddles may be, they imply or make definite allusion to many things; a settled community, a king, an army trained and disciplined, economic foresight, dramatic changes in social rank, laws of natural inheritance, acute reflections on the fate of man and on human character—surely a picture too elaborate for pre-historic years? Certainly, and for these particular proverbs, no such claim is advanced: the lingering trace of a forgotten world is in their form, *numerical* proverbs. Those just quoted are, as it were, links in a long chain, which we may follow backwards

---

[1] The dots indicate words missing from the Hebrew text or of unknown meaning.

Studies in Life from Jewish Proverbs

or forwards. The former process will lead to the result we seek; but first, for convenience and in further illustration, let us notice some, still later, examples of these proverbs. Two more are included in the Book of Proverbs, one of which will be quoted below (p. 51): here is the other.

SEVEN HATEFUL THINGS.

There be six things Jehovah hates,
Yea, seven which he abominates—
Haughty eyes, a lying tongue,
And hands that innocent blood have shed,
A mind devising wicked plans,
Feet that be swift to do a wrong,
A witness false declaring lies,
And he who stirs up friends to strife (Pr. 6[16-19]).

Though cast in the same mould, this saying with its insistence on justice, truth, honesty of purpose and humility of spirit, certainly reflects a later and more complex stage of thought than the naive conundrums quoted above from Pr. 30. Indeed, it may be no earlier than the third century, the golden age of proverb-making, to which period belongs also the following sentence from Ben Sirach's book: *There be nine things that I have thought of and in my heart counted happy, and the tenth I will utter with my tongue—A man whose children give him joy: a man that liveth to see his enemies fall: happy is he whose wife hath understanding, and he that hath not slipped with his tongue, and he that hath not had to serve an inferior man: happy is he that hath found prudence · and he that discourseth in the ears of them that listen. How great is he that hath found wisdom! And above him that feareth the Lord is there none. The fear of the Lord surpasses all things; and he that holdeth it, to whom shall he be likened ?* (E. 25[7-11]) [1]

---

[1] Cp. also E 25[1,2], 26[5].

Forgotten Years

Turn next to the *Sayings of the Fathers*, a treatise of Jewish ethical reflections, compiled in the first and second centuries A D., and in the fifth chapter will be found a series of " numerical " observations. It must suffice to quote but one : *There are four types of moral character. He that saith " Mine is mine and thine is thine " is a character neither good nor bad, but some say 'tis a character wholly bad* [1] *He that saith " Mine is thine and thine is mine " is a commercially minded man.*[2] *He that saith " Mine and thine are thine " is pious :* " *Mine and thine are mine," the same is wicked.* For a last and latest example a modern saying current among the Jews and Arabs of Syria, can be cited · *There are three Voices in the World—that of running water, of the Jewish Law, and of money.*

So much for the later links in the chain, but what of its beginning ? Why give thoughts in stated number ? Is it a writer's trick to catch our fancy ? *That* it may be in the later, but certainly not in the early instances. There is only unconscious art in such an unsophisticated, childlike verse as the FOUR STATELY THINGS. "Child-like," that is the word we require to describe these riddles. True ; but when were the Jews and their Semitic ancestors children ? Before Abraham was called, when almost the world itself was young.

For a moment permit your thoughts to be drawn back a very great way, and consider the rude and inefficient life of early man. Unaided by the numberless resources, mental and material, that enrich our civilised life, dwelling in forests, caverns and rude huts of stone or earth, well-nigh defenceless against the larger animals, haunted and harried by a

[1] lit. " the character of Sodom."

[2] *i.e.*, He thinks the world requires nothing more than the interchange of commodities. As to the way of putting it, be it remembered that in the Orient business transactions are, politely, " gifts " ; cp. Gen. 23[10-16].

Studies in Life from Jewish Proverbs

thousand perils real and imaginary, so man once lived and worked and thought, and by his thinking accomplished marvels. "From the moment," writes A. R. Wallace, "when the first skin was used as a covering, when the first rude spear was formed to assist in the chase, when fire was first used to cook his food, when the first seed was sown or shoot planted, a grand revolution was effected in Nature, a revolution which in all the previous ages of the earth's history had had no parallel; for a being had arisen who was no longer necessarily subject to change with the changing universe—a being who was in some degree superior to Nature, inasmuch as he knew how to control and regulate her action, and could keep himself in harmony with her, not by a change in body, but by an advance in mind."[1] But it was not enough that the individual should think. The secret of human success has lain in the ability to communicate ideas. Yet, to this day, with what effort we find words to body forth our thoughts and feelings ! Try to conceive how difficult was the formulation and transmission of ideas in those forgotten centuries. Imagine the tribesmen gathered home for the day and seated around their fire. Here is one who has had a thought when out hunting, which would amuse or interest the rest, if only it could be made articulate. But none can read, and none can write, and language is in its infancy. How then can he find a way to tell it, and they perceive his meaning, and all *remember* ? By means of proverbs; not the neat epigram of later ages, but yet sayings which for all their simplicity were embryonic proverbs. Earliest and easiest type of all was the bare comparison—*this is like that*—a type which, it is interesting to note, may be illustrated by one of the oldest phrases in the Bible: *Like Nimrod a mighty hunter before the Lord* (Gen. 10^9). And the method of comparison never ceased to be a favourite mould for

[1] A R Wallace, *Natural Selection*

Forgotten Years

the formation of proverbs, as some polished examples from *Proverbs* will serve to show: *As the swallow ever flitting and flying, so the curse that is groundless alighteth not* (Pr. 26²). *The way of the wicked is like the darkness: they know not whereon they stumble* (Pr. 4¹⁹). Another device for communicating thought and storing wisdom was the riddle, and this also, under slight disguise, has its lineal descendants in the Biblical proverbs. Thus Pr. 16²⁴, *Pleasant words are as an honeycomb, sweetness to the soul and health to the body*, was once most probably a reply to the question, *What is sweet as honey?* Another example is Pr. 22¹: someone would ask, *What is worth more than gold?* and when the listeners had guessed in vain give his answer, *A good repute*. But better than any one comparison, more memorable than the single question, was the *numerical riddle*; for instance this—*What four things are beyond our power to calculate?*

> *There be three things too wonderful for me,*
> *Yea, four which I do not comprehend—*
> *The way of an eagle in the air;*
> *The way of a serpent upon a rock;*
> *The way of a ship in the midst of the sea;*
> *And the way of a man with a maid.*—(Pr. 30 ¹⁸,¹⁹).

By sayings such as these were thought and experience acquired and transmitted in forgotten years. When complex thinking was impossible, when minds were dull and expression feeble, these primitive proverbs by the barb of their wit or fancy, fixed themselves deep in the memories of men.

(2). The last quotation has in early Indian literature a close parallel beginning thus:

> *The paths of ships across the sea,*
> *The soaring eagle's flight, Varuna knows* . . .

Studies in Life from Jewish Proverbs

and another of the numerical sayings from the same chapter of *Proverbs* has an even closer parallel:

> *There be three things unsatisfied,*
> *Yea, four that say not " Enough ":*
> *Death, and the barren womb,*
> *Earth, never sated with water,*
> *And fire that says not " Enough."* (Pr. 30^{15,16}),

compared with:

> *Fire is never sated with fuel;*
> *Nor Ocean with streams;*
> *Nor the God of death with all creatures;*
> *Nor the bright-eyed one (i.e., woman) with man.*
> (Hitopadeça 2, 113).

These resemblances of thought and phrase between India and Palestine provide another hint of far-past days by raising the question of the wandering of proverbs. Variations of the same tales and sayings occur among so many different peoples throughout Europe and Asia, that the possible rise of similar ideas, finding somewhat similar expression, in the various races, seems insufficient to account for the phenomena; rather we must suppose that tales and phrases circulated from tribe to tribe over an amazing stretch of territory and in very early times. What, for example, may be inferred from the correspondence between these Jewish and Indian sayings? Does it preserve a glimpse of some one man, interested in the reflections and questionings of his people, who once ages ago travelled out of India, following the immemorial trade-routes westwards across Arabia till he reached Palestine, and in the mind of some kindred soul left a memory of his wise words? Either that, or perhaps many minds were needed to transmit the thought from East to West or West to East; so that almost one might think of the words as having had wings on which they

Forgotten Years

flew from camp to camp along the routes, alighting wherever men gathered for trade and found time for friendly intercourse. The subject might be developed at some length; but, try as we may, the details of these migrations hide themselves in the mists of a too distant past, and we catch but a glimpse of scenes we can never more make clear. It is better to give more time to certain general characteristics of the Jewish proverbs.

II

The abnormal aptitude of the Jews for proverb-making and their love of concrete expression are ultimately due to the conditions of early centuries. Of these two features it will be convenient to consider the second first.

The land of Palestine, home of the Jews from about 1200 B.C., lies between an ocean of water and an ocean of sand: on the west its coasts are washed, but not threatened, by the Mediterranean Sea; on the east and on the south it has to wage incessant warfare against the indrifting sands. The country is an oasis snatched from the great deserts and kept from their insidious grasp only by the toil and ingenuity of man. Behind Palestine looms Arabia, and beneath the Jew is the Arab. Throughout the last five thousand years the population of Palestine (excepting the Philistines on the coast) has been formed by layer after layer of Arabian immigrants, who have invaded the fertile lands, sometimes by the rush of sudden conquest, but also by steady, peaceful infiltration. Despite much intermarriage with the earlier Canaanites there was always a passionate strain of the desert in Jewish blood, and throughout its whole history in Palestine Israel had to live in uneasy proximity to its kinsfolk, the wild nomads who roamed the deserts to the east and south. Consequently the ultimate background of the Old Testament writings is not Palestine but Arabia, a land which sets a deep and lasting impress on its

Studies in Life from Jewish Proverbs

children. A life wild yet monotonous in the extreme, rigid in its limitations but unbridled in its licence within those limitations : such is the rule imposed by the vast wilderness on the men who have to wander its blazing solitudes. Arabia produces four paradoxes in the intellect and characters of its nomadic tribes.[1] First, " the combination of strong sensual grossness with equally strong tempers of reverence and worship." Second, " a marvellous capacity for endurance and resignation broken by fits of ferocity : the ragged patience bred by famine. We see it survive in the long-suffering, mingled with outbursts of implacable wrath, which characterises so many Psalms. These are due to long periods of moral famine, the famine of justice." Third, ingenuity of mind and swift perception, but without that power or inclination for abstruse or sustained argument which the Western world has inherited from the Greeks. Fourth, a subjective attitude to the phenomena of nature and history, combined with an admirable realism in describing these phenomena.

For thousands of years before Israel entered Canaan and became a nation its ancestors were nomads of Arabia. It would be strange indeed if the great desert which so subtly and irresistibly sets its spell upon the human spirit had left no trace on Jewish proverbs. Yet the trace is not evident in points of detail. Most of the sayings we shall study in this volume represent the thoughts of certain post-exilic Jews. Where then does the mark of the desert linger ? First in the peculiar *concreteness* of the proverbs. All proverbs tend to concrete expression, but in this respect the Jewish ones are only equalled by those of the Arabs themselves ; and this quality is shown not only in the early but also in the later sayings. Let us illustrate the point before suggesting its ultimate cause. The Jew said, " Two

[1] G. A Smith, *Early Poetry of Israel*, p. 33 ; and cp. Kinglake, *Eothen*, ch. 17.

Forgotten Years

dogs killed a lion,"[1] where we say, "Union is strength." We say, " Familiarity breeds contempt " ; they said, " The pauper hungers without noticing it."[2] Our tendency is to consider riches and poverty, but they talked of the rich man and the poor. The most remarkable example of this tendency is the conception that gives unity to the *Book of Proverbs*, namely the idea of Wisdom. Here, if anywhere, one would expect the abstract to be maintained. But the individualising instinct has conquered, and in the loftiest passages of *Proverbs* we shall find Wisdom praised, not as an idea, but as a person, represented as a woman of transcendent beauty and nobility. Such abnormally concrete thinking may have its disadvantages, but at least it will have one satisfactory quality—*humanism*. Men who thought not in generalisations but in particular instances, who saw not classes but individuals, could not help being great humanists. If now we ask whence the Jewish mind received this tendency, our thoughts will have to travel back till we discern a group of black hair-cloth tents out in the Arabian Wilderness. In the tents are men who have learnt to pass safely across the deserts and are at home in them as a seaman on the seas ; wild men and strong and confident, yet never careless, knowing that they can relax vigilance only at the risk of life. For these wastes are not empty but treacherous ; apparently harmless, in reality full of peril. Security in the desert depends on acute and untiring observation. No amount of abstruse reasoning, no ability in speculative thought, will save life and property there, if the first sign of a lurking foe is passed unnoticed in the trying and deceitful light. Every faculty must be trained to the swift perception of concrete facts, faint signs of movement, the behaviour of men and beasts. The great sun in heaven may be trusted to rise and set : why speculate on the mystery ? While we are lost in thought the sons of

[1] Cohen, *Ancient Jewish Proverbs*, 88   [2] *op. cit* 13.

Studies in Life from Jewish Proverbs

Ishmael may fall upon us. "The leisure of the desert is vast, but it is the leisure of the sentinel . . . To the nomad on his bare, war-swept soil few things happen, but everything that happens is ominous."

Keen observation, then, more than any other quality, is required by Arabia from its children. But observation is the quintessence of the art of proverb-making, provided it be combined with practice in the expression of one's thoughts. As for practice in talk, one might readily suppose that the solitudes would have made their peoples tongue-tied. In point of fact the contrary is true, and the skill of the Jews in the devising of proverbs, no less than their love of concrete expression, goes back to habits engendered by this desert existence. Arabian life provided not only long leisure for reflection but also opportunity for social intercourse in the small tribal groups ; so that the nomads came to have a passion for story-telling and for all manner of sententious talk, witness the customs of the Bedouin to this day and the immense collections of Arabian proverbs. Hour after hour, with Eastern tirelessness, the tribesmen, gathered at the tent of their sheikh, would listen approvingly to the eloquence bred of large experience and shrewd judgment. Here is the scene painted in the words of Doughty's *Arabia Deserta :* " These Orientals study little else [than the art of conversation and narrative], as they sit all day idle in their male societies ; they learn in this school of infinite human observation to speak to the heart of one another. His tales [referring to a Moorish rogue, Mohammed Aly], *seasoned with saws which are the wisdom of the unlearned*, we heard for more than two months ; they were never-ending. He told them so lively to the eye that they could not be bettered, and part were of his own motley experience." The Israelites carried this habit with them from Arabia into their settled homes in Canaan. Here is a similar scene in the hall of a modern Palestinian village-

Forgotten Years

sheikh: "We were seated on mats, spread with little squares of rich carpet round three sides of a hollow place in the floor, where a fire of charcoal burned, surrounded by parrot-beaked coffee pots. This was the hearth of hospitality, whose fire is never suffered to go out; near it stood the great stone mortar in which a black slave was crushing coffee-beans. The coffee, deliciously flavoured with some cunning herb or other, was passed round. But the conversation which followed was the memorable part of that entertainment. In the shadow at the back the young men who had been admitted sat in silence. The old men, elders of the village community, sat in a row on stone benches right and left of the door. The sheikh made many apologies for not having called on us at the tents—he had thought we were merchantmen going to buy silk at Damascus. Then followed endless over-valuation of each other, and flattery concerning our respective parents and relations. . . . The elders sat silently leaning upon their staves, except now and then, when one of them would slowly rise and expatiate upon something the sheikh had said—perhaps about camels or the grain crop—beginning his interruption almost literally in the words of Job's friends: "Hearken unto me, I also will show mine opinion. I will answer also for my part, I also will show mine opinion. For I am full of matter, the spirit within me constraineth me."[1] So has it been in Palestine time out of mind, and it is in settings of this description that we must imagine the art of proverb-making developing in Israel.

Such, then, is the significance of these features which we have been considering — the numerical proverbs,

[1] Fulleylove and Kelman, *The Holy Land*, pp 103, 104. Note the "Scriptural" language. Such talk, when we find it in the Bible, is neither pedantic nor is it a "religious" dialect To a Western it seems affected, but let us remember that to an Eastern our manner of speech, with its tortuous sentences, might savour of an unholy cunning.

Studies in Life from Jewish Proverbs

parallels with sayings of other nations, the love of the Jews for proverbs with their consequent skill in making them, and their remarkable *penchant* for concrete expression. Otherwise, antiquity has left few traces in the Jewish proverbs. That, however, is but natural, since proverb-making was a living art among the people. New maxims kept coming into use, and they crowded out of memory the favourites of byegone generations. Doubtless a few of the sayings in the *Book of Proverbs* are ancient, though just how old we cannot tell. For example, P. 27^{20} *Sheol and Abaddon are never filled, and the eyes of man are never sated* may be co-æval with the fear of death and the passion of greed. Cheyne discovers a relic of " that old nomadic love of craft and subtlety " in the saying (Pr. 22^3), *A shrewd man sees misfortune coming and conceals himself, whereas simpletons pass on and suffer for it;* but his interpretation of the verse seems somewhat forced. The following, however, in matter and perhaps in form also may be nearly as ancient as the settled occupation of the land:

Remove not the ancient landmark which thy fathers set up.
(Pr. 22^{28}).

Nothing could well be easier than the removal of those landmarks—insignificant heaps of stone, set at the end of a wide furrow. But from earliest times the East has counted them adequate guardians of the fields, and from generation to generation, by consent of all decent-minded men, they have stood inviolate. Other nations, as well as Israel, called them sacred. Greece, and Rome too, gave them a god for their protection, Hermes of the Boundary, beside whose shrine of heaped-up stones travellers would stay to rest, and, rested, lay an offering of flowers or fruit before the kindly deity:

" *I, who inherit the tossing mountain-forests of steep*

Forgotten Years

Cyllene stand here guarding the pleasant playing-fields, Hermes, to whom boys often offer marjoram and hyacinths and fresh garlands of violet."[1]

Even the thief and murderer, we are told, would hesitate before the wickedness of moving these simple, immemorial heaps of stone: such was their sanctity. What unutterable contempt for the laws of God and man is therefore revealed in the multiple witness of the Old Testament[a] against the rich and powerful in Israel, that *they* scrupled not to remove the landmarks of their poorer brethren? Thieves and murderers would have kept their hands clean from such pollution:

> *Remove not the landmark of the widow,*
> *Into the field of the orphan enter not;*
> *For mighty is their Avenger,*
> *He will plead their cause against thee* (Pr.23^{10,11}).

---

[1] Appius Planius, 188 (McKail's translation).

[a] e g , *Hosea* 5^{10}, *Isaiah* 5^{8}, *Deut* 27^{17}, *Job* 24^{2}.

CHAPTER IV

The Day of Small Things

POPULAR as the custom of making and of hearing " wise words " may have been in ancient Israel, it is not surprising that only five or six proverbial sayings are recorded in the early writings of the Old Testament. For proverbs are not likely to receive mention in literature. They are too plain for the poet, too vague for the historian, too complaisant for the law-maker. And even these five or six, it appears, have been preserved not for any merit they possess as proverbs : one is of local interest only, two are picturesque, but obscure, two are the merest truisms. The right question, therefore, is not " Why are there so few ? ", but " Why have *these* sayings been rescued from oblivion ? "; and, being preserved, " Why should they receive our attention ? "

Suppose that in Britain fifty or a hundred years hence men should quote " It's a long, long way to Tipperary," when they seek an expression for the pathos and heroism that mark the acceptance of a difficult and perilous task— if those words live, why will they live ? Obviously for no intrinsic merit, but for the undying memory of men who counted not their lives dear unto themselves. So with these early proverbs in the Bible. Each of them came into quickening contact with a great personality, or played a part in one of those fateful moments when the fortunes of a people or the trend of human thinking has been determined this way or that. They have lived because each has

The Day of Small Things

been touched by the passion of humanity. Therefore we have to study them not in isolation from the context, but in close connection with the scene or circumstance that gave them unexpected immortality.

(1) In days when Jerusalem was not yet Jerusalem, City of David, but only *Jebus*, a stronghold of the Canaanites, there had been built in the limestone uplands of Judæa an Israelitish village, *Gibeah*, situated (as the name implies), on a hill-top, doubtless for such security as the rising ground afforded.

At the time we are concerned with, Israel stood in sore need of every protection her settlements could find. Baffled by the great Canaanite fortresses, the invading Hebrews had never become absolute masters of the land, and of recent years their fortunes had altogether failed under the counter-pressure of new invaders, the Philistines, who had seized the coast of Canaan and whose restless armies came sweeping up the valleys that lead to the highlands from the plain along the sea. The raiders harried the Judæan villages, slaying the men and carrying the women, children and cattle captive to the lowlands. The villages were an easy prey, and the spirit of the Israelites was broken by the miseries of these repeated ravages. Wandering bands of religious devotees, preaching remembrance of the power of Jehovah, kept the embers of corporate feeling from flickering out ; but, at the best, their wordy warfare must have seemed a feeble answer to the mail-clad giants of the Philistine hosts.

Imagine that we are standing on the hill of Gibeah, looking down the steep pathway which leads up to the village. A few days ago a young man, accompanied by a servant, went out to search the countryside for some strayed animals. All in Gibeah know him well, Saul, the son of Kish, a proper man, tall and powerful, one who in happier

Studies in Life from Jewish Proverbs

days might have been a leader in Israel. Saul and his servant are returning and have almost reached the foot of the ascent to the village. Last night they were with Samuel at Ramah, and at day-break secretly the seer had anointed the youth to be king over Israel; but of these events we are ignorant as yet; we do not know that the Saul who went out will return no more. Idly watching from the hill-top, we observe a company of devotees, who have spent the night in Gibeah, descending the slope towards Saul. As they approach, Saul stops and, to our faint surprise, is seen to be in speech with them. Question and answer pass. Suddenly our listless attention changes to astonishment. Below, excitement is rising, and on none has it fallen more than on Saul! He begins to talk and gesticulate like a man inspired. We raise a shout and the folk come running, and, as they see beneath them Saul now in an ecstasy, the incredulous cry breaks forth *Is Saul also among the prophets?*

What is the interest of this famous scene? That a proverb was born that day in Israel? That it marked the commencement of a new stage in the national life of Israel? More than that. The real interest is in the transformation effected by the recognition of a personal duty. Young men like the Saul who went out to seek the lost animals are useful members of a State, but, had Saul remained unaltered, what waste of his latent, unsuspected power! Saul had met devotees many times before, but their words had roused no energies in him. One touch of the faith of Samuel, one illuminating moment of consciousness that *to him* God had spoken, and—Saul was a king, and Israel again a people; despair became hope, and hope achievement. It has always been so, whenever men have listened to the summons of personal religion. We go upon our ordinary path a hundred times and return as we went, uncomprehending; but if once God meets us on the way,

The Day of Small Things

whether He speak by the mouth of a prophet, or, as now, by the shock of war, the miracle is effected : we are changed into another man.

(2) The scene of the second of these early proverbs is the steep and rugged country that mounts from the floor of the Dead Sea valley near Engedi. But the setting of the incident matters little ; its point is all in the play of character between two great personalities—Saul, now nearing the dark finish of his reign and haunted by the thought that at his death the throne will pass from his house ; and David, with youth and a good conscience to support him but fleeing for his life from the jealous king and hard pressed by the royal soldiery. Saul has entered a cave, unaware that David is hiding in its recesses. David suffers him to go out unharmed and still ignorant of his peril ; but quietly he follows Saul to the sunlight at the cave's mouth, and standing there, as the King moves off, he calls, " O my lord the King ! " At the clear, musical, voice of the man he half-loves, half-hates, and cannot kill, Saul in astonishment turns to hear these words : " *Wherefore hearkenest thou to men's words saying ' Behold David seeketh thy hurt ' ? Behold this day the Lord had delivered thee into mine hand in the cave : and some bade me kill thee ; but mine eye spared thee and I said ' I will not put forth mine hand against my lord, for he is the Lord's anointed.' Moreover, my father, see, yea, see the skirt of thy robe in my hand : for in that I cut the skirt of thy robe and killed thee not, know thou and see that there is neither evil nor transgression in my hand, and I have not sinned against thee, though thou huntest after my soul to take it. The Lord judge between me and thee, and avenge me of thee : but mine hand shall not be upon thee. As saith the proverb of the ancients,* **Out of the wicked cometh forth wickedness** : *but mine hand shall not be upon thee.*" We can see how David meant it, that proverb of the ancients. It leapt to his lips in eager protestation.

63

Studies in Life from Jewish Proverbs

How could Saul deem him capable of a deed of foulest treachery? Why could he not see that only out of the basest of men could such dire wickedness proceed? But into the mind of Saul the saying sank with double edge. What had *he* done towards the making of this scene—that red mist of passion when he flung the javelin; those cold and cunning plots to lure David into adventure that would be his death; the unrelaxing hunt to catch and kill? Saul for an instant saw his soul laid bare by the ancient proverb: he at least was a man from whom great wickedness had come, and "A good tree cannot bring forth corrupt fruit, neither can a corrupt tree bring forth good fruit." *And Saul lifted up his voice and wept. And he said to David, " Thou art more righteous than I, for thou hast rendered unto me good, whereas I have rendered unto thee evil."* A few years later the King lay dead and vanquished on Mount Gilboa. From that day to this men have not ceased to find in him a text for moralising, with some justice but with strangely little sympathy, seeing that he sinned in one thing and paid a heavy penalty. Which was the real Saul? The King crazy with murderous hatred, or the man who answered David's generosity in those noble words, who once " was among the prophets," who had made Israel again a people and so long time had held the Philistines at bay? It does not greatly matter if men reply " the mad Saul, who died believing himself forsaken of God "; and so push their moralisings home. But on which Saul does the Divine judgment pass? One man, more than all others, had reason to condemn, and he did more than pardon. He sang of Saul slain on Gilboa, *How are the mighty fallen? . . . Saul and Jonathan were lovely and pleasant in their lives, and in their deaths they were not divided.*

(3) In the books of Jeremiah and Ezekiel two popular sayings are mentioned, which may be considered together, for their burden is one.

The Day of Small Things

(a) *Behold, everyone that useth proverbs shall use this proverb against thee saying,* As is the mother, so is the daughter (*Ezekiel* 16:44).

(b) *But it shall come to pass that like as I have watched over them to pluck up and to break down and to overthrow and to destroy and to afflict; so will I watch over them to build and to plant, saith the Lord. In those days they shall say no more,* The fathers have eaten sour grapes, and the children's teeth are set on edge. *But every one shall die for his own iniquity: every man that eateth the sour grapes his teeth shall be set on edge (Jeremiah* 31:28-30); and to the same effect, this from Ezekiel, *The word of the Lord came unto me saying, What mean ye that ye use this proverb concerning the land of Israel, saying,* The fathers have eaten sour grapes, and the children's teeth are set on edge? *As I live, saith the Lord God, ye shall not have cause any more to use this proverb in Israel. Behold, all souls are Mine: as the soul of the father so also the soul of the son is Mine: the soul that sinneth,* IT *shall die. But if a man be just, and do that which is lawful and right . . . hath spoiled none by violence, hath given his bread to the hungry, and hath covered the naked with a garment . . . he is just, he shall surely live, saith the Lord God (Ezekiel* 18:1ff).

Heredity, the question at issue in these passages, presents a more complex and stringent problem to the modern mind than to the ancient. But it would be a great error to suppose that the Jewish thinkers were less concerned about it, or that its consequences seemed to them less bitter. Indeed for the Hebrews the problem had a sinister background which for us has sunk far out of sight. The solidarity of the tribe or family was a fearsome reality in days when for the sin of one member vengeance would fall upon the whole community or household. Recollect the story of Achan, who stole from the sacred spoil a Babylonish mantle, silver, and a wedge of gold: *Wherefore Joshua and all Israel with him took Achan* AND *his sons and his daughters and his oxen*

Studies in Life from Jewish Proverbs

and his asses and his sheep and his tent and all that he had, and burned them with fire and stoned them with stones.[1]
There was a grim wisdom in the ancient procedure. Man has had a stern fight for existence. How far can he tolerate " handicaps " in the contest ? What can be expected from children of corrupt and vicious parents ? Good citizens ? " Men do not gather grapes of thorns." Yet who could fail to see that the children were so far innocent ; and therefore, whilst Achan died unpitied and forgotten, perhaps their young voices and terror-stricken looks remained an uneasy memory in the minds of those who stood consenting unto their death ? Was it necessary that the child should be irretrievably ruined through his father's guilt ?

By the time of Jeremiah and Ezekiel, as the quotations show, the problem had deepened and become general. In the perils, hardships, and disasters which marked the decline and fall of the Judæan kingdom men felt that the whole nation was suffering the consequences of their fathers' iniquities, and bitterly they quoted the saying *The fathers have eaten sour grapes, and the children's teeth are set on edge.* That way lay despair : Let us too eat of the grapes and drink of their wine and be merry, since to-morrow we die ! Even the prophets experienced the temptation to hopelessness; as when Ezekiel, wrestling with Judah sunk in the old sins, thinks that in future days men will still have to cast at her the charge of idolatries handed down from the ancient Canaanites : *as is the mother so is the daughter.* But Jeremiah and Ezekiel both fought their way through to a new conception of life, and this it is which is proclaimed in the two chief passages quoted above. Deliverance from the entail of evil is, they declare, possible ; man is not

---

[1] Cp *Joshua* 7[24,25] The earliest form of the narrative clearly implies that all, and not Achan alone, were destroyed by burning or stoning.

The Day of Small Things

immovably fastened in chains which his ancestors have forged.

So stands religion to-day, claiming power in the building of human character. Fuller recognition and much deeper comprehension of the works of heredity (as also of environment) are desirable and are not inimical to a religious interpretation of human nature. Religion lays stress on these two points. First, the fact that if there is an entail of evil there is also an entail of good, together with the judgement that the inheritance of good is the greater and ought to be made supreme : that as St. Paul insisted *Where sin did abound, grace doth much more abound*[1]. And, secondly, religion insists on the reality of that power of self-determination which would seem to be characteristic of every living being and in Man to be of primary importance. All that we may become does not follow inexorably from what we now are. What we have become was not wholly involved in what we were. Crude determinism is either an Eastern idleness or a pedant's nightmare, and freedom, though it slips through the meshes of our clumsy analysis is a reality. To each in measure it is given, though one may misuse it into the atrophy of evil habit, whilst another may use it unto the liberty of the children of God. We inherit, but, inheriting, we also originate. We are created, but are also creators. We are pressed by our environment, but our environment may become Christ, whose service is perfect freedom.

(4) One other embedded proverb occurs in a passage of *Ezekiel* ($12^{21, 22}$) : *And the word of the Lord came unto me saying,* " *Son of man, what is this proverb that ye have in the land of Israel saying,* **The days are prolonged, and every**

---

[1] Not but what the belief is at least as old as the Hebrew Law, *I the Lord thy God am a jealous God, visiting the iniquities of the fathers upon the children unto the third and fourth generation of them that hate Me, and shewing mercy unto the* thousandth *generation of them that love Me and keep My commandments.*

Studies in Life from Jewish Proverbs

vision faileth?" Other lands besides Israel have echoed those despairing words. It is hard not to feel in a city-settlement that "the days are prolonged"; hard in a half-filled church not to wonder if "every vision faileth." But a true man will still hold to the instinct that somehow his hopes are certainties, and will make answer with Israel's prophet thus: *Tell them therefore, "Thus saith the Lord God: I will make this proverb to cease, and they shall no more use it as a proverb in Israel; but say unto them, 'The days are at hand, and the fulfilment of every vision.'"*

A man who finds himself without confidence in God or man might save himself from pessimism by a study of the intellectual, moral and spiritual achievements of the Hebrew prophets.[1] Looking back on Jewish history it is manifest that the spiritual longings of these great personalities were realised to a wonderful extent and in ways impossible for themselves or their contemporaries to perceive or anticipate. Things did work together for good to those Jews who sought to discover the will of God and, despite perplexity and hardship, refused to abandon their imperfect but advancing faith. Thus even the Exile, apparently the dissolution of Israel's life, proved to be the very means of its preservation and subsequent extension to a position of world-wide influence. No one who has realised on the one hand the overwhelming difficulties against which the prophets had to contend, the frankness with which they faced the naked facts, their own agonising struggle of soul against doubt and despair, and on the other side the ultimate vindication of their faith; no one with that knowledge clear before him will find it easy wholly to despair of men, or to cast from him for ever the hope of God.

Besides these few incidental proverbs, the pre-exilic literature of the Old Testament fortunately has preserved

[1] A *study*, not a half-hearted perusal of the text in the English Bible.

The Day of Small Things

occasional glimpses of the *makers of proverbs* in Israel, and to these we now turn. We shall then be prepared to study the special development of Jewish proverbs which furnishes the chief interest of our subject. It will be convenient first to set down the evidential passages consecutively, and afterwards to consider their significance.

(*a*) The narrative in 2 *Samuel* 14^{1f} relating the stratagem by which Joab succeeded in reconciling King David to his son Absalom begins thus: *Now Joab the son of Zeruiah perceived that the king's heart was towards Absalom. And Joab sent to Tekoa and fetched thence* a wise woman.

(*b*) The second passage is in 2 *Samuel* 20$^{16-22}$—Joab, as David's general, having pursued the rebel Sheba into the North of Israel, has compelled him to take refuge in the town of Abel, and is on the point of breaching the wall and capturing the city, when *there cried unto him* a wise woman *out of the city . . . and she said unto him " There is a saying,* To finish your business ask counsel at Abel."[1] *Thou seekest to destroy a city and a mother in Israel. And Joab answered and said, " Far be it from me that I should swallow and destroy. But . . . Sheba the son of Bichri . . . deliver him only, and I will depart from the city." And the woman said unto Joab, " Behold, his head shall be thrown to thee over the wall."* Then the woman went unto all the people in her wisdom . . .

(*c*) The famous passage in which the wisdom of King Solomon is extolled, 1 *Kings* 4$^{29-34}$: *And God gave Solomon wisdom and understanding exceeding much and largeness of heart, even as the sand that is on the sea shore.* And Solomon's wisdom excelled the wisdom of all the children of the East (*i.e.* Arabia) and all the wisdom of Egypt. *For he was wiser than all men: than Ethan the Ezrahite, and Heman, and Calcol, and Darda, the sons of Mahol: and his fame was in*

---

[1] Cp. *Numbers* 21^{27}, *Wherefore they that speak in proverbs say* " *Come ye to Heshbon,*" . . .

Studies in Life from Jewish Proverbs

all the nations round about. **And he spake three thousand proverbs :** *and his songs were a thousand and five. And he spake of trees, from the cedar that is in Lebanon unto the hyssop that springeth out of the wall ; he spake also of beasts and of fowl and of creeping things and of fishes.*

(d) *Isaiah* 29^{13,14} : *And the Lord said, Forasmuch as this people draw nigh with their mouth, and with their lips do honour me, but have removed their heart far from me and their fear of me is a commandment of men which hath been taught them ; therefore behold I will again do a marvellous work among this people . . . and* the wisdom of their wise men *shall perish, and the understanding of their prudent men shall be hid.*

(e) *Jeremiah* 18^{18} (cp. 8^8 and 9^{23}): *Then said they, Come and let us devise devices against Jeremiah ; for the law shall not perish from the priest, nor* counsel from the wise, *nor the word from the prophet.*

Of these passages the first two show that there was a " Wisdom " in Israel before Solomon, that it was concerned with prudential counsel as to the conduct of life, and was associated with the use of maxims, some of which had passed into well-known proverbs ; and further that certain persons (often, perhaps generally, women) were recognised as of pre-eminent skill in this giving of advice ; and that townships (doubtless with a shrewd eye to the increase of their commerce) vied one with another in vaunting their respective sages. Slight as this evidence may be, it is sufficient, because it is in accord with the facts of later periods and with that liking for sententious talk which we have noted as characteristic of the Semites from very early ages. Observe also how in the third passage the wisdom of Solomon is not regarded as a quality peculiar to himself. True, he possessed wisdom in a rare or superlative degree, but it was *comparable* with the " Wisdom of the East " (Arabia) and the " Wisdom of Egypt." Nor was Solomon

The Day of Small Things

alone in his wisdom. To him the first place; but he had great rivals whose names posterity thought worth preserving. One suspects that the King's reputation for sagacity may have been enhanced by his royal estate, and that in the passage quoted from the *Book of Kings* we see him through the haze of grandeur with which later generations encircled his reign. Even so, the tradition of his wisdom stands, and like all firm traditions has a basis in fact. What inferences should we draw? Not that the three thousand proverbs with which tradition credited Solomon are those preserved in the *Book of Proverbs*, despite the fact that the main sections of the Book are prefaced by titles ascribing them to him.[1] A few of the proverbs may have been spoken by Solomon himself or at his court by persons renowned for sagacity, but nothing more than that is probable.[2] Two

[1] For these titles see Chapter II., p. 37. That such a phrase as *The proverbs of Solomon, the son of David, king of Israel* (Pr. 1¹) at the head of a section does not necessarily imply or even claim authorship, may seem astonishing to those unacquainted with ancient literature, but it is easily understood by those who have made so much as a moderate study of the subject. The ancient title in modern parlance would be represented by some such heading as the following, "A collection of sayings representative of Hebrew wisdom dedicated to the memory and example of that royal lover of Wisdom, King Solomon." To suppose that the propriety of the ancient procedure ought to be judged by modern canons of literary right and wrong would be both unjust and foolish. Similarly from the heading prefixed to Pr. 25-29, *These also are proverbs of Solomon which the men of Hezekiah, king of Judah, copied out*, it does not follow that the proverbs in those chapters were old in Hezekiah's time. Probably Hezekiah, like Solomon, showed special interest in literary work, and it may be that a collection of proverbs formed in his reign is the nucleus of the present chapters 25-29 (So Volz, *Weisheit*, p 95). On the other hand it is possible that nothing more should be inferred than that, there being a tradition of literary activity in Hezekiah's reign, the compilers of the Book of Proverbs made use of the tradition in order to indicate (by this title) that in their opinion the proverbs of chaps. 25-29 were later than or secondary to the "Solomonic" proverbs which precede in chs 1-24 (So Toy, *Proverbs*, § vi., and p. 457); and see also Driver, *Literature of the Old Testament*, p. 405.

[2] Detailed proof is impossible, and the question must be argued on general evidence, which any modern commentary on the Book

Studies in Life from Jewish Proverbs

positive conclusions seem tenable. First, that King Solomon made a profound impression on his contemporaries by reason of his subtle judgment, and his ability to express his thoughts in just such moralistic maxims, comparisons, parables, and fables, as the Wise were wont to use. In fact, the King was a Wise-man and a Wise-man was King.[1] No wonder that his renown grew until he became, so to speak, the patron saint of Wisdom in Israel, with whose authority any " Wise " words might fittingly be associated. But further in view of the aptitude shown by the King for the art of the Wise, it is reasonable to believe that their prestige at this period must have been greatly enhanced in the estimation of all classes. The man of Wisdom was *persona grata* at Court. And what more is needed to secure a reputation ?

Hence it is not unexpected, though very interesting, to find two or three centuries later that when Isaiah and Jeremiah speak of the Wise they refer to them as an influence in the land ranking with the prophets and the ceremonial religion. To the true prophets it appeared to be an influence not always for good, or even inimical to their moral idealism. Thus Isaiah declares that in the glorious day when Jehovah reveals His truth *the Wisdom of the wise men shall perish* (*Isaiah* 29[14]) ; and Jeremiah gives as the reason why his enemies consider that his death or imprisonment would be small loss to the nation their belief that " *the law shall not perish from the priest, nor counsel from the wise, nor the word from the prophet* (*Jer.* 18[18]).

---

of Proverbs will supply Toy, *Proverbs*, § vi is emphatic in his view that no authority whatever attaches to titles ascribing proverbs to Solomon Volz (p 95) is non-committal : " Whether small fragments of Solomon's work have been transmitted to us cannot be determined." Driver, *Literature of the Old Testament*, p 406f, is of much the same opinion ; but, remarking that the " proverbs in 10[18] exhibit great uniformity of type," he remarks that " perhaps this type was set by Solomon "

[1] Compare the way in which the Greeks tended to associate all fables with the name of Æsop.

The Day of Small Things

This evidence might be augmented by passages in the *Book of Job*, where, for instance, the wisdom of Israel is described as an ancient, though living, tradition : it is *that which wise men have told from their fathers* (*Job* 15^{18}.) But enough has been said. To sum up, it appears that the Hebrews, like their near kinsmen the Arabs, loved to listen to the conversation of those, who, having ripe experience, shrewd wits, and a sharp tongue, were able to cast their reflections on life into parables and maxims which the hearer could readily remember. Persons with an aptitude for such discourse were acknowledged among their fellows as " wise." Anyone with the necessary intelligence and dignity might acquire this reputation. The Wise were never sharply differentiated from the rest of the community ; they did not become a strict order or a caste like the priests, but remained a type or class ; a class, however, of such importance that it could be spoken of in the same breath with the prophets and the priests. Egyptian analogies suggest that the Wise may have taken on themselves duties in the instruction of the young : but just what these early sages said and thought we cannot ascertain. Nor is it likely we have lost much in consequence Some of their favourite sayings may eventually have been incorporated in the *Book of Proverbs*, but the antagonism of the great prophets shows that they were not enthusiasts for reform, and doubtless the bulk of their maxims were prudential counsels suitable to the standards of the age. In short, their teaching must have been desultory, lacking the inspiration of a definite purpose and a clearly conceived ideal. Thus far we find nothing that matters to the modern world, nothing to awaken more than a flicker of our interest. No reason has yet appeared to prompt the hope that Israel would make more of her Wisdom than Edom or Egypt of theirs, and that was little enough. In all this we find only " the Day of Small Things," and need dwell no

Studies in Life from Jewish Proverbs

longer on its trifles. But equally we ought to avoid the folly of despising it. The Hebrews, after all, were not precisely as their neighbours of Philistia, Edom, or Egypt. Behind them they had, as a people, an astonishing history, and in their midst a succession of amazing men, the prophets who had prophesied to them words which it was not possible should die, seeds of the ultimate Wisdom. In Judah there was growing up a capacity for faith, a spiritual interpretation of life and an enlightenment of moral conscience unique in the ancient world. Hence Israel's Wise-men were not as other Wise-men; they had great potentialities. At length, after the exile, circumstances came to pass which favoured the development of latent genius in these men. All that had been needed was an immediate stimulus, a liberating idea, a flash to kindle the flame.

CHAPTER V

Iron Sharpeneth Iron

LIFE is very jealous of its secrets, and it is only by irrepressible questioning that man has read what he has read of the truth. The insurgent "Why?" of our early years is perhaps the one childish thing we ought to cherish to our dying day. All sorts of evil things—surface-familiarity, routine, but above all self-satisfaction—combine to stifle and to end our curiosity; at length we acquiesce in and forget our ignorance, and thereafter stand with our prejudices cumbering the ground for those who would go further. Questioning is health to the soul, and perhaps success is to be measured not by the fulness of the answers we receive but by our eagerness in asking.

Almost everyone knows that there is in the Bible a *Book of Proverbs*. A few of its sayings are in daily use. Most men have read a chapter or two. But at that point knowledge is apt to flag. What lack of enterprise! It is like giving up an excursion at the first mile-stone. Why should there be a *Book of Proverbs*? Why did men think it worth transmitting, and why did they finally count it sacred literature? Why has it just the form it has? How comes it, for instance, that single sayings have sometimes blossomed into little essays, and brief comparisons grown into finished pictures? What is the note of clear intention which pervades the chapters and gives them a certain unity and individuality? Zeal and energy characterise the Book. Zeal for what? The previous chapter indicates that the

Studies in Life from Jewish Proverbs

answer to that last question may be stated concisely in the one word "Wisdom," the meaning of which subsequent pages will unfold. The aim of the present chapter is to discover an adequate reason for the *zeal*.

Not seldom it happens that enthusiasm for a cause is first provoked by opposition. For example, belief that international relationships ought to be governed by ethical principles was generally and genuinely held by the vast majority of English-speaking people in 1914; but the belief lacked energising force. It seemed enough to entertain it. Of the existence of a fundamentally different conception —that Might is the ultimate right in national affairs—we were of course aware, but the knowledge did not disturb us greatly. We fondly imagined that after some more debate, and a little more reflection, so unenlightened and unneighbourly a notion must disappear. When, however, Germany suddenly put false theory into infamous practice, mark how our amiable opinion became not only an urgent and indispensable ideal, but a definite policy which must at all costs be upheld and made effective, if humanity was to be saved from the yoke of an utterly immoral tyranny. In a moment we realised the awful immediacy of the issue that had been at stake. The debate was not as we supposed, on paper. Here was no wordy strife. Nay! the battle at our gates was not confined even to the quick bodies of men; it penetrated to the very mind and spirit, so that almost St. Paul's words seemed again in place: "Ours is not a conflict with mere flesh and blood, but with . . . the spiritual hosts of evil arrayed against us in the heavenly places."[1]

Similarly it was an insistent menace that roused the fervour of the Wise-men of Israel. Subtle but deadly opposition compelled them either to champion their cause or see it fall. Wisdom in consequence acquired a firmer outline. Because another Creed was in the air, it also

[1] *Ephesians* 6:12 (Weymouth's translation).

Iron Sharpeneth Iron

became a definite "Way of life." The issues were clarified, the trend of things revealed. It was felt there were but two paths for a man to choose, now sharply defined and seen to lead in opposite directions:

Hear, O my son, and receive my sayings,
And the years of thy life shall be many.
I have taught thee in the way of Wisdom,
I have led thee in paths of uprightness
When thou goest thy steps shall not be straightened,
And if thou runnest thou shalt not stumble.
Take fast hold of instruction; let her not go:
Keep her, for she is thy life.

Enter not into the paths of the wicked,
And walk not in the way of evil men.
Avoid it, pass not by it;
Turn from it, and pass on.
For they sleep not except they have done mischief;
And their sleep is taken away unless they cause some to fall.
For they eat the bread of wickedness
And drink the wine of violence.

But the path of the righteous is as the shining light,
That shineth more and more unto the perfect day.
The way of the wicked is as darkness
They know not at what they stumble. (Pr. $4^{10\text{-}19}$)[1].

What then, was Wisdom's opponent? Not Folly in the perennial sense, else where was the novelty of the situation? The foe was Folly masquerading as Wisdom, a specious spurious Wisdom which, said the Jewish moralists, despite appearances was No-Wisdom. But if it was not the reality, it was very like it; for the false Wisdom was beautiful, brilliant, and exceedingly effective, had all the rights of sovereignty save one, all the qualities of permanence save one—a firm basis in morality. It lacked only the "fear

[1] Cp the similar but more poetic description in *Psalm* 1.

Studies in Life from Jewish Proverbs

of the Lord," which the Jew defined as "to depart from evil," and which he held to be the one possible foundation for the truly wise life. Not having that, it was but the devil robed as an angel of light, Folly of Follies, a Temple of Wisdom founded upon the sand.

In order to do justice to the efforts made by the Jews of the third and second centuries B.C. to maintain an intellectual, moral and spiritual independence in face of the new learning, or rather the new manner of life we are about to describe, it is necessary to appreciate not only the force of the attack but also the limited resources of the defence. Let us begin therefore by striving to realise the position of the Palestinian Jews in the ancient world.[1] The overwhelming religious importance of the Jews has so distorted the proportions of that world that even the professed student of antiquity finds it difficult to recover the true perspective and realise their geographical and historical insignificance. Without pausing to reflect, answer this question, "Which were the chief nations of antiquity?" "The Jews, the Greeks, the Romans," is perhaps the reply that would rise most readily to your lips. But as well might one classify the inhabitants of the modern Western world into Manxmen, Europeans, and Americans! "Which were the famous countries of the pre-Christian era?" "Palestine, Egypt, Assyria, and Babylonia," might be our response. But the Egyptians and Babylonians did not hang with breathless interest on the fortunes of Palestine, as we are naturally prone to imagine. They cared no more for the fate of Jerusalem than modern Europe does for the fortunes of

[1] What follows is without reference to the ancient civilisation of the far East, India or China. The "world" we are here considering means the civilisation of the lands bordering the Mediterranean Sea. A few pages later, the terms "Eastern" and "Western" will be used with similar latitude · "Eastern" or ("Oriental") denoting the peoples of Egypt, Arabia, Palestine, Syria, Mesopotamia, and "Western" the peoples of Greece Macedonia, and the old Greek colonies of the Ægean islands and the coast of Asia Minor.

Iron Sharpeneth Iron

Monaco. Now and again a king of Egypt marching north along the Philistine plain, or a grand monarch of Babylon, sweeping south to the borders of Nile, might turn aside a fraction of his host to ravage and overcome the Judæan highlands. But, as a rule, Jerusalem, not being on the main track of conquest, was not vitally affected by the coming and going of the huge armies that issued periodically from the northern and southern Empires.

And next consider how unimportant even in Palestine were the Jews of post-exilic days. The history of that country is familiar to us only from the records of the Jewish Scriptures. If with the same fulness we could hear the story from the standpoint of Israel's neighbours the proportions of things might seem immensely changed. How hard it is to remember that Solomon in all his glory had no authority in Philistine towns thirty miles away ; and that Hiram of Tyre doubtless considered himself every whit as great a lord as the ruler of Jerusalem, and perhaps more highly civilised, certainly his superior in the matter of arts and crafts. In 722 B.C., with the capture of Samaria, the northern kingdom of Israel passed out of history, and with the influx of alien settlers into its desolated territory the district became semi-heathen. In 586 B.C. a like fate befell the little kingdom of Judah, the Temple of Jerusalem being burnt, the city walls destroyed and the upper classes carried off to Babylonia. Thereafter for a period of a century and a half Jerusalem existed only as an enfeebled, unfortified township. The return of exiles from Babylon in the reign of Cyrus (537 B.C.), though the fame of it bulked large in Jewish tradition, was no great increase of strength, perhaps little more than the accession of a few influential families. Not until a century later in the time of Nehemiah, about 432 B.C., did the Jews feel that their political history had recommenced ; and, even so, the work of Nehemiah was not the creation of a kingdom for his people but the

Studies in Life from Jewish Proverbs

circumvallation of their one city. With its walls restored Jerusalem might again be said to exist, a defenced city, no longer dependent on the mercy of petty and jealous neighbours. But the territories of the Jews remained much as before; namely the fields and little villages to a distance of some ten or fifteen miles around Jerusalem. Nor was there any considerable extension of purely Jewish land until the successes of the Maccabees were gained in 166 B.C. To sum up. Even after the work of Nehemiah had been accomplished, the Jewish State in Palestine was still no more than an insignificant upland community, a drop in the ocean of pagan races enclosing it; a tract some fifteen miles in length and breadth with Jerusalem as its only city. Doubtless the Jews were encouraged by the prosperity of their kinsfolk in the great cities of Babylonia, Syria and Egypt. But that was a source only of moral or financial help, not of physical protection: and to the east were the wild nomadic tribes, and south of Jerusalem the treacherous Edomites, and to the north the worse than alien Samaritans, whose Temple on Mount Gerizim challenged Jerusalem's last glory, its spiritual pre-eminence. Galilee was heathen land; on the west were the splendid heathen cities of the coast; and far to the distant south beyond mysterious Nile and away to the most distant north ranged the vast territories of heathen monarchs before whose military power and worldly splendour Jerusalem was altogether less than nothing and vanity.

In 332 B.C. a thunderbolt smote all the countries of the near East. In that year a European army, led by the young king of Macedonia, Alexander the Great, invaded Asia Minor—with such astonishing effects that the events marks the commencement of a distinct epoch in history, the Greek or Hellenic age. Military conquests prove sometimes to be of small consequence in the great movement of human affairs, and famous battles often have

Iron Sharpeneth Iron

decided no more than that so many thousand men should die untimely deaths and that this royal house instead of that should hold the throne: an almost meaningless result. Only those wars are decisive which, like the present one, involve the dominance of one or other of two divergent conceptions or ideals of human life. Now the conquests of Alexander were of this latter character; and, that being so, their significance has to be measured not only from the standpoint of events but also from the history of ideas. At this point then—the coming of the Greeks to the East—let our narrative be checked for a moment that we may reach the same event by following up a different line of thought, namely the history of the development of human society. What is the significance of Alexander from that point of view? Our aim in examining the question will have to be threefold; to present (of course, in simplest outline) *first*, the ruling principles of the Eastern or Oriental manner of life; *secondly*, the Western—that is, the Greek or Hellenic—ideals; and *thirdly*, the attempt of Alexander and his successors to impose this Hellenic culture upon the Easterns and, in particular, upon the Jews in Palestine.

1. First, of ancient Oriental life. In a previous chapter it was said that behind Palestine looms Arabia and beneath the Jew is the Arab. From before the dawn of history the immense grass-lands of Arabia have been peopled by small nomadic tribes who derived a sufficient livelihood from the flocks they possessed and followed. All the organised life of the Semitic races, with whom alone we are here concerned, has its instincts rooted in this nomadic existence, about which much might profitably be said; but only one point is essential, and to that our remarks will be confined. It is that these pastoral communities have solved the problem of life under existing circumstances. The rigid limitations of their physical surroundings dictates a narrow circle of ambitions beyond which they do not pass, so long

Studies in Life from Jewish Proverbs

as the conditions remain unchanged. For not only have they discovered how to live, but they have found out the best way of living, within their simple, monotonous world. Therefore they continue, but they do not change. Progress was practically unthought of, certainly undesired ; and in fact the life of the modern Bedouin of Arabia is still in its essentials the same as that depicted in the *Book of Genesis*. But about 3000 B.C., for the first time though not the last time in history, Arabia became overcrowded, in the sense that its pasturage was insufficient to sustain the population, and multitudes of nomads, hunger-driven, poured forth into the fertile territories bordering the deserts. There the arts of agriculture and of building were learnt, settled communities formed, tribal organisation yielded to larger groups, kingdoms arose, and eventually great empires. But the civilised life of the Semites proved to be as lacking in the instinct for progress, whether material, moral or intellectual, as in its simpler way the original pastoral existence has been. Life in Semitic towns became richer and more complex up to a certain point, but there ambition faded, and the ingrained habit of acquiescence in existing circumstances prevailed, hindering and preventing further growth. Thus, politically, this eastern civilisation was characterised by the mass of the people seeking no share in their own government. They were content to be ruled by authorities whom they seldom created and never effectively controlled. It has been truly said that the kings of the East fought over the heads of their subjects. The affairs of a baker in Jerusalem, a merchant in Gaza, a craftsman in Tyre (provided the victorious army left him alive) were unaltered by the rise and fall of his rulers. To the bulk of the inhabitants of the Palestinian towns it mattered little whether they were temporarily independent or were under the heel now of Babylon, now of Egypt, now of Persia. Men hoped for no more than that trade should be possible,

Iron Sharpeneth Iron

food obtainable, and that the injustice in the realm should be —not abolished (no one was so mad as to entertain the notion) but—kept within tolerable bounds. For the rest, what more could a man desire than to live as had his father before him ? Ancestral custom held the whole of life in its paralysing grasp, and choked initiative. The potter sought no new patterns ; what was wrong with the old ? Why devise a new method of ploughing, when the old way grew the crops ? Innovation was an altogether hateful thing. Hence, however populous Eastern towns might grow, however active and prosperous their commerce, life in them was essentially stationary, its ambitions limited, its possibilities achieved. In all Palestine there was but one spark of unexhausted thought ; namely, the conception of God which the great prophets of Israel had discovered and transmitted to their people. Evidently a nation which remembered such words as these : *I hate, I despise your feasts, and I will take no delight in your solemn assemblies. Yea, though ye offer me your burnt offerings and meal offerings I will not accept them : neither will I regard the peace offerings of your fat beasts. Take thou away from me the noise of thy songs ; for I will not hear the melody of thy viols. But let justice roll down like waters, and righteousness as a mighty stream*[1]— that nation is not finished ; it has living seed within its soil. Yes, but against this confident assertion recall how shrunken and enfeebled the Jewish community had become. Further, remember that in all things except their religion and their morality these Jews were part and parcel of the general Oriental civilisation. In their civil occupations, their commercial and agricultural methods, they also were just as much slaves of tradition and as content with their bondage, as were their neighbours. " Slaves of tradition," how much the words cover ! If even dimly we could realise the misery, disease and squalor of the poor,

[1] *Amos* 5^{24}.

Studies in Life from Jewish Proverbs

the degradation of womanhood, in those tradition-ridden Eastern towns; if we could taste like gall and bitterness in our own experience one thousandth part of the injustice and cruelties of those " contented " despotisms ; " A stationary civilisation, having reached the limit of its ambitions " —how easily the phrase is framed !—if we could feel how much that meagre consummation left to be desired, the words would seem to be written in blood and blotted with tears !

2. Meanwhile in Europe, across the blue seas of the Eastern Mediterranean, a new thing had come to pass: an organisation of human life different in form and in intention because different in mind and spirit. By its means the intellectual powers and artistic achievements of man were swiftly to be raised to an unimagined splendour, and, even so, *to remain unexhausted:* we say " unexhausted " because the inspiring and energising ideas which Greek genius was the first to realise and accept have never ceased to operate, being in fact the intellectual principles upon which Western civilisation has been constructed, and providing the ideal towards which the development of society is still directed. Doubtless there is terribly much to deplore in modern life ; we are far from wisdom, peace and true prosperity ; it may be doubted whether the conditions of the poor under modern industrialism are not, in places, worse than anything even the East can show. And yet there is one incalculable difference revolutionising the whole prospect. Unlike the East, we do not acquiesce in existing evils. We are not exhausted, not apathetically willing to accept things as they are. We spurn as nonsense and cowardice any suggestions that the limit of human development has been attained. Vehemently and hopefully we insist on the achievement of better things. Not all the errors of the past and the resultant evils of the present daunt us. We are rebels against our failures, and our discontent is the measure of our vitality. This instinct

Iron Sharpeneth Iron

for improvement, which is the characteristic of Western life, we owe—an infinite debt—to the people whose coming into history we have now, briefly, to relate.

As early as before 2000 B.C., the islands of the Eastern Mediterranean, together with certain parts of the mainland of Greece, were the home of a vigorous sea-faring people, possessing remarkable artistic talent. Their civilisation is now known by the name Minoan. Somewhere between 1200 and 1100 B.C. catastrophic disaster befel this race. Out of the immense grass-lands which stretch from the plains of Hungary in Europe eastward right across central Asia there issued a multitude of men, moving southward with their wives and families. The invaders swept down into Thessaly and Greece, filling the mainland and pressing onwards across the sea to the Ægean Isles, massacring or enslaving the Minoan inhabitants. But if the newcomers at first brought ruin to a more highly developed race, they had their own virtues. They carried with them a fresh vigour, like a breeze from the north. Hardy and simple, they were not rude savages; they had learnt the use of wheeled vehicles, they had tamed the horse, and above all they possessed, as individuals, a certain sturdy independence and an uncommon open-mindedness. Fortunately, the older population was not extinguished; large numbers survived as slaves, and from these in time the " horse-tamers "—as the conquerors loved to style themselves—learnt for themselves the secrets of the Minoan arts and crafts. With astonishing rapidity they were to improve upon their teachers.

Owing to the mountainous character of Greece and the indentations of its coast, the invaders were split into many separate communities, each easily controlling the small plains and valleys in the immediate neighbourhood, but finding it difficult, if not unnatural, to extend its rule beyond the mountain passes. For defensive purposes the members of these small groups naturally tended to inhabit a single fortified town, which became the all-absorbing centre of the tiny state; the town being, as it were, a stronghold and its territories a garden round it. Thus there came into existence what is known as " the Greek City-State." Like the Arabian tribes who also had passed from nomadism to settled life, each of these new communities fell for a time under some form of despotic government, now the rule of one man, a King or " Tyrant," now of a clique of rich and powerful persons, an Aristocracy. But there was something in the character of the Greeks which proved intolerant of such organisation, and, unlike the Arabians, they passed beyond that experience and developed a novel and, as events were to prove, an invaluable social system to which they gave the name " Democracy." The foundation principle of the democratic state lay in the conviction that every adult free-born citizen, being an integral part of the state, contributing to its prosperity and security, was entitled to a share in its government. Slaves were outside the franchise, but all others whether base-born or noble, rich or poor, clever or stupid, were citizens—each with a vote and a voice in the direction of public policy, internal and external. To this citizen-body belonged the power of electing from among themselves officers, both civil magistrates and military commanders, to whom administration was *temporarily* entrusted, and who were ultimately responsible for their actions to the citizen-body. Under happy fortune this system was adopted as the constitution of society in the leading Greek cities. Mark the mental and moral qualities thereby engendered. In the first place men became exhilaratingly conscious that they possessed individual freedom combined with corporate strength. Each citizen felt himself to be of political importance, an organic part of the state, entitled on the one hand to a share in its glory and

Iron Sharpeneth Iron

its privileges, and on the other responsible himself for the general welfare. How can the epoch-making importance of this fact adequately be emphasised ? In primitive patriarchal society the individual had been free but only within the narrow limits imposed by the rigidity of custom and the bare simplicity of rudimentary life. And civilised town-life of the Eastern type, as we have seen, was complex and magnificent in many ways, but nevertheless had missed the secret of advancing freedom. Intellectually it hated novelties. Politically it made men either kings or the slaves of kings, giving them either too great importance or none at all. Hence the larger the Eastern town, the more powerful and extensive the State, the less was the mass of the people personally concerned in their civil or military affairs. "Freedom" in an Eastern city meant anarchy. The Greeks succeeded in bringing freedom and civilisation into organic union. So far from choking liberty, the connection of each Greek citizen with his city was perceived to be the very cause of the freedom he enjoyed, the means by which his privileges were multiplied and secured. Hence the greater the organisation of society the greater the opportunities each citizen acquired for the development of personal talent and inclination. It is assuredly no exaggeration to describe such an achievement as "epoch-making."

Along with political freedom went mental freedom. Interchange of opinion took place easily and continually between all grades of the free community. The general obligation to promote the social, commercial, and military well-being of the state stimulated discussion and gave to debate the piquancy and solemnity of serious issues. A Greek might be poor, but he could hold up his head with the richest as a member of the citizen army and the citizen electorate ; and in the citizen assembly he need not be a gray-beard to be reckoned wise. Mental ability became the test of worth, and the benumbing tyranny of tradition was overthrown; at least its unquestioned rule was at an end. Custom must henceforth submit to criticism and seek to justify itself. Enterprise, enquiry, innovation became the order of the day. It was the emancipation of the human intelligence.

Moreover, since the rough work of society was performed by the slave population, Greek citizens found much leisure at their disposal. Herein was obviously a danger, but also an opportunity; and fortunately the genius of the people was not found wanting, so that, in the early days the Greeks turned their leisure to good purpose, physical and intellectual. Part of their leisure was devoted to physical exercises, running, wrestling, boxing, throwing the *discus*, chariot-racing; and in the healthful competition of these games in stadium and hippodrome they found continual pleasure. But their ardour for mental exercise was even keener. They began to think with restless energy and with brilliant results; men of genius, poets, historians, philosophers, and artists, by their matchless achievements raised the intellectual interests of their contemporaries to an extraordinary extent. In general, the Greeks acquired a wonderful feeling for proportion and natural rhythmic beauty. "Nothing in excess" became their motto, but what was meant thereby was no timid mediocrity, but an avoidance of extreme, wherever the extreme was grotesque or foolish. Men sought an equipoise of perfection, and felt infinite delight in the increasing measure of their success. Within a few hundred years the Greeks had produced masterpieces of art and literature which few nations have been able even to rival, none to surpass.

In short, three characteristics distinguished Greek or Hellenic civilisation: First, *Emulation*. Men vied one with another, vied with their own past efforts. They sought to

Iron Sharpeneth Iron

excel and achieved excellence. Second, *Intellectualism*. The critical faculties of the mind were increasingly released from the trammels of tradition. Reason became the touchstone of life in all its aspects; and thus, just as in our own age, the immense destructive and constructive energies of the free intelligence were ceaselessly set to work. Third, *Patriotism*. This third quality calls for fuller comment, for it was the main source of Greek morality. Greek religion contributed something to the growth of moral principles, but less than one might imagine. Its ethical interest for the most part was limited to inculcating the fear lest Divine vengeance should follow *gross* outrage of the normal decencies of life. Doubtless also the artistic sense fostered love of the good, since, as a rule, what is wicked appears to men to be ugly; yet the fruits from this source also were not much to boast of. But from the intense patriotism fostered by the City-States came great moral consequences. The interests of the State claimed men's allegiance, and the claim was nobly answered. Not only great-hearted leaders but also masses of ordinary men were willing to set the public weal above their individual prosperity or security. In striving to be noble citizens men became noble men. Thousands and thousands were conscious that they could not live unto themselves—without shame. Altruism was a searching reality in their lives, and its burdens were loyally, even gladly, accepted. Men were very zealous for their city, longing for its honour and renown, ready to toil for it, to face hardship and peril on its behalf, and for its safety to die unflinchingly. And no less measure of sacrifice was all too frequently required from the citizens of these ambitious and war-like little States. Let their own words tell how they met the supreme call : " Through these men's valour, the smoke of the burning of wide-floored Tegea went not up to heaven, who chose to leave the city glad and free to their children, and themselves to die in the forefront of the battle."[1] Or, best of all, take Simonides' epitaph on the Athenians fallen at Plataea :—

> " If to die nobly is the chief part of excellence,
> To us of all men Fortune gave this lot ;
> For hastening to set a crown of freedom on all Hellas,
> We lie possessed of praise that grows not old."

Surely no one can fail to hear in those words and in the spirit of this Greek life the music of familiar things, things which we have taken to our heart. That is because the thoughts of Hellas are the source from which our own intellectual and social ideas have been derived.

But Hellenic life was not sunshine without shadow. For all its power and brilliance Greek society was exposed to many perils and was guilty of serious mistakes. These, however, we have here no need to discuss in full. It is enough to note that, when-and-where-soever the necessity for ardent patriotism was absent or unfelt the Greek conception of life lacked adequate moral incentive, and sinister conditions which were a very black shadow in a fair world could and did arise. Much might also be said regarding the jealousies of the petty cities, whence came warfare constant, embittered, and suicidal. Nevertheless it remains absolutely true, that compared with the stagnation of Eastern civilisation, Hellenism was life and health. Judge from one token, the epitaphs just quoted. Men could not write like that in Palestine or Babylon, because they never died for such a cause.

In the years between 359 and 338 B.C. the independent Greek cities were all forced to admit the suzerainty, first of Philip II., king of Macedon, and, after his assassination in 336, of his son Alexander, who was to be remembered throughout history as Alexander the Great. The humiliation was not in any way a crushing blow to the spirit of

[1] Simonides (MacKail's translation, *Greek Anthology*, pp. 149, 151.)

Iron Sharpeneth Iron

Greece. To the yoke of Philip and Alexander the city-states could submit with a good grace, for the Macedonians were of the same ancestry as the Greeks, and for years had been to all intents and purposes a part of the Greek world ; and Alexander was wholly Hellenic in his upbringing and his ideas. Had he not been educated by the great philosopher, Aristotle ? In 334 B.C., the young king organised an army of Macedonians and Greeks and set forth to make a grand assault upon the nations of the East : a stupendous task, but the enterprise appealed to the Greeks as a poetic requital of the awful peril one hundred and fifty years before when Xerxes of Persia at the head of a horde of Orientals had crossed to Greece and almost blotted out its rising life. If the task was colossal and the force to achieve it tiny, the results staggered the imagination of the world. The huge Persian Empire crumbled at the touch of Greek military prowess, directed by the genius of Alexander. In three years the young Macedonian had become absolute master of Western Asia Minor, of Egypt, Syria, Babylonia, and Persia. In 326 B.C. he pushed his conquests to the Punjab, and in 325 he died; but *Hellenism did not die with him*. The East had seen many conquerors rise and sweep through its lands in triumph, and had continued to dream its long dreams. But the military achievements of Alexander were only the beginning of his work. What stirred the East to its depths was the fascination of the ideas that had accompanied him and that he deliberately sought to establish among the conquered peoples ; with what measure of success it now remains to consider.

3. A stormy period followed Alexander's death. Eventually his Eastern dominions were divided between two of his generals ; Ptolemy, who took possession of Egypt, and Seleucus, who became ruler of Syria and the Mesopotamian territories. Happily it is not necessary to follow the confused struggles that ensued between them and their

successors — struggles in which Palestine, situated between the rival kingdoms, was continually involved. The point to be observed is that both Ptolemy and Seleucus were Hellenes, as also were most of their leading men, and both they and their successors prosecuted, with all possible energy, Alexander's policy, the Hellenising of the East. Consider the forces directed to the attainment of that object.

The powerful influences of the royal courts in Egypt and Syria saw to it that throughout the length and breadth of their kingdoms places of honour were reserved for Greeks and such Orientals as might show themselves capable of appreciating and adopting Hellenic culture. To be a Greek, if not by race, then by imitation, became the only avenue to wealth or fame or royal favour.

Alexander, however, had seen that if Hellenism was permanently to subdue and recreate the East it must touch not only the interests of such as are clothed in soft raiment and in kings' courts live delicately, it must be made a reality daily affecting the life of common folk; and with the foresight of genius he himself pointed the way to secure that end. Realising the organic connection between the Greek ideals and the Greek city, he established at strategic points of his Empire new cities planned on the Hellenic model. The Ptolemaic and Seleucid kings persevered in this scheme. New cities of the Grecian type were founded in their realms, and the old towns were conformed to the new order of things so far as might be. In all important centres the essential accompaniments of Hellenic life were introduced: new political organisation for the election of magistrates, and buildings to meet the system; a hall for the Senate, shady pillared galleries where the free citizens might gather to lounge and talk, baths and gymnasia, a stadium and a hippodrome for the games, and for the drama a theatre. With such interests and amusements the imagination of

Iron Sharpeneth Iron

the common folk was stirred and pleased. The youth of the cities became enthusiastic for the gaieties and glories of the competitive games. Guilds of athletes were formed and received the privilege of wearing a special dress, " a broad-brimmed hat, a fluttering cloak broached about the shoulders, and high laced boots."[1] In great public processions these young men marched as a special class, wearing crowns of gold, and bearing witness to the wealth and pride of their respective cities by the colours and rich embroideries of their attire. But staider folk than the young and fashionable were also caught in the wide-spread nets of Hellenism. The wealth of the Greek cities and the royal favour shown them attracted commerce, and sleepy Eastern merchants discovered that if they wished to do business they must conform to the prevailing tastes ; so that Greek became the language of the market-place as well as of the Court. Finally, the learning and skill of the East confessed its conqueror. Greek art and Greek literature, Greek science and philosophy made the older Eastern styles seem worthless in comparison. Within two centuries following the death of Alexander the near East had been transformed. Hellenism had cast its spell over the whole of life.

The period is one of profound interest for the study of humanity. On the one hand it did much to secure the perpetuation of the intellectual methods of the Greeks, which might have perished had they not been extended beyond the frontiers of the small Greek States in Europe ; and on the other hand it showed that the East can change. Human nature is not, as some would have us believe, divided for ever into irreconcilable sections. There are no unbridgeable gulfs between the Eastern and the Western mind. If the modern Westernising movements in China or India should fully succeed, they will but demonstrate anew what was proved long ago in Asia Minor during the three critical

[1] Bevan, *Jerusalem under the High Priests*, p. 35.

Studies in Life from Jewish Proverbs

centuries before Christ. The challenge these facts present to those who suppose that Christianity cannot become a universal faith is obvious. We must not attempt to give a detailed picture of Hellenism. But even these outlines are enough to show how thoroughly and dramatically the immemorial fashions of the East had been upset and new ambitions kindled, so that men must have felt as if they had been emancipated from the dead past and told to make trial of a new form of life, one that was already brilliant and delightful, but was most of all thrilling in its unknown possibilities. The peoples that walked in darkness thought they had seen a great light.

One fact, however, and that of prime importance, has been left out of count in this description of the situation. Hellenism in the East had a fatal deficiency; it lacked the keen patriotism that inspired the life of the old Greek cities. In Athens men had known that only by the maintenance of their best ideals could Athens lead the intellect of Greece, only by discipline and self-sacrifice could the foe be driven from Athenian fields, could Athens rule the seas, could Athens be free and Athens glorious. But citizens of some Hellenised city of Syria experienced no such sentiments. Their politics were urban not imperial, academic not matter of life and death. To be a captain in the armies of Ptolemy or Seleucus might be a convenient way of gaining a livelihood and might lead to fame, fortune and favour; but after all, to fight in those ranks was to fight for kings' glories, not for hearth and home. The ambitions of the petty states of Greece had had certain evil aspects; strifes, jealousies, envyings were ever present among them, bleeding the higher interests of their common civilisation. Nevertheless the need for passionate devotion to one's city had been the root of Hellenic virtue, and *that* not even Alexander's genius could transplant to Asiatic soil.

Moreover, even such faint assistance as Greek religion

Iron Sharpeneth Iron

gave to morality failed the Hellenism of the East. By Alexander's time the early conceptions of the gods had been riddled by criticism, and as yet neither philosophy nor mysticism had discovered for morality a basis intelligible and acceptable to ordinary men. The earnest spirits of the day were aware of the danger ahead. They foresaw that, if society continued on its present course unchecked, its moral bankruptcy must bring disaster. For not all the Greeks were eating, drinking, and making money: some were asking questions about life to which a *demoralised* Hellenism could give no satisfying answer. And the problem was more than merely intellectual. The perils and pains of actual life made the enigma a personal agony for many men, who saw that " they were being carried onward into a future of unknown possibilities, and whatever might lie on the other side of death, the possibilities on the hither side were disquieting enough. Even in our firmly ordered and peaceful society, hideous accidents may befall the individual, but in those days when the world showed only despotic monarchies and warring city-states, one must remember that slavery and torture were contingencies which no one could be sure that the future did not contain for him." In the old days it had been possible to appeal for succour to deities not wholly inhuman in their ways and thoughts. " If now that hope faded into an empty dream, man found himself left naked to fortune. With the mass of passionate desires and loves he carried in his heart, the unknown chances of the future meant ever-present fear."[1] The situation called for remedy. Hellenism itself evolved the Stoic philosophy as a possible solution for its urgent problems.[2]

[1] Bevan, *Stoics and Sceptics*, pp 25, 26.

[2] Stoicism whilst it offered the thinker immunity from the fears of life, was also adapted to the needs of the generality of men whom it sought to provide with principles for the stable and successful conduct of ordinary life. Bevan (op. cit.) points out that the

Studies in Life from Jewish Proverbs

Our contention is that in their own sphere and in their own fashion the Jewish proverbs, as used at this period by the Wise in Jerusalem, were, like Stoicism, an answer to the moral instability which contemporary Hellenism had spread abroad.

But even if Hellenism could have entered Syria in its purest form, it would have needed all its nobility to overcome the vices ingrained in the East. When it came to the task with faith in the high gods shaken and falling, with the spur of patriotism left behind in Greece, no wonder that the ugly elements hitherto held in check in the city-states fed themselves fat amid the ancient evils of the Oriental world. Particularly in Syria did the baser tendencies of Hellenism run riot. Life there did indeed become richer, richer in iniquity. If facts have any meaning, then the history of Syria and Egypt in the Hellenic age cries aloud in witness of the futility of a civilisation, however brilliant, that lacks a basis of moral idealism: "Other foundation can no man lay than that which is laid." The fine culture of the Hellenised lands was dependent on the wrongs and miseries of countless slaves; the cities were filled with glittering, venal women; and the general population sank deeper and deeper in corruption, gluttony, and license. Even the games in Syria were made to pander to the base side of human nature; and, although ideally the cult of athletics might be an excellent thing, "in its actual embodiment it could show all degrees of degradation." Life in the Syrian towns became for the most part a studied gratification of the grosser senses. Here is the accusation of an eye-witness, a Syrian Greek named Poseidonius, who lived about

---

system shows signs of hasty construction, reflecting the urgency of the problems it sought to meet. Its strongly practical character is seen in the tendency to find expression in brief, pointed, *formulæ*, catch-words, and maxims, evidently designed to make its doctrines easy for the average man to comprehend The resemblance to Hebrew Wisdom-teaching is interesting and obvious.

Iron Sharpeneth Iron

100 B.C.: " The people of these cities are relieved by the fertility of their soil from a laborious struggle for existence. Life is a continual series of social festivities. Their gymnasiums they use as baths, where they anoint themselves with costly oils and myrrhs. In the public banqueting halls they practically live, filling themselves there for the better part of the day with rich foods and wines; much that they cannot eat they carry away home. They feast to the prevailing music of strings. The cities are filled from end to end with the noise of harp-playing."

And yet it was a great and wonderful age. Although the nobler qualities of the Greek cities could not be made to grow in the new soil, the genius of the Greek intellectual attitude to life was rescued from the bickerings and fatal factions of the little states and was successfully communicated to the larger world, to become in time the priceless heritage of Western civilisation. Rightly conceiving that the spiritual aspect of human life is the supreme thing, we are accustomed to divide history into the period before and the period after the birth of Christ; but were attention to be confined solely to the mental development of mankind, the dividing line would be found in the coming of the Hellenic methods of thought.

The bearing of these facts upon our subject is not far to seek. In face of the subtle influences that were transforming their environment how fared it with the Palestinian Jews? Jerusalem was sheltered by its outlying position from the full tide of Hellenism. Had it not been so, its special characteristics could scarcely have been preserved; it would have become as one of the cities of the coast. But if Jerusalem was not swept away by the flood, that does not imply that the rain of new ideas was not falling in its streets and markets. From 300 to 200 B.C. Palestine was controlled by the Ptolemaic Kings of Egypt, from 198 B.C. by the Syrian Seleucids. This change of authority imposed no

Studies in Life from Jewish Proverbs

check upon the progress and vigour of the Hellenistic movement. Greek cities sprang up throughout the land, and older towns were eager to adapt themselves to the new models. Shortly after the death of Alexander, Samaria and Ptolemais (Acco) had already become centres of Greek influence, and there was a group of Greek cities beyond Jordan. Imagine too how quickly and how effectively the ideas of the Jews in Jerusalem would be affected by intercourse with the flourishing colonies of their brethren now thoroughly at home in the great centres of Greek dominion in Egypt, Syria and Babylon. It is not surprising therefore to find a Greek writer about 250 B.C. observing that " many of the traditional ordinances of the Jews are losing their hold." And if any reader wishes further confirmation, he need only turn to the works of *Josephus,* and note the relish with which that writer tells the story of Joseph the son of Tobiah, nephew of the High-Priest, who by his insolent wit won favour at the Egyptian Court, and battened for a while on the extortionate taxes he wrung from the towns of southern Syria: a repulsive character but quite evidently a popular hero in the estimation of many of his Jewish contemporaries. Picture the coming and going of Greek traders in the bazaars of Jerusalem, and the journeying of Jewish merchants to and from the markets of the Hellenic cities. Consider what it meant that the immense mercantile centre of Alexandria, with its tempting opportunities to the acute and enterprising Jew, lay only a few days' journey to the south. In short, Hellenism was swiftly becoming the very atmosphere men breathed. Certainly its manifold allurements were only too visibly and temptingly displayed before the eyes of the young and ambitious in Jerusalem. And yet Hellenism had met its match in the strange city of Zión. Greek met Jew, and in the struggle the Wise-men of Israel played no insignificant part. For they marshalled and moulded their proverbs till they represented the Wisdom

Iron Sharpeneth Iron

of Israel set over against the worldly-wisdom[1] of Greece. They counselled a way of life which was *not* the seductive Greek way. They sturdily opposed another doctrine to the fashionable immorality of Hellenism with its overwhelming prestige and ostensible success. For several generations the attack of the new civilisation came by way of peaceful penetration, which was perhaps harder to resist than open enmity, since nobody could deny the good in Hellenism, its beauty, and its cleverness, if only it had been pure in heart. Later, as we shall see, the campaign was to be conducted with all the devices of reckless and inhuman violence. Hebraism against Hellenism! All Egypt, Syria, and Persia had made scarcely an effort to resist the spell of the new learning and the new ways. At first sight then how unequal the contest! A stiff moralism preaching against the pleasures of sin to hot-blooded, able, and ambitious men. A clique of obscurantists arrayed not against a kingdom or an empire but against a magnificent, world-conquering civilisation. The Jews maintain their ground ? Impossible! No, not wholly so; for this battle, like another which touches us more closely, was ultimately spiritual; and because the Jews held a conception of the nature and destiny of man deeper, truer, than even the Greeks had found, Hebraism in the end proved stronger than Hellenism with all its genius and all its works.

---

[1] We have to use the term "worldly-wisdom" and not "wisdom," because the Greeks also had their seekers after true wisdom at this period, as may be seen in the gnomic verses of Solon, Phocylides and Theognis, many of whose maxims, as well as the sayings of Stoic philosophers, might be quoted to show that Hellenism was not without the protest from within itself of noble souls. The contrast suggested above is therefore not one between Greek and Hebrew Wisdom-teaching, but between the Hebrew Wisdom and the *general* "unwisdom" of ordinary Hellenic life.

CHAPTER VI

A Sower went forth to Sow

LET us imagine two of the Wise-men meeting in the streets of Jerusalem and conversing. That is easier proposed than effected: bold words, to be followed by small performances. For the outlines of ancient Jerusalem are none too clear, and again in what tongue shall our Wise-men converse? In ancient Hebrew or in modern English? Modern English from their lips will seem incongruous, and Hebrew is not so widely known as it deserves. Before we can make so much as a beginning we are compelled to compromise: let them talk in Hebraic English. But the difficulties need not discourage us overmuch, for in this case even a half-done task will be worth the doing, and there are some circumstances in our favour. The topography of old Jerusalem may be uncertain, but our knowledge of the influences, events and tendencies of the period in question is considerable. Therefore although the conversation between the Wise-men must be imaginary, it need not be fancy-free. We can make them say such things as can be inferred from the historical situation, and the talk can be so directed as to help our immediate purpose, discovering what were the dominant fears and ambitions of the Wise. Moreover, however imperfectly this aim be realised, the picture can hardly fail to help us across the gulf which divides the abstract or general conception from the concrete or particular embodiment, a matter of vital importance for the comprehension of these Jewish proverbs. It is not sufficient to imagine the Wise as a class. Doubtless most Wise-men

A Sower went forth to Sow

conformed to a type, and they were a class in the community in that they shared a general attitude towards life; but this bond of union was loose enough to leave room for great variety of interest, beliefs, and moral qualities. And just this diversity within the unity is the point on which stress should be laid; for it explains the individualism of the Jewish proverbs, and is the secret of their broad humanity.

It is the month of June in the year 203 B.C. Ptolemy Philopator, the ruler of Egypt, has died the previous year, and is succeeded on the throne by Ptolemy Epiphanes, a child of four years old. The situation points to the renewal of warfare between the great Empires. Embarrassed by the weakness of its young king, Egypt is in obvious danger from the restless ambition both of Philip of Macedonia and of Antiochus III of Syria. But although the East is uneasy, the storm has not yet broken. Palestine is still controlled by the Egyptians, and a garrison of Ptolemy's soldiers lives at ease in the citadel of Jerusalem. Zion is at peace; her harvests of barley and wheat have been gathered in; the first-ripe figs have fallen and already are on sale in the markets, and there is prospect of a plentiful later crop. Imagine that we are watching the city, as the day is about to break. The last hour of the night is ending. Low down in the Eastern sky a faint tinge of blue appears, with shades of purple and pink above it, fading upwards into the dark of the night sky overhead. Soon the horizon flushes into red, changing swiftly to deep yellow as the first rays of the sun rise over the hills.[1]

The guard of the Levites on duty at the Temple stands watching for the dawn, and as soon as the sunlight touches Hebron, just visible to the south, they raise a shout, heralding the day and summoning the people to hasten

[1] See G. A. Smith, *Jerusalem*, vol. i., ch. i., where a beautiful description of night and dawn in Jerusalem may be found.

to the celebration of the morning sacrifice.[1] From the citadel the trumpets of the soldiers take up the sound and call the garrison from sleep. Soon the whole city is astir. Day has begun, and its hours are precious before the sun grows hot beyond endurance. The gates open, and first the cattle-dealers and money-changers begin to pass along the narrow lanes, hurrying ahead of the people to the Temple-court. Shopmen appear and busy themselves preparing their booths in the bazaars. From his house in one of the narrow streets a dignified man of rather more than middle age, Judah ben Zechariah, comes out and, turning in the direction of the Temple mingles, with the stream of worshippers who purpose to be present at the offering of the sacrifice. Let us keep him in sight. When the ceremony at the temple is ended, he makes his way without haste through the tangle of streets towards the Northern wall and the Fish gate. There in the open space near the gate, just inside the city, he stops, and stands watching the passers by. A company of Tyrians, pagans all of them, files in through the gate, bringing fish for Jerusalem from the Phoenician markets. They are followed by a long caravan of forty or fifty mules laden with wheat from the north, and their drivers, like the Tyrians, are also pagan. Judah is Hebrew of the Hebrews, and the sight does not please him. After a while as he stands there a friend approaches and gives him greeting—Joseph ben Abijah, one who, like Judah, had reputation as a Wise-man. " Peace be to thee, Judah." " And may Jehovah bless thee, my brother," answered Judah, " and may He increase thee to a multitude ; for truly there be few this day in Israel such as thou, who keepest faith before God and before men. Behold now this long time stand I here, Joseph, to see them that pass by, and I swear unto thee that for one man of Israel there be nine from the ends of the earth, worshippers of

[1] Mishna, *Yoma*, 3 1

A Sower went forth to Sow

strange gods. Men call this city Zion; but where are Zion's children? From end to end the streets are full of these Gentiles. Moreover, look yonder!" (a company of the garrison came swinging down to change guard at the Gate)—"these soldiers of Ptolemy! Mark well their heathen insolence, their pride and their contempt for us. Are we not the bondservants of Egypt, even as our fathers were? I tell thee, Joseph, it is not well with Israel."

"Nay! thou art over-anxious, Judah. The land is at peace. The harvests are good, trade prospers and extends; we and our wives and our children dwell in safety. None hinders us in our worship. Why then take so sore to heart these Gentiles? *They* are the slaves, who in their folly worship dumb and senseless images. Is not Israel free in her God? Moreover—a word in thine ear—how thinkest thou, Judah? Will Ptolemy much longer lord it over us in Zion? Or are his times come near to an end?"

"Hush! see that none hear thee. I also think his day is at an end. But for what then shall we look? For the dreams of the prophets? For the Day of the Lord? Ah, would that the Lord might rend the heavens and come down, but I, for one, do not look for these things to come to pass at this time, Joseph. And except the Lord deliver us wherein shall we hope? Nay, Zion, is still far from salvation. We shall change the bondage of Egypt for the yoke of Syria, and her little finger will be thicker than the loins of Egypt. Antiochus is ten times more Greek than Ptolemy. Verily, the whole world becometh Greek. Traders and talkers, how they throng in our streets and multiply in our midst! And whether they be rich and noble or poor and the servant of servants, behold how they despise us and make mock of us, the people of the one true God! And how with their vainglory and their wicked wisdom—for, as the Lord liveth, 'tis not the wisdom of God —they do bewitch fools and entice them away. Thou

Studies in Life from Jewish Proverbs

sayest, 'Israel is free in its God'; but I say 'How long shall God find faith in Israel?' If then Ptolemy be cast down and Antiochus be lifted up over us, wherein is our advantage? How wilt thou save this people from following wholly after the thoughts and customs of the Greeks? Again, thou speakest of peace and good harvests, but how long shall peace and prosperity be permitted us? If that whereof we speak should come to pass, it shall not be without war and desolation. Who knows but that Jerusalem shall soon be a besieged and captured city? As for the Day of the Lord, the prophet hath said 'The Lord will hasten it in His time' and his word is good; but alas! I fear that ours is better: *Hope deferred maketh the heart sick.*"

Said his friend, "I also—thou knowest it, Judah—am not of the dreamers, and know well that they who in our days see visions are prophets in name and not in truth. And the true prophets did not live for ever. Nevertheless their word liveth; and have not we that are Wise learnt from them that fear of Jehovah which is to turn from evil and do good, so that in measure their mantle is fallen upon us and we are become their successors, and according to their commandments so we teach? Yea, I say that their word *hath* overtaken this people, not for evil but for good; since of all the Jews who is there that doth not from the heart know that the Lord our God is one God, and that the gods of the heathen are nought and their images wood and stone? Wherefore, Judah, I fear not the Greeks so much as thou. For if a Jew from among us go forth unto them and learn their skill and follow their fashions, yet he will not reverence their gods. Moreover, remember, Judah, those that fight for us in the strife. If God hath not raised up a prophet in Israel these many years, are not the Priests and Levites become a strong tower of defence? In all their interpretation of the Law of Moses, they do well: for they seek to establish justice and mercy between a man

A Sower went forth to Sow

and his brethren, and to confirm the fear of Jehovah's Name. It is written, *The Law of the Lord is perfect, making clean the heart*; and these men love its statutes wholly. Thou dost not think that *they* will become Greeks?"

"Not all of them, Joseph; yet of the great priests many are evil. They live for place and power, not for the pure service of their God, and if the day come when it shall profit them these would surpass the Greeks in the fashions of the Greeks. But concerning the Levites and the Scribes thou sayest right; for they truly have set their hearts upon their work: albeit zeal for the Law will not save Israel. If only the ritual be observed and the services in the Temple maintained, if the feasts be duly kept, they deem all things are well. They would have all men more Levite than themselves. But what answer is that to the young who crave for fortune, favour, and fulness of pleasures like the unbridled heathen? Some it may satisfy, but thou knowest that more turn empty away; and all of them understand that the Greeks will feed their desires full. Come now: tell me, I pray thee: this very year how many are gone hence to seek fortune in the markets of Ptolemais? How many to the court of Antiochus, aye! from the noblest of our families? How many to be made captains in his armies and in Ptolemy's? Perchance it is well for thee, Joseph, whose son is a scribe well spoken of and one day will be counted a Wiseman and a fearer of God even as thou, his father, art: but my son, my son, is in Alexandria, though I besought him with tears that he would not go."

"Judah, I verily knew that it was for this cause thine heart was sad. Nevertheless I would comfort thee, my friend. Hear now my words. They are not all lost to Zion that are gone forth from Zion's gates. Thou knowest there is no evil in thy son. Take heart. Are not the families of our people there in Egypt many and prosperous? Thy son will be a loyal Jew in Egypt, not forsaking his

Studies in Life from Jewish Proverbs

father's faith. I am persuaded he will send his tribute to the Temple when the time comes round. Aye! and thine eye shall see him again ere long returning to keep the feast at Jerusalem and to make glad thine heart. My brother, hear thou the thought which the Lord hath given me concerning this thing. It is written that all flesh shall come to worship before the Lord in His holy hill; but how shall this thing come to pass? They chant in the Temple of His outstretched arm and His mighty acts. What if the stretching out of His arm is in the going forth of these His children unto the ends of the earth; seest thou not how that already praise is offered to His Name in many lands, and His glory is exalted among the heathen? In the Temple they sigh for the day when all peoples shall come crouching to Zion; but what if thy son, and others even as he, have gone to prepare the way of the Lord and to make straight His paths, and in Alexandria, Babylon, and Antioch are beginning the victory of our God, a victory which shall be (as saith Zechariah) '*not by might, nor by power, but by my Spirit,' saith the Lord?* So shall thy son's going be turned to God's glory, and perchance it hath happened in accordance with His will. Saith not Isaiah that *His ways are not our ways, nor His thoughts as our thoughts?* And when thou sayest of the priests and scribes that all their care is for the Law and the Temple, and that they know not how to speak unto the heart of these young men, in truth thy reproach is just. But herein is our work. *We* have the answer for this need in Israel. Have we not counsel for success in life *with* allegiance to our God; so that our words are from the Lord, though we praise not the Law daily neither make mention of the prophet's hopes? If then we be found faithful and our task well done, none in Israel shall reckon that Wisdom is of the Greeks only, but rather that their Wisdom is found folly in the latter end. Honour, long life, and riches are in our words and they

A Sower went forth to Sow

that hearken unto us shall find them and yet shall not depart from justice nor hate mercy. He that heareth our words and learneth our Wisdom shall even dwell with the Greeks and be wiser than they, being delivered from the snares of their iniquities and the vanity of their faiths. So shall it be with thy son, my brother. He will not forget thy instruction. And like him there shall be many who, though they go forth from Jerusalem, will yet give diligent heed unto our precepts, and with them shall go Wisdom to be a guide unto their feet that they shall not stumble. Yea, even of those that in Zion seem to heed us not, some perchance shall remember in a distant land, and so be saved from falling. But, come, thou knowest this even as I, though sorrow for a moment had hidden it from thine eyes. With the blessing of God we do not labour in vain."

"Friend, thou comfortest well; and in my soul I know that these thy words are true, and that our work is of God, and that our children's children shall see the reward of all our labours. But as for this generation many there be that scorn and few that hear."

"Be our zeal the greater then!" responded Joseph, "What saith the prophet ?—*Precept on precept, line upon line*; and for us therefore ' Proverb on proverb.' "

The older man smiled at him gently, pleased by the words and spirit of his friend : " Thou art a true friend and wise counsellor, ben Abijah. And now let us leave this place, and, if it seem good to thee, let us pass through the streets and take note of them that buy and sell; for the heat is not yet upon us and the markets are full this day. Comest thou with me ? "

" I come gladly. Thou shalt see—we shall find one here, one there, that hath need of our wisdom; and perhaps to-day we shall even catch the ear of the multitude, and many will give heed both to hear and to receive our teaching."

CHAPTER VII

Men and Manners

STUDENTS of the Old Testament do not require to be told that the universalism of the *Book of Proverbs* is a remarkable fact. But even those whose knowledge of Jewish history is not exact, and who have not made a comparative study of the post-exilic writings, need have no difficulty in perceiving how strange it is, if they will give the briefest consideration to the following points. Just how free are these sayings from indications of the national aspirations or religious peculiarities of the Jews ? Never once in the whole *Book of Proverbs* is mention made of Israel or of any synonym for Israel ! Not a word is said of the nation's past history or present fears and hopes ; the word " prophet " never once occurs, although the influence of prophetic teaching is frequently manifest ; Priests, Levites, Temple and even Jerusalem are absolutely ignored ; " sacrifice " is mentioned four times in disparagement ; *To do justice and judgement is more acceptable to the Lord than sacrifice* (Pr. 21^3; cp. 15^8; 17$^{1(mg)}$; 21^{27}) : and " offerings " once incidentally : *I have peaceofferings with me* (Pr. 7^{14}) Even the divinely appointed Law is passed silently by ; it is neither commended nor condemned. True, the word " law " is often found in *Proverbs*, but the law which men are there bidden to observe is not the precepts, ritual or moral, of the great Pentateuch, not the Law of Moses, but the doctrine laid down by the Sage and his *confrères* ! Ben Sirach differs from the Sages represented in *Proverbs* to this extent that once or twice he identifies the Law of

Men and Manners

Moses with the Divine Wisdom, and asserts that Wisdom has chosen Zion for her resting-place.[1] Otherwise his book has precisely the same broadly humanistic and supernational character.

Clearly one need not be an expert in Jewish history to see that all this is startling; but it seems little less than astounding as soon as it is brought into comparison with the passionate patriotism and religious exclusiveness that characterise other books of the Old Testament, not only those that set forth the Law, but also such prophecies as *Isaiah* 40-66, or again the *Psalms*. For example, contrast the ecclesiastical version of Israel's history given in the Books of *Chronicles, Ezra, Nehemiah*, which in its present form is the work of a Levite of Jerusalem writing about 350-250 B.C., *i.e.*, at the very period of this Wisdom preaching. A glance will show that the narrative of the Chronicler is consistently intended to set forth the praises and virtues of the holy city, Jerusalem, and its inhabitants, the true " Israel." From first to last his work burns with national devotion, and the events of history are by him so related as to make prominent the honours due to the divine Law of Moses, wherein he sees the nation's eternal hope and sure defence. Greater contrast there could scarcely be. The seeming indifference of *Proverbs* and Ben Sirach would be explained if the Sages had been irreligious or mere worldly-wise men, contemptuous of altruistic, national sentiment. But their doctrine is in no way anti-national: there is absolutely no whisper of polemic against Judaism or even depreciation of its special tenets. Neither were they irreligious; that is quite certain. Although on the surface there is no warm glow of religious zeal, again and again " the fear of Jehovah," said they,

[1] See p. 174 and 198. Of the *Book of Proverbs* Toy remarks that " if for the name Jehovah we substitute ' God,' there is not a paragraph or a sentence which would not be as suitable for any other people as for Israel " (*Proverbs*, p. xxi.)

Studies in Life from Jewish Proverbs

" is the foundation of Wisdom." The Sages, at least the majority of them, were respectable, earnest, and God-fearing Jews. It seems to the present writer psychologically incredible to suppose that such persons in Jerusalem of 300-200 B.C. were, in their heart of hearts, unmoved by the extraordinary distinctive sentiments of their race. Why then the apparent apathy shown in their proverbs?

It is true that a taste for aphoristic ethical teaching was manifesting itself at this period in various countries besides Judæa, and that such moralistic teaching always tends to be cosmopolitan, but we find therein no adequate explanation of the astonishing facts just mentioned. It is more to the point to follow up a hint suggested by the conversation of the two Wise-men depicted in the preceding chapter. Hellenism seemed to be in the ascendant, as no observant person in Jerusalem of the third century could fail to perceive; equally, no sober-minded pietist of the old school could be blind to its demoralising tendencies, and no patriot fail to dread its disintegrating effect on Judaism. How to encounter the insidious and attractive force that threatened the overthrow not only of Jewish nationality but of Jewish virtue: that was the problem for every loyal Jew. The Priests and Levites of the Law of Moses were fighting the foe in one way. The Wise had chanced on another weapon for the fray. In the old, common-sense maxims of their fathers, which being rooted in Israel's religious faith and enriched by the ethical idealism of the great prophets presented a general moral standard, or at least a moral ardour, clearly superior to the normal tone of the neighbouring Hellenic cities, the Wise perceived they had an instrument for countering the peril on its more mundane side. Their duty was to teach men that in order to get on in life it was not necessary, even in the clamorous confident Hellenic atmosphere, to fling morality overboard and laugh at the fear of Jehovah. To suppose that all, or even the

Men and Manners

majority, of the Wise-men consciously formulated this point of view is of course not essential: many of them may have been actuated by an instinctive rather than a reasoned antagonism to the spirit of the age. The point is that, viewing the teaching of wisdom on the one part and the circumstances of the period on the other, this is the *rôle* the Wise in actual fact fulfilled. Now it is evident that the nature of the work presented to them was such as to make the advocacy of nationalism or even of the duty of conformity to the Law somewhat irrelevant for them. It was for others to enjoin these things. The Wise kept to their own path. Broad-minded yet loyal Jews, they were engaged on a task that happened to be naturally independent of the ritual injunctions of the Law and of any immediate political concerns.[1] It was their business to urge morality, and to be very practical in so doing; to tell men how to get on and not be blackguards; to persuade men that the wages of sin is not victory but death—a noble task, however matter-of-fact the means they used for its achievement.

We believe, then, that the universalism of these proverbs is to be explained chiefly as the mark of the Wise-men's ability to keep to the point, not as evidence either of lack of patriotism or of indifference to the national faith. They were speaking to the heart on the common things of daily life that men of all races necessarily share with one another. Consequently—perhaps without their knowing or intending it—what they said transcended time and country. It was none the less work for their people. As we hope to show later, there is good reason to believe that the plain, common-sense morality of the Wise preserved for Judaism the res-

[1] The Jews seem to have had an unusual aptitude for confining themselves to particular points of view Mark to what an extent the Prophets ignore the Priests, and the Priests the Prophets. This makes it less surprising to find that the Proverbialists should ignore both.

pect and affection of many ordinary men, whom the Levites, with all their enthusiasm for the specific forms of the national worship, would have lost. Religion has no right to despise or overlook even the least of its advocates. There was One who said, "He that is not against us is on our part."

Reviewing the argument of these pages and the suggestions of the last chapter, we conclude that, whilst the ranks of the Wise were wide enough to include men of diverse character and outlook, they must be credited with having had a definite standpoint and a method of their own well suited to the circumstances of their times.

Let us now turn our attention from the Wise themselves to the men they observed. Let us walk with Judah and Joseph through the busy streets, and take our stand with them in the open spaces by the city-gates, and overhear their comments on the scenes of human intercourse which met their eyes. Let us, as it were, join some group that has gathered round to enjoy their talk, to applaud their maxims and their morals, to laugh as the characteristics of this man or of that are hit off in some shrewd epigram, and perhaps— —if need be—to take to heart the lesson.

In the popular talk there were doubtless many sayings concerning the habits of the various craftsmen and traders —the potter, the sandal-maker, and so forth—but (perhaps because the purpose of the Wise was so broadly humanistic in its outlook) such specialistic sayings are rare in the literature the Sages have left us. A few, however, do occur in which men are pictured from the standpoint of their external relationships, and with these we may conveniently begin.

First, then, an observation so faithful to human nature that it has never lost its spice and is appropriate in all countries, although it must always have had peculiar

Men and Manners

pungency in the deceitful, haggling, Eastern marts. Behold the bargain-hunter drawn to the life:

"It is nought, it is nought," saith the buyer;
But when he is gone on his way then he boasteth (Pr. 20^{14}).

Not a man in old Jerusalem but must have felt the dry humour and the accusing truth. But here is the other side of the transaction:

A merchant shall hardly keep himself from doing wrong,
And a huckster shall not be acquitted of sin.
Many have transgressed for the sake of gain,
And the fortune-hunter requires a blind eye.
As a nail will stick fast between the joinings of stones,
So will sin thrust in between buying and selling (E. 26^{29}-27^{2}).

Six of one and half a dozen of the other, but perhaps neither buyer nor seller were such rogues as they are painted! Let us allow a discount for the epigram.

Of the man in debt, a problem for society in all periods, the Sages said plainly but sufficiently:

The rich man lords it over the poor,
And the borrower is the lender's slave (Pr. 22^{7}).

Ben Sirach, however, was much more graphic; says he,

Many have treated a loan as a windfall,
And have been a plague to those that helped them.
Till the loan is lent, he will kiss a man's hand,
And for his neighbour's money will speak right humbly;
But when payment falls due, he prolongs the days,
And girds and grumbles and says, "Hard times" (E. 29^{4,5}).

Support for Ben Sirach's description might still be obtained.

The rendering of assistance to unfortunate members of the community has always been a prominent and admirable feature of Jewish society, and quotations to be given

Studies in Life from Jewish Proverbs

later on will bear witness to the esteem in which the Sages held the practice of charity. But the alms-giving was not wide enough, or else not deep enough or (it may be) not wise enough—as our own is not yet—to succour the lowest *stratum* of society. Remember Lazarus at the rich man's gate: apparently there were such as he in Ben Sirach's time, whether brought low by misfortune or by fault:

> *My son, lead not a beggar's life;*
> *It is better to die than to beg.*
> *A man that looketh unto the table of another,*
> *His life is not to be counted life* (E. 40^{28-29}).

In E. 38, Ben Sirach discusses an ancient and unsettled controversy—subject, the doctor. As he devotes half a chapter to the matter, we may reasonably assign it a paragraph.

It would seem that in those days the medical profession was under a slight cloud. Some people (and for these we have no mercy: they were doubtless prescribing for others, not for themselves) were of opinion that all sorts of healing were an invention of iniquity and an attempt to thwart God's will. Ben Sirach enters a healthy-minded protest against these fanatical obscurantists, insisting on the healing properties of plants: *Was not water made sweet with wood to acquaint every man of God's power?* (E. 38^5); an allusion to *Exod.* 15^{25}). More damaging is the unspoken but obvious implication of the sober-minded Chronicler when he records concerning King Asa that *in the thirty and ninth year of his reign Asa was diseased in his feet; his disease was exceeding great; yet in his disease he sought not to the Lord, but to the physicians. And Asa . . . died in the one and fortieth year of his reign* (2 *Chron.* 16^{12}). But to this the physician may make a weighty answer. Until later times than Asa's it seems possible that orthodox medical practice was in the hands of the priestly classes, and therefore it may be

Men and Manners

suspected that Asa is censured for having committed the unpardonable wickedness of daring to call in one of the non-priestly practitioners, dealers in herbs and incantations, outsiders, quacks, charlatans, impostors all of them. But unfortunately, whatever the rights and wrongs of Asa's case, it must be admitted that the profession did not wholly succeed in quelling the doubts about its merits. *Physician, heal thyself*—so ran the proverb in our Lord's time (*Luke* 4^{23}), and is it not written of a certain poor woman that *she had suffered many things of many physicians, and had spent all that she had, and was nothing better, but rather worse* (*Mark* 5^{26}) ? Moreover, reluctantly, we have to notice that the *Mishna*, still later, gives utterance to the disconcerting opinion that *the best of physicians is deserving of Gehenna* (*Kidd*, 4^{14}). Well, well, it is a vexed question. With relief let us turn, in conclusion, to Ben Sirach's altogether cheerier view. *The Lord*, says he, *created medicines out of the earth, and a prudent man will not despise them. Wherefore, honour a physician as thou needest him with the honours due; for verily the Lord hath created him. For from the Most High cometh his healing, and from the king he shall receive a gift. . . . My son, in thy sickness be not negligent, but pray unto the Lord, and He shall heal thee. Put away wrong-doing, and order thine hands aright, and cleanse thine heart from all manner of sin. Offer a sweet offering and a memorial, set in order a fat offering, as best thou art able. Then give place to the physician, and let him not go from thee, for thou hast need of him. There is a time when in their hands is the issue for good : they also shall beseech the Lord that He may prosper them to find out what is wrong and to save the life* (E. 38$^{1-15}$)—then, as the conclusion of the passage, in the Greek text come these words which read like a very doubtful compliment,

> *He that sinneth before his Maker—*
> *Let him fall into the hands of the physician.*

Studies in Life from Jewish Proverbs

But Ben Sirach must be acquitted of malice, for the Greek text turns out to be a mistranslation of the original Hebrew which fortunately has here been recovered; and all ends happily thus:

> *He that sinneth before his Maker*
> *Will behave himself proudly before a physician.*

Good doctrine! Sound therapeutics and sound theology are allies, not enemies.

Reference to the special trades may be few, but some of those few are memorable. Thus the only allusion in *Proverbs* to the unskilled labourer is one of the poignant sayings of the Book:

> *The labourer's appetite laboureth for him,*
> *For his mouth constrains him to toil* (Pr. 16^{26}):

Hunger! that unwearying goad of men, so beneficial to the race, so pitilessly cruel to the individual.

Ben Sirach gives us a glimpse of many men in some graphic verses—the ploughman, the cattle-driver, the engraver, the smith, the potter:

The wisdom of the scribe cometh by opportunity of leisure,
And he that hath little business shall become wise.
How shall he become wise that holdeth the plough,
That glorieth in the shaft of the goad,
That driveth oxen, and is busied in their labours,
And whose discourse is of the stock of bulls?
He will set his heart upon the turning of furrows,
And his wakefulness is to give his heifers their fodder.
So is every artificer and workmaster
That passeth his time by night as by day,
Cutting gravings of signets,
And his diligence is to make great variety:
He will set his heart to preserve likeness in his portraiture,
And will be wakeful to finish his work.

Men and Manners

So is the smith sitting by the anvil
And considering the unwrought iron ;
The vapour of the fire will waste his flesh,
And with the heat of the furnace will he contend ;
The noise of the hammer will be ever in his ear
And his eyes upon the pattern of the vessel :
He will set his heart upon perfecting his works,
And he will be wakeful to adorn them perfectly.
So is the potter sitting at his work,
And turning the wheel about with his feet ;
Who is alway anxiously set at his work,
And all his handicraft is by number ;
He will fashion the clay with his arm,
And bend its strength in front of his feet ;
He will apply his heart to finish the glazing,
And he will be wakeful to make clean the furnace.

All these put their trust in their hands,
And each becometh wise in his own work.
Without these shall not a city be inhabited
And wherever they sojourn they will not hunger.
They shall not be sought for in the council of the people,
And in the assembly they shall not mount up on high ;
They shall not sit on the seat of the judge,
Nor understand the covenant of judgement,
Neither shall they declare instruction and judgement,
And among them that speak proverbs they shall not be found.
But they will maintain the fabric of the world,
And in the handiwork of their craft is their prayer (E. 38^{24-34}).

The passage is so interesting an illustration of the attitude of the educated Jews towards manual labour that a digression is irresistible. Among the Greeks all humbler forms of labour were heartily despised. In ancient society so much of the rough work was performed by slaves that the fortunate classes could and, as a rule, did find occupation in military, political, commercial, and literary or artistic affairs. Even the farmer was reckoned of small account, because, despite the honest worth of his occupation, his busy life and practical interests denied him the intellectual leisure of the town population. The Romans had certain incidents in their historical traditions that gave to agriculture a measure of honour, at least in theory. Otherwise their standpoint was much the same as that of the Greeks. But the Jews maintained a more generous and a very sensible attitude, as is exemplified by this quotation from Ben Sirach. They recognised the limitations imposed by hard toil, but at the same time they saw that it had an essential part to play in the economy of the whole, and therefore they freely acknowledged its merits:

Hate not laborious work,
For toil hath been appointed of God (E. 7^{15}).

Nevertheless Ben Sirach is well pleased that God had not made him a farmer or a smith. It is evident that he did not deem the art of the craftsman compatible with learning; and, since he loved his scribe's life, his satisfaction at having full leisure to prosecute the search for Wisdom is very human and pardonable. All the same, some may feel there is a touch of intellectual snobbery in his tone. If so, his successors, the Rabbis of later Judaism, did not follow him in the fault. They took the view that the degrading tendencies of certain occupations must be frankly recognised, but that there were many trades requiring manual toil which ought to be highly esteemed.[1] In that most interesting

[1] Further reference may be made to Delitzsch, *Jewish Artisan Life in the time of Christ*, and also Büchler, *Der galiläische 'Am-ha-'Arets des zweiten Jahrhunderts*. Some of the trades then reckoned ignoble seem by no means so to us; for example, tanners, weavers, and hairdressers were particularly despised. One Rabbi quaintly remarks: "Ass-drivers are mostly wicked, camel-drivers mostly honest, sailors mostly pious, the best of physicians is destined for Gehenna, and the most honourable of butchers is a partner of Amalek."

Men and Manners

work of the first and second century A.D., *The Sayings of the [Jewish] Fathers*, we read that Shemaiah said, *Love work*. Rabbi Meir, however, said cautiously, *Have little business, and be busy in the Law*. It is said in the Talmud (*Kidd*, 99a) that *Whosoever doth not teach his son work, teacheth him to rob*. These remarks scarcely carry the question beyond Ben Sirach's view. But many of the Rabbis went much further and urged that religious and intellectual studies were not profitably undertaken unless accompanied by some acquaintance with manual labour. Thus, said Rabbi Gamaliel (about 90 A.D.), *An excellent thing is study of the Law combined with some worldly trade . . . but all study of the Law apart from manual toil must fail at last and be the cause of sin*. Another, and a powerful, saying is this: *Flay a carcase in the street and earn a living, and say not, " I am a famous man, and the work is beneath my dignity."* St. Paul will doubtless occur to many as an instance of a great scholar who was proud to know and to exercise the trade of tent-making. Recall how earnestly he protested to the Christians of Corinth his independence of their monetary help (cp. *Acts* 18$^{1-3}$; 1 *Cor.* 4^{12}, 2 *Cor.* 11^9). This admirable association of labour and learning persisted among the Jews, and their history contains many examples of splendid men who combined the virtues of great scholarship with the pursuit of some humble means of livelihood. Some of the best-known Rabbis of the Middle Ages supported themselves by labouring as carpenters, shoemakers, builders, bakers, and so forth.

Of the numerous sayings concerning wealth and poverty we may mention some that bring before us the concrete picture of men rich and poor. Here is one that is eloquent of the bitterness of the contrast:

> *The rich man's wealth is his strong city;*
> *The poor man's poverty is his undoing* (Pr. 10^{15}).

Studies in Life from Jewish Proverbs

Even to-day, in a land where Justice is designed to be even-handed, but must needs be approached through the lawyer, who imagines that the rich and the poor stand on level terms? Even among the well-to-do the majority of men would think twice before engaging in legal warfare with a millionaire or a railway company.

Of the friendlessness of the poor there are these pathetic proverbs:

Wealth addeth many friends,
But the poor is separated even from the friend he hath
(Pr. 19⁴).

The poor is hated even of his own neighbour,
But the rich hath many friends (Pr. 14²⁰).[1]

And this from Ben Sirach:

My son, deprive not the poor of his living,
And make not the needy eyes to wait long (E. 4¹).

Do not those eyes stare hungrily from the proverb, and seem to gaze after us as we hurry on?

A sterner note is heard in this almost ironical observation:

A rich man toileth in gathering money, and when he resteth he is filled with his good things:
A poor man toileth in lack of substance, and when he resteth he cometh to want (E. 31³).

Two beautiful passages in the *Book of Proverbs* recognise that the problem of success goes deeper than riches:

Better a dinner of herbs where love is,
Than a fatted ox and hatred therewith (Pr. 15¹⁷).

[1] It is good to feel that, whatever the Christian centuries have not yet achieved for the regeneration of society, the "poor man's neighbour" has redeemed his reputation from this terrible charge.

Men and Manners

Remove far from me vanity and lies :
Give me neither poverty nor riches ;
Feed me with the food that is needful for me :[1]
Lest I be full, and deny Thee, and say, " Who is the Lord ? "
Or lest I be poor, and steal,
And use profanely the name of my God (Pr. 30[8, 9]).

Both grand sayings. The last is a really noble prayer for the Golden Mean, and at the same time an effective accusation which we know to be only too true of many self-confident rich men on the one hand, and many embittered poor men on the other.

Finally, let us ruminate on the fact that wealth and dyspepsia are old acquaintances: *Better is a poor man, being sound and of good constitution, than a rich man that is plagued in his body,* says Ben Sirach (E. 30[14]); and doubtless he had plenty of shocking examples to confirm his opinion, if there be any truth in Poseidonius' description of the Hellenic cities whose citizens "practically lived in the banqueting halls," and were wont to pocket what they could not there devour.

In the next place we may turn to proverbs dealing with character. Fastening upon one outstanding quality, for the moment they identify the personality with it. And if that is never entirely fair to any human being—because even the best of us is, for instance, never perfectly brave, nor the worst of us wholly mean—nevertheless it is good to be told bluntly whither the bias of our nature tends. To isolate the Virtues and the Vices and to hold them up for praise or blame has ever been a favourite and a successful method of moral education.

The quotations that follow are, as it were, swift portraits, some of them only lightning sketches, seizing in outline some obvious feature; but others (for all their brevity) are so

[1] Cp. Matt. 6[11], *Give us this day our daily bread.*

Studies in Life from Jewish Proverbs

full of life and colour, and often so tellingly correct, that no comment is needed to enforce the justice or importance of what is said. They have been compared to " Meissonier pictures: minute, graphic, realistic, unromantic; pictures drawn not by Fancy but by Observation "[1]:—

THE MEAN MAN

Riches are not comely for a niggard,
And what shall a covetous man do with money?
He that gathereth by miserliness gathereth for others,
And others shall revel in his goods (E. 14 ^{3,4}).
The miser hasteth after riches
And knoweth not that want shall come upon him (Pr. 28 ^{22})

AND THE GENEROUS

There is that scattereth, and increaseth yet more;
And there is that withholdeth, and it tendeth only to want.
The liberal man shall prosper the more,
And he that nourisheth others shall himself be nourished
$\qquad$ (Pr.11 ^{24,25})—

But appearances are sometimes deceptive:

There is that feigneth himself rich, yet hath nothing;
And there is that feigneth poverty, yet hath great wealth (Pr. 13 ^{7}).

There are numerous sayings dealing with the tale-bearer and the mischief-maker, for slander was a prominent evil of the crowded Oriental cities:

THE SLANDERER

The liar disseminates strife:
The whisperer parteth friends (Pr. 16 ^{28}).
For lack of wood the fire goes out,
And where there is no whisperer, contention ceaseth
$\qquad$ (Pr. 26 ^{20}).

[1] Lyman Abbott, *Life and Literature of the Ancient Hebrews*, p. 278.

Men and Manners

The Mischief-Maker
An evil man digs a pit of mischief
And on his lips is a fire that burns[1] (Pr 16²⁷).
An evil man, a sinful man, deals always in crooked speech.
He winks his eyes and shuffles his feet,
And his fingers make secret signs:
His thoughts are all plots,
He plans ceaselessly mischief;
A spreader of discord.
Wherefore, his ruin shall come in an instant.
Like a flash he'll be broken, and that beyond mending
(Pr. 6¹²⁻¹⁵).

The Boaster
As clouds and wind that yield no rain,
So is he who brags of gifts ungiven (Pr. 25¹⁴).

The Self-Confident Man.
The fool is quite certain his way is right,
But the wise man listens to counsel (Pr. 12¹⁵).
Seest thou a man wise in his own conceit?
There is more hope of a fool than of him (Pr. 26¹²).

—the last, a saying that increases in force when a little later we come to note just what the Wise-men thought of a fool! With these proverbs on the Proud we may conveniently group some sayings on the man whose tongue runs away with his discretion:

The Garrulous Man
The tongue of the Wise distils knowledge,
But the mouth of fools poureth out folly (Pr. 15²).
A fool's mouth is his destruction,
His lips are the snare of his soul (Pr. 18⁷).
A fool's vexation is instantly known,
But a prudent man ignores an affront (Pr. 12¹⁶).

[1] *i.e.*, his slanders, which scorch his victims.

Studies in Life from Jewish Proverbs

How true! Most normal persons have acquired the power to delay or suppress the answer that rises to the lips in anger, but which of us would not confess that it was hard to learn this wisdom and that it is never easy to observe its teaching? The temptation to blurt out all our thought in time of trouble or vexation is always with us. In the hot-tempered East restraint was even more necessary than it is amongst ourselves, and one is therefore not surprised to find the absence of this virtue receiving the same fearsome condemnation as self-confidence:

Seest thou a man that is hasty of speech?
There is more hope of a fool than of him (Pr. 29^{20}).

Next, a group of proverbs concerning certain persons who to their own great surprise have missed success in society. The list may begin with a character one scarcely expects to meet in Scripture:

The Practical Joker
As a madman that casteth firebrands, arrows and death,
So is he who deceives his neighbour and cries, " I was only in
        jest " (Pr. 26^{18,19}).

Then some advice to

The Boor in Society[1]
When thou sittest to eat with a ruler
Bear in mind his lordship's presence;
And if thou be a hearty eater,
Put a knife to thy throat (Pr. 23$^{1-3}$).

[1] Compare the unintentionally funny passage in E. 31^{12}ff. *If thou sittest at a great man's table, be not greedy at it, nor say, " What a lot of things are on it ! " . . . Stretch not your hand wheresoe'er your glance wanders, nor thrust yourself forward into the dish. Eat like a man* [i.e., do not gnaw or gobble as an animal would do] *what is set before thee, and do not bolt your food, lest you be loathed. Be first to leave off for the sake of good manners, and be not insatiate lest you offend.* Cp E 8 which also treats of " How to behave."

Men and Manners

And, thirdly, in two proverbs,

THE INOPPORTUNE MAN

As one that taketh off a garment in cold weather,
And as vinegar upon a wound;
So is he that singeth songs to a heavy heart (Pr. 25^{20})[1].

He that blesseth his friend with a loud voice, rising early in the
    morning;
It shall be counted a curse unto him (Pr. 27^{14}).

The last saying prompts the thought that Mr. E. V. Lucas is also among the Sages, for has he not given it as his opinion that " early rising leads to self-conceit, intolerance, and dulness after dinner " ? " The old poet," says he, " was right—

> ' When the morning riseth red
> Rise not thou but keep thy Bed ;
> When the Dawn is dull and gray
> Sleep is still the better way :
> Beasts are up betimes, but then
> They are beasts and we are men.' "

The last of the social failures is the Flatterer, oily and ingratiating, but treacherous and in the end exposed :

THE FLATTERER

The words of a flatterer are like dainty morsels
Going down to the innermost parts of the body (Pr. 18^8).
A man that flattereth his neighbour
Spreadeth a net for his feet (Pr. 29^5; cp. 26^{28}).
He that rebuketh a man shall afterward find more favour
Than he that flattereth with the tongue (Pr. 28^{23}).

Theophrastus, a Greek writer, has left us certain character-sketches of Athenian society about 300 B.C., many of

[1] The Hebrew text of the first two lines is uncertain.

Studies in Life from Jewish Proverbs

which might profitably be studied in relation to these Hebrew epigrams. His essay on *The Flatterer* is a case in point. Here is the Greek conception:—

"Flattery may be considered as a mode of companionship, base but profitable to him who flatters. The flatterer is a person who will say as he walks with another, 'Do you see how people are looking at you? This happens to no man in Athens but you.' . . . With these and the like words he will remove a morsel of wool from his patron's coat; or, if a speck of chaff has been laid on the other's hair by the wind, he will pick it off, adding with a laugh,' Do you see? Because I have not met you for two days, you have had your beard full of white hairs—although no one has darker hair for his years than you?' Then he will request the company to be silent while the great man is speaking, and will praise him too in his hearing, and mark his approbation at a pause with 'True'; or he will laugh at a frigid joke and stuff his cloak in his mouth as if he could not repress his amusement. He will request those who pass by to 'stand still until His Honour has passed.' . . . When he assists at the purchase of slippers, he will declare that the foot is more shapely than the shoes. If his patron is approaching a friend, he will run forward and say 'He is coming to you'; and then, turning back, 'I have announced you' . . . He is the first of the guests to praise the wine, and to say as he reclines next the host, "How delicate is your fare,' and (taking up something from the table) 'Now this—how excellent it is' . . . He will take the cushions from the slave in the theatre and spread them on the seat with his own hands. He will say that his patron's house is well built, his land well planted, and that his portrait is excellent."[1] Even when full allowance is made for the unity of authorship and the conscious and careful artistry of the Greek writing, it must be felt that

[1] Theophrastus, *Characters* (Jebb's translation), pp. 82, 83.

comparison between the Hebrew portrait and the Greek is scarcely possible, the advantage is so entirely with the latter. The Wise were perhaps unusually dull in their *dicta* concerning the Flatterer, but at their best they never come within sight of the brilliant detail that makes the Greek portrait live before our eyes. It is all the more significant therefore that the Hebrew has hit the one point that the Greek ignores or overlooks: the moral issues of flattery. Theophrastus, the artist, observes that flattery is a base employment; with its evil and disastrous consequences he does not trouble himself. The Wise miss almost everything except that: *A man that flattereth his neighbour*, said they, *spreadeth a net for his feet*. They offer an unadorned assertion; but, taken to heart, it would prove more useful to society than all the subtlety of the Athenian delineation. Note then in passing how the contrast is an epitome of the struggle between the two world-ideas, Hellenic and Jewish; on the one hand the overwhelming charm and skill of the Greek, and on the other the unfailing instinct of the Hebrew for the one thing the Greek world lacked.

The Lazy Man

In the lazy man the Wise found a subject that stirred not only their wit but also their eloquence. In two instances proverb has expanded to become a parable and a picture, both of which arrive at the same conclusion. The parable is very famous—

> *Go to the ant, thou sluggard,*
> *Consider her ways and be wise,*
> *Which, having no chief, overseer or ruler,*
> *Provideth her meat in the summer*
> *And gathereth her food in the harvest.*
> *How long wilt thou sleep, O sluggard ?*
> *When wilt thou arise from thy slumber ?*

Studies in Life from Jewish Proverbs

> *Yet a little sleep, a little slumber,*
> *A little folding of the hands to sleep—*
> *So shall thy poverty come as a robber,*
> *And thy want as an armed man* (Pr. 6$^{6\text{-}11}$).

But the picture deserves to be no less familiar:

> *I passed by the field of the slothful,*
> *By the vineyard of the witless man:*
> *And lo! it was all grown over with thorns,*
> *Its surace was covered with nettles,*
> *Its stonewall was broken down.*
> *Yet a little sleep, a little slumber,*
> *A little folding of the hands to sleep—*
> *So shall thy poverty come as a robber,*
> *And thy want as an armed man* (Pr. 24$^{30\text{-}34}$).

Besides these longer sketches there are several brief and pithy words about the lazy man. First, a delightful "hit" at him to whom any excuse for idleness is better than none:

The sluggard saith, "There is a lion outside. I shall be slain in the streets!" (Pr. 22^{13}).

And here are two beautiful verses which breathe the very air of indolence:

As the door turneth upon its hinges,
So doth the sluggard upon his bed.
The sluggard burieth his hand in the dish;
It wearyeth him to bring it to his mouth again (Pr. 26^{14,15}).

The verse immediately following (Pr. 26^{16}) will serve to conclude this topic, for it shows the sluggard to be own cousin to the type of man whom next we shall consider:

> *The sluggard is wiser in his own conceit*
> *Than seven men that can render a reason.*

Men and Manners

As the Wise went through the streets of Jerusalem and stood to teach in its open spaces, they observed certain men of various occupations, differing one from another both in social rank and in mental ability, whom nevertheless they classed under one category—THE SONS OF FOLLY. There were, of course, distinctions in the nature of their folly. The Authorised and Revised Versions are content to differentiate only three types, namely—Simpletons[1] (whether from lack of brain or lack of instruction, "Dullards"), Scorners[2], and Fools. The Hebrew text goes further and classifies the last named, the Fools, into (1) *Ivvillim*, those whose folly is due chiefly to the unrealised weakness of their nature—ignorant, vain, confident, headstrong, infatuate persons: in a word, "stupid fools"; and (2) *Kesilim*, whose is the folly of a gross and sensual nature, men who are morally, rather than mentally, unresponsive to the finer aspects of life—insensate, brutish persons, "coarse fools"; and (3) the *Nabal*, the man who is deliberate in his wrong-doing, the "Fool of Fools," but whose folly is only folly, provided the moral instinct of Humanity is sound and the law of the Universe is ultimately against evil and Man was meant for God and goodness. He it is of whom a Psalmist, getting to the very root of the problem, says *The fool hath said in his heart: "There is no God."* Having made the fundamental error, his whole judgment of life has become perverted. Probably he is an astute person; but the greater his ability, the greater and more pernicious will be his folly. Naturally, this fool and the scorner were often one and the same person. The Wise speak little of him, except in his capacity as a scorner; but they recognise that he is terrible. One of the four things that cause the earth to tremble, say they, is when a man of this sort is filled with meat (Pr. 30[22]). Elsewhere (Pr. 17[7]) they remark sarcastically that *Honest words do not become a fool*—decency would be out of

[1] In Hebrew, *Pethāīm*.   [2] Hebrew, *Lētsīm*.

Studies in Life from Jewish Proverbs

keeping with his character. So much for "the Fool *par excellence.*"

The rest of the sayings about "fools" are concerned with those of the first and second types. If it were our intention to go into the teaching fully, the nice distinctions of the Hebrew would have to be observed with care.[1] But now that the *Nabal* has been considered, it will be sufficient to follow the classification of the English Bible—scorners, simpletons, and fools—allowing the precise distinction between the *weak* and the *coarse* fool to lapse.

The *Simpleton* is one type; his folly may, and should be, cured by instruction. But he is disappointingly dull of hearing and "slow at the uptak": *How long, ye simple ones, will ye love simplicity?* cries Wisdom to them (Pr. 1^{22}). Nevertheless, although the teacher may fail to give them efficient brains, he can perhaps save them from evil and, in a quiet, humble way they may learn that fear of the Lord which is a sufficiency of true Wisdom. Wherefore on the whole the Wise spoke to these men sympathetically and hopefully: so in the exordium which states the purpose of the *Book of Proverbs* we are told that it is meant *to give prudence to the simple* (Pr. 1^4).

To the average fool the Wise were severe. Were they fair in being so? Surely many of these fools were either weak-willed or coarse, as the case might be, because they were just uninstructed "simpletons?" No! These are they who have opportunity but refuse or neglect it Therefore their condition is culpable, and the Wise do well not to mince matters concerning the folly of their conduct.

---

[1] Sometimes the whole point of a saying lies in the use of different terms Thus Pr 17^{21} seems merely redundant in the R.V., "He that begetteth a fool doeth it to his sorrow; and the father of a fool hath no joy." But the "fool" of the first clause is in the Hebrew *Kesîl*, a coarse fool, and the "fool" of the second is *Nabal*; *i.e*, to have the first as a son will involve some regrets, but the second robs his father of all joy.

Men and Manners

Such persons require to be kicked into sense, and the Wise were of opinion that in some instances the kicking might with advantage begin by being physical. Hold! Of whom are we speaking? Of the inhabitants of Jerusalem? Yes, but, suppose we were analysing the population of our own times, would there not be more than a few found guilty of just such folly—men and women *undisciplined* in mind and soul? Possessing plenty of wits and much capacity for moral feeling, they fling their chances aside. It is a perilous attitude towards the realities of life, for refusal to learn grows ever easier as life goes on. What chance do thousands give themselves of acquiring Christian faith, or even of maintaining or improving their intellectual and moral qualities? Do they seek for the good in the Christian Churches, or for the faults, and so miss the good? How much study have they given to the knowledge of God in Christ? Many have consulted their Bradshaw more often than their Bible. What efforts do they make to apprehend the meaning and value of Christianity in face of modern knowledge and in view of modern conditions? " Last Sunday you managed to evade the message which God sent you: that makes it much easier to evade the message He sends you to-day. Next Sunday you will be almost totally indifferent. Soon you will get out of reach of His word altogether, saying it does you no good. Then you will deny that it is His word or His message."[1] This reference to Church-going is of course but one point out of many: the principle at issue is one which vitally concerns the whole of a man's attitude to life. The fool is almost unteachable, and that of course is his supreme peril. He is so self-confident, so unreasonable, so certain he is right and others wrong. He does not dream of becoming wiser, because already he knows himself to be as wise as Solomon. Therefore the Sages are justified in their unsparing rebukes.

[1] Horton, *Proverbs* (Expositor's Bible), p. 347.

Studies in Life from Jewish Proverbs

What is wrong with the fool, is primarily his moral condition ; and accordingly for the moment we need not trouble to distinguish be ween the weak fool and the coarse. What is censured in them both is neither their present silliness nor their grossness, but their unwillingness to learn. They have what amounts to an error of moral vision, and they desperately need to realise the fact. Mr. Chesterton has somewhere said, " The fool is one who has an impediment in his thought. It is *not*, as the modern fellows say, put there by his grandmother. I have wandered over the world (so to speak) trying to find some faithful, simple soul who really believed in his own grandmother. He does not exist. The first act of the fool, when he is articulate, is to teach his grandmother how to suck eggs. Fools have no reverence. Fools have no humility." Doubtless a man must not be blamed for the initial quality of his mind, and possibly the Wise were too caustic to the congenitally stupid. But then the Wisdom they were teaching was not intellectually difficult to acquire ; it was not book-learning but that Wisdom which is from on high and can be revealed to babes and sucklings.

As for the third class, the Scorner or Chief Fool ; he too suffers from corruption of moral vision. But with him the distortion is desperate : he calls white black and black white For this alert, deliberate Fool, the Wise had little hope or none at all ; he has chosen the path of Folly with his eyes open. All they can do is to meet his scorn with a greater scorn, and make their appeal in his hearing. One does not wonder that the Wise were baffled by this type of man. There is hope of such a person, but the hope is in the fact of Christ. This Fool has wit enough to rethink the situation, if he chose. He may some day have imperative cause to reconsider his view of life, and so may discover first that Christ is truth, and then learn that Christ can pardon.

Men and Manners

We turn now to the sayings themselves, or rather to a selection from them, for the sons of Folly provoked very many proverbs.

A number are humorous and spicy—the sort of phrases that might catch the ear of a crowd, raise a laugh at the fool's expense, and remain fixed in the hearer's memory by the barb of wit. Think, for instance, of the feeble, vacillating eyes that so often accompany and reflect a weak intellect or character:

Wisdom stands ever before the mind of a prudent man,
But the eyes of a fool are in the ends of the earth (Pr. 17^{24}).

and for comment on the mind behind the eyes, this will do:

The mind of a fool is like a cartwheel,
And his thoughts like a rolling axle-tree (E. 33^5).

The Wise laid their finger with much accuracy on the salient features of the foolish character. Thus in the dullard they point to his credulity, *The simpleton believeth every word, but the prudent looketh well to his going* (Pr. 14^{15}), The fool is apt to be greedy of reward, *The fool will say " I have no friend and I have no thanks for my good deeds* (E 20^{16}); and grudging in his charity, *To-day he will lend but to-morrow he will ask it again* (E. 20^{15}), although himself a spendthrift, *Precious treasure abides in the Wise man's house, but a foolish man swallows it up* (Pr. 21^{20}, cp. Pr. 14^1). He is a blusterer, *A Wise man is cautious and avoids misfortune, but the fool rageth and is confident* (Pr. 14^{16}); shallow and frivolous, *As the crackling of thorns under a pot, so is the laughter of a fool* (*Ecclesiastes* 7^6); garrulous, saying what he thinks before he thinks what he says, *The heart of fools is in their mouth, but the mouth of wise men is in their heart.* (E. 21^{26}); changeable and unreliable, *The foolish man changeth as the moon* (E. 27^{11}); *Take not counsel with a fool, for he will not be able to conceal the matter* (E. 8^{17}).

Studies in Life from Jewish Proverbs

He is a bully often, but his courage is unstable, *Pales set on a high place will not stand against the wind; so the cowardice in a foolish heart will not bear up against any fear* (E. 22[18]). He aspires to be witty, but seldom has wit enough, *The legs of the lame hang loose: so does a parable in the mouth of fools* (Pr. 26[7]).

Nevertheless the fool's pride and self-confidence is complete, *The way of the foolish is right in his own eyes* (Pr. 12[15]; cp. 14[3], 28[26]); so that he loses sense of the awfulness of evil and even enjoys it, *It is as sport to a fool to do wickedness* (Pr. 10[23], cp. 13[19]); sneering at those who fain would give him guidance, *A fool despiseth his father's correction . . . a fool scorns his mother* (Pr. 15[5, 20]); and hating information, *A fool hath no delight in understanding* (Pr. 18[2]). Thus it is almost useless to attempt to instruct a fool—here is a counsel of despair, *Speak not in the hearing of a fool, for he will despise the wisdom of thy words* (Pr. 23[9])—and here is the sigh of the weary teacher, *Wherefore is there a price in the hands of the fool to buy wisdom, seeing that he hath no wits?* (Pr. 17[16]). *The inward parts of a fool are like a broken vessel, and he will hold no knowledge* (E. 21[14]). *He that teacheth a fool is as one that glueth a potsherd together* (E. 22[7]). The fool, in fact, is in uttermost peril of being incorrigible, *He that discourseth to a fool is as one discoursing to a man that slumbereth; at the end thereof he will say "What is it?"* (E. 22[8]). Altogether it is hard to suffer fools gladly:

> *A stone is heavy and the sand weighty,*
> *But a fool's vexation is heavier than both* (Pr. 27[3]).

Wherefore the Wise dealt them some shrewd blows, being well aware that the skin of the dullard and the scornful was tough:

> *A whip for a horse, a bridle for an ass,*
> *And a rod for the back of fools* (Pr. 26[3]).

Men and Manners

*As a dog returneth to his vomit,
So a fool repeateth his folly* (Pr. 26¹¹).

*A rebuke entereth deeper into a sensible man
Than a hundred stripes into a fool* (Pr. 17¹⁰).

*Though thou shouldst bray a fool in a mortar,
Yet will his folly not depart from him* (Pr. 27²²).

It may be thought that some of these words are over-bitter and even savage. If so, the plea can be advanced that there was probably much provocation. The Scorner seems to have been a familiar figure, and he was doubtless clever enough to upset with his mockery many an audience to which the Wise-man was holding forth. *He that correcteth a scorner getteth to himself insult, and he that reproveth a wicked man getteth himself reviling* (Pr. 9⁷)—that sounds like the fruit of experience, and there is much that is suggestive in this saying also—*The proud and haughty man, scorner is his name, he worketh in the arrogance of pride* (Pr. 21²⁴). But if the Wise suffered at times, one gathers that they found no small consolation for their hurt dignity in such reflections as these:

> *Answer not a fool according to his folly
> Lest thou be like unto him* (Pr. 26⁴).

> *Judgements are prepared for scorners,
> And stripes for the back of fools* (Pr. 19²⁹).

CHAPTER VIII

The Ideal

THE Wise were not cynical persons intent on the faults and failings of humanity. The sayings recorded in the preceding chapter give their comments on the abnormal elements of society, and do not represent their general outlook on life. The real centre of their interest was the ordinary man. They were well aware that for one incorrigible fool or one notorious flatterer there are a hundred, or a thousand, average persons who, if they do not grow better, will assuredly grow worse; and to these the bulk of their instruction was directed. The Wise therefore ought not to suffer in our estimation, because we have arbitrarily chosen to set their critical opinions in the foreground. And if it be insisted that, in point of fact, criticism of others is a prominent feature of the proverbs, the reply is first, that we are not endeavouring or expecting to prove the Wise innocent of all censoriousness or occasional snobbery; and secondly, that criticism is an almost indispensable weapon for practical moralists. Human beings hate to be lectured directly on their weaknesses; yet when the faults of others are being exhibited they will listen merrily and attentively, notwithstanding the possibility that some shrewd blow may come knocking at the gates of conscience. Every teacher knows that the average man will be left only offended and unbelieving if he is told bluntly how much his small failings leave to be desired; but show him by a shocking example whither the way of pride or

The Ideal

folly tends and he will often take to heart the lesson. It might therefore be claimed that in a sense all the proverbs were addressed to the normal, teachable man, even those which rebuke an extreme fault in an extreme manner being meant for the ears of others besides the hardened sinner against whom they were ostensibly directed.

Certainly the great majority of the proverbs are applicable to the affairs of the rank and file of men. So keen were the Wise on the task of admonishing and encouraging very ordinary men that they uttered many a commonplace in a fashion too simple to be memorable or even momentarily interesting to any person of alert intelligence. Nevertheless such material cannot be neglected here, and ought not to be despised. It must not be neglected, just because it is actually a large section of our subject matter ; it ought not to be despised, for it all helps to show the humanism of the Wise, testifying that they were honest and practical teachers rather than clever writers anxious only to compile a book of skilful proverbs. *That* teacher is to be condemned who cannot, or will not, relate his thinking to the capacities of his hearers. The Wise deserve praise because they said a great deal that even the simpleton could not plead was beyond him.

We have begun, it seems, by tasting some of the spices with which the Wise seasoned their counsel We come now to the solid matter of their doctrine. By noting the qualities they praised or blamed, the deeds which won their approval or their censure, we shall gain a general conception of their aspirations. What were their ideals for men as individuals, as members of a family, as citizens of a State ?

I.—The Individual

The threefold division just suggested—man in his individual, domestic and political relationships—seems simple and natural, but proves difficult to maintain, because the

Studies in Life from Jewish Proverbs

first category in reality trespasses on the other two. Strictly speaking, none of the virtues and the vices concern the individual alone. If a man ruin his health by intemperate indulgence of fleshly desires, doubtless he is himself the prime sufferer, but obviously the State loses something thereby and woe betide his family! Still, such a quality as Temperance may reasonably enough be classed as a personal virtue, being primarily an aspect of Man's duty to himself. But what shall be said of duties such as Generosity, Forbearance, Deceitfulness, the exercise of which might be reckoned almost as much Man's duty to his neighbours in family or State as to himself? In which division shall we reckon these? For convenience, let these also be considered under the first heading as personal, rather than social, qualities. Enough material will still remain for use in the second and third sections of our topic.

(a) VIRTUES OF RESTRAINT. A convenient starting-point for our review of the characteristics the Wise desired to see in the individual is provided by certain negative virtues of restraint, which the proverbs frequently enjoin.

The duty of Moderation in eating and drinking is sufficiently, though not urgently, commended: *He that loveth pleasure shall come to want, and he that loveth wine and oil shall not be rich* (Pr. 21^{17})—*A companion of gluttonous men shameth his father* (Pr. 28^7). Again, *Wine is a mocker, strong drink a brawler, and whoso erreth therein no wise man is he* (Pr. 20^1; cp. 23$^{29\text{-}35}$). Not that the Wise were advocates of an ascetic abstinence: they did no more than commend moderation.[1] Thus Ben' Sirach, who certainly enjoyed banqueting on good food and good wine, contents himself with advising the inexperienced "not to eat greedily lest he be hated"; *How sufficient*, says he, *to a*

I
OF THE
APPETITE

---
[1] See below, ch. X, p 184f.

The Ideal

well-mannered man is a very little, and he doth not breathe hard upon his bed. Healthy sleep cometh of moderate eating; he riseth early and his wits are with him. The pain of wakefulness and colic and griping, these go to the insatiable man (E. 31$^{19-20}$).

The duty of curbing anger is emphasised in several telling proverbs. Doubtless the evil consequences of unbridled passion are more evident among the quick-tempered peoples of southern and eastern lands; but the northerner is apt to be sullen, and perhaps what he gains by initial restraint he loses through the permanence of his indignation. Who dare affirm that a warning against wrath is not sorely needed in all lands and all centuries? What havoc has been wrought in human affairs by passion, be it sullen or sudden! Not even poverty is chargeable with causing more pain and misery. In delivering their admonitions the Wise took up no specially exalted standpoint: they were content to note the plain consequences of anger—its disastrous effect on society, *An angry man stirreth up strife and a wrathful man abounds in transgression* (Pr. 29^{22}, cp. 15^{18}); and how that the angry man (too weak to conceal his emotions, *A fool uttereth all his anger but a wise man keepeth it back and stilleth it* [Pr. 29^{11}]), must himself suffer in the end, *He that is soon angry will deal foolishly and a man of wicked desires is hated* (Pr. 14^{17}). And again to much the same effect they said in a phrase that has become immortal, *He that is slow to anger is better than the mighty, and he that controlleth his temper than he that taketh a city* (Pr. 16^{32}). How excellent that last proverb is! "So hot, little man, so hot?" The British Government has discovered the uses of advertisement for thrusting facts before the unobservant: one may disapprove the practice but not on the ground that it is ineffective. What if this proverb (and a few other valuable sayings that the Jewish Sages could supply) were to appear

(marginal note: II OF ANGER)

Studies in Life from Jewish Proverbs

one fine day on a million placards throughout the Kingdom ? Would the money go wasted, or would there be the swiftest and most economical reform on record ?

Closely associated with restraint of passion is restraint of speech, a duty which is considered in several forceful proverbs : *Death and life are in the power of the tongue, and they that love it shall eat the fruit thereof* (Pr. 18²¹)—*He that guardeth his mouth keepeth his life, but he that openeth wide his lips shall have destruction* (Pr. 13³). Of the specious dignity that silence for a time confers, they said with truth and humour : *Even a fool when he holdeth his peace is counted wise ; when he shutteth his lips he is esteemed as prudent* (Pr. 17²⁸). On the other hand, speaking the right word at the right time won their keen approval. Was it not the very art in which they themselves sought to excel ? *A man hath joy in the answer of his lips, and a word in due season how good it is* (Pr 15²³).

III OF SPEECH

(*b*) THINGS TO AVOID. Much can be learnt regarding the ideals of the Wise by observing what they counselled men to shun. Thus the sayings on the Sluggard (p. 128) might be used to show how they hated Indolence : *As vinegar to the teeth and as smoke to the eyes, so is the sluggard to them that send him* (Pr. 10²⁶). They censured Disdain and Pride: *He that despiseth his neighbour is void of wisdom* (Pr. 11¹²)—*Pride goeth before destruction and a haughty spirit before a fall* (Pr. 16¹⁸). Ingratitude is dealt with in a restrained but memorable saying, *Whoso rewardeth evil for good, evil shall not depart out of his house* (Pr. 17¹³) ; and there are these two splendid proverbs against Revenge, *Say not, " I will recompense evil " : wait on the Lord, and he will save thee* (Pr. 20²²)—and *Rejoice not when thine enemy falleth, and let not thine heart be glad when he is overthrown, lest the Lord seeing it be displeased, and transfer his anger from him to thee*

The Ideal

(Pr. 24$^{17\text{-}18}$)[1]. Recall, by way of contrast, the terrible Italian proverbs quoted in Chapter I. (p. 23) ; remember the innate ferocity, derived from the ancient custom of the Desert vendettas, that has always characterised the quarrels of the near East ; and the wonder of such generous and noble exhortations as these in the Jewish proverbs cannot fail to be perceived.

Here is a vice which the Wise counted worse even than anger : *Wrath is cruel and anger is overwhelming but who can stand against Jealousy* (Pr. 27^4) ? They repeatedly point out the evil of contentiousness : *As coals to the hot embers and wood to fire, so is a quarrelsome man to inflame strife* (Pr. 26^{21})—*It is an honour for a man to keep aloof from strife, but every fool sheweth his teeth* (Pr. 20^3). One proverb makes use of two curious similes to enforce the lesson, *Lay thine hand upon thy mouth ; for, as the churning of milk bringeth forth butter, and as wringing of the nose bringeth forth blood, so the forcing of wrath bringeth forth strife* (Pr. 30^{33}) and another with a touch of dry humour remarks, *He seizes a dog by the ears who meddles with a quarrel not his own* (Pr. 26^{17}), *i.e.*, having once taken hold he cannot let go !

What the Wise thought of Slander and of Flattery has been indicated sufficiently in the preceding chapter.

Dissimulation and Treachery stirred them to a fine contempt : *Fervent lips and a wicked heart are an earthen vessel plated with silver. He that hateth dissembleth with his lips, but layeth up deceit within him : when he speaketh fair, believe him not ; for in his heart are seven abominations. Though his hatred cloak itself with guile, his wickedness shall be shown openly before the congregation* (Pr. 26$^{23\text{-}26}$)—brave

[1] Toy justly remarks, " The motive here assigned—fear of Jehovah's displeasure—belongs to the ethical system of *Proverbs* But this motive does not impair the dignity of the moral standard presented. Jehovah's displeasure is the expression of the moral ideal : it is one's duty, says the proverb, not to rejoice at the misfortunes of enemies This duty is enforced by a reference to compensation, but it remains a duty."

Studies in Life from Jewish Proverbs

words and vigorous! One feels very sure that the Empire which betrayed its mind in the Hymn of Hate would need to show more than the penitence of fair words on fervent lips before it could hope for clemency from this Sage.

(c) THE VIRTUES. So much for the Vices. It is time to consider the positive qualities that the Sages praised, and the foregoing picture of guile raises thoughts of its opposite. Let us begin therefore with the praises of True Friendship. Ben Sirach expands the subject into a little essay: *If thou wouldest get thee a friend, get him by dint of trial, and be not in haste to trust him For there is a friend that is such for his own occasion, and he will not continue in the day of thine affliction. And there is a friend that turneth to an enemy, and he will be openly at strife with thee to thy confusion. And there is a friend that is a companion at the table* (*i.e.*, a "cupboard-lover"), *and he will not remain in the hour of thy distress. . . . A faithful friend is a strong defence, and he that hath found him hath found a treasure. There is nothing can be exchanged for a faithful friend, and his excellency is beyond all price. A faithful friend is a medicine of life, and they that fear the Lord shall find him* (E. 6⁷ff). To match any single proverb against such words is a hard test, yet there is one that not only can bear the ordeal but is perhaps the finest of all epitomes of friendship: *A friend is always friendly, born to be a brother in adversity* (Pr. 17¹⁷, mg. R.V.).

Seeing that the Wise saw in the fool's pride and self-sufficiency his worst and fatal error, it is only to be expected that they should lay constant stress on the duties of preserving an open mind and continuing amenable to instruction and reproof: *Take fast hold of instruction; let her not go, for she is thy life* (Pr. 4¹³)—*Whoso loveth correction loveth knowledge, but he that hateth reproof is a boor* (Pr. 12¹) —*He that being often reproved hardeneth his neck shall suddenly be broken, and that beyond mending* (Pr. 29¹).

The Ideal

No less prominent and much more remarkable (seeing how profoundly and persistently falsehood in speech has beset the Oriental character) is the demand for Truthfulness: *A righteous man hates deception* (Pr. 13^5). We are told that only truth endures: *The lip of truth shall be established for ever, whereas a lying tongue is but for a moment* (Pr. 12^{19}). Sincerity of character is often extolled in plain speech and in metaphor: *The righteousness of the perfect shall make straight his way* (Pr. 11^5)—*The mouth of the righteous is a fountain of life* (Pr. 10^{11})—*The tongue of the righteous is like choice silver* (Pr. 10^{20})—*The lips of the righteous feed many* (Pr. 10^{21})—*The thoughts of the righteous are just* (Pr. 12^5)—*The heart of the righteous studieth what to answer, but the mouth of the wicked poureth out evil things* (Pr. 15^{28}).[1]—*The fruit of the righteous is a tree of life* (Pr. 11^{30}). Integrity of purpose is even more beautifully commended in this memorable proverb: *He that loveth pureness of heart, and on whose lips is grace, the king shall be his friend* (Pr. 22^{11}).

Perhaps not a few of the Wise wore an air of superiority to their neighbours; some may have given God thanks that they were not as other men; but assuredly not all fell victims to what was for them a natural temptation, and justice demands that full weight be assigned to the numerous sayings in which they castigate Vanity or praise Humility. For instance, *When pride cometh*, said they, *then cometh shame, but with the lowly is Wisdom* (Pr. 11^2).

To be temperate in body and mind, energetic, peaceable, honest and truthful, teachable, sincere, loyal and honourable—evidently the Wise made no small demand on human nature. But above and beyond these qualities, and very wonderful in the old Oriental world, are these virtues,

[1] "The antithesis is ethical, not merely intellectual. The meaning is not that the righteous speaks cautiously, the wicked inconsiderately; but that the good man takes care to speak what is true and kind, whilst the bad man, feeling no concern on this point, follows the bent of his mind and so speaks evil." (Toy *ad. loc.*).

Studies in Life from Jewish Proverbs

which the Wise expected good men to possess and show—consideration for others, helpfulness, mercy, kindness of word and deed, and even forgiving love. They declare that, *Whoso mocketh the poor reproacheth his Maker, and he that is glad at calamity shall not go unpunished* (Pr. 17^5). The righteous ought to be a guide to his neighbour (Pr. 12^{26}); and (as an arresting passage insists) the obligation must not be shuffled off or wilfully ignored: *Deliver them that are carried away unto death and them that are tottering to the slaughter see that thou hold back. If thou sayest, "Behold we knew not this," doth not He that weigheth the hearts consider it? And he that keepeth thy soul doth He not know it? And shall he not render to every man according to his work* (Pr. 24$^{11, 12}$)? As regards the broad social applications of this proverb, the deep guilt of all nations leaves little to choose between them. But taking the command on its more intimate and individual aspect, does it not utter a warning that the average Briton has peculiar need to hear? For our national character is such that we hate interfering with another man's way of life, we are even shy of rebuking the young. There is, of course, a virtue in our natural tolerance, for men cannot be school-mastered into mending their ways. But conscience will admit that much of our non-interference is mere shirking of duty, a passing-by on the other side. If we were less frightened to warn or to help others, less anxious how our words would be received and whether we might be snubbed and made uncomfortable or called a Pharisee, it may be that, whenever we did so warn or help, we should do it with a better grace and therefore more effectually. Since nine out of ten are wont to err on the side of silence, we reiterate the injunction . . . *them that are tottering to the slaughter see that thou hold back*. There are times when diffidence may be a sin, and the fear of contention cowardice.

Concerning Mercy in deed or thought and Honesty in

The Ideal

speech the Wise said, *Let not mercy and truth forsake thee. Bind them upon thy neck, write them on the tablet of thine heart ; so shalt thou find favour and good repute in the sight of God and man* (Pr. 3³،⁴). There are phrases concerning Kindness which live in the memory and touch the heart : *The healing tongue is a tree of life* (Pr. 15⁴)—*There is that speaketh rashly like the piercings of a sword, but the tongue of the Wise is health* (Pr. 12¹⁸), and a saying that for all its gentleness holds the conscience in a vice-like grip : *A soft answer turneth away wrath* (Pr. 15¹)—so hard to believe when occasion presses, but proved true a thousand thousand times. And here, in conclusion, are three, wonderful, winged proverbs, which haunt one with the magic of their moral challenge : *Say not, " I will do so to him as he hath done to me, I will render to the man according to his work "* (Pr. 24²⁹)—*If thine enemy be hungry give him bread to eat, if he thirst give him water to drink ; for thou shalt heap coals of fire on his head, and the Lord shall reward thee* (Pr. 25²¹).

> *Hatred stirreth up strife,*
> *But love covereth all transgressions* (Pr. 10¹²).[1]

So much for Man, the individual. To finish the outline of the Wise-men's ideal we have still to consider the proverbs concerning family life and the wider relationships of the State.

II.—Family Life

A slight acquaintance with Oriental life will suggest the probability that in the family, as the Wise conceived it, fathers and sons were the only important figures ; and Jewish proverbs at first sight confirm the conjecture : " Daughters," says Kent[a], " are passed by with a silence that is significant." But, significant of what ? Not that they were ill-used or neglected or unloved in Hebrew

[1] cp. *Romans* 12¹⁰, and also p 268 [a] *Wise Men of Israel*, p. 158.

Studies in Life from Jewish Proverbs

homes, but that the Wise not unnaturally acquiesced in the normal conditions of Oriental existence which inevitably made a daughter of much less importance than a son. A girl was debarred from the manifold interests of commercial, social, and political affairs; she could not, like a son, perpetuate the family name; nor could the parents hope to see in her the support and strength of their old age. The Wise never attempted to ignore facts, and they never aimed at nor imagined revolutions in the fundamental circumstances of society as they found it. But we have to confess that Ben Sirach does more than acquiesce in the recognised limitations of daughters. He was reprehensibly querulous upon the subject, and we fear lest some who read may find it difficult to forgive him for such a ridiculous exhibition of masculine stupidity. Says Ben Sirach (and from the slow shake of his head we infer this to be no hasty *dictum*, but the result of his mature and cautious consideration), *A daughter is a secret cause of wakefulness to a father, and anxiety for her putteth away sleep. . . . Keep a strict watch over a headstrong daughter, lest she make thee a laughing-stock to thine enemies, a byword in the city, and notorious among the people* (E. 42$^{9\text{-}11}$).

Closer scrutiny of the Wise-men's thoughts about family life reveals something surprising and gratifying. It might have been expected that in any Eastern society Woman would continue all her days to be held in small esteem, carrying a heavy yoke for scant reward. But the Hebrew proverbs testify on the contrary that when a Jewish woman grew up and became wife or mother she stepped at once into a noble and influential position, enjoying a real share in the honour or prosperity of her husband, and entitled equally with him to the obedience and devotion of her children. No less than the father she was reckoned by the Wise to be the children's guide and counsellor. She had reasonable opportunity for social intercourse with

The Ideal

other persons than the members of her own household, and within her own house was trusted with responsibilities that gave her a large share in the making or marring of its happiness and fortunes. The Wise-men's ideal of married life is presented in a famous panegyric, which deserves to be given at length, for some writers have declared—not unreasonably in view of the immemorial inferiority to which the women of the East have been condemned—that it is the most remarkable feature of the *Book of Proverbs*.

THE WISE AND LOYAL WIFE[1]

A virtuous woman who can find ?
For her worth is far above rubies.
The heart of her husband trusteth in her,
And he shall have no lack of gain.
She doeth him good and not evil
All the days of her life.
She seeketh wool and flax,
And worketh it up as she pleaseth.
She is like the merchant-ships,
Bringing her food from afar.
She riseth also while it is yet night,
And giveth food to her household
She examines a field and buyeth it ;
With her earnings she planteth a vineyard.
She girdeth herself with strength,
And maketh strong her arms.
She perceives that her profit is good ;
Her lamp goes not out by night.
She puts out her hand to the distaff,
And layeth hold on the spindle.
She extendeth her hand to the poor ;
Yea, she reacheth forth her hands to the needy.

[1] (Pr 31[10-29]). The poem is in the Hebrew an alphabetical acrostic, which accounts for certain repetitions and roughnesses in the movement of the thought.

Studies in Life from Jewish Proverbs

She feareth not snow for her household,
For all her household are clothed with scarlet.
She maketh her cushions of tapestry;
Her clothing is fine linen and purple.
Her husband is distinguished in the gates,
When he sitteth among the elders of the land.
She maketh linen cloth and sells it,
And delivereth girdles to the merchants.
Strength and dignity are her clothing,
And she laughs at the time to come.
Her speech is full of wisdom,
And kindly instruction is on her tongue.
She looketh well to the ways of her household
And eateth not the bread of idleness.

Industrious, skilful, wise, provident and kind, she is rewarded by the praise and affection of husband and children—

Her husband also, and he praiseth her saying:

" Many daughters have done excellently
But thou excellest them all."

Wherefore despite the despondent query, *A virtuous woman who can find?* which somewhat quaintly introduces this eulogy, we may believe that the ideal thus pictured was a reality in many Jewish homes. To be critical, the poem has a touch of the *Hausfrau* conception which is none too pleasing, but it does not set out to say everything about Woman, and one might fairly read some romance between the lines; certainly the enthusiasm of the last verse has a note of something deeper than " thanks for value received." To give further assurance, if that be required, we may also quote this happy saying, *Whoso findeth a wife findeth a good thing, and obtaineth favour from the Lord* (Pr. 18²²).

The Ideal

The treatment of children advocated by the Wise is accurately, although too succinctly, summarised in the notorious "Spare the rod and spoil the child" doctrine (cp. Pr. 13[24]). Thus we are told, *The rod and reproof give wisdom, but a child left to himself causeth shame to his mother* (Pr. 29[15])—*Withhold not correction from a child, for if thou beat him with the rod he shall not die. Thou shalt beat him with the rod, and shalt deliver his soul from Sheol* (Pr. 23[13, 14]). All this sounds merely harsh. But the splendid records of Jewish family life make one suspect that the Wise were sterner in their words than in their deeds, that at least their justice was often tempered with mercy and their discipline with genuine affection. Ben Sirach, the most severe, is also the most encouraging. Here is a truly forbidding passage: *Pamper thy child, and he shall make thee afraid; play with him and he will grieve thee. Laugh not with him, lest thou have sorrow with him and thou shalt gnash thy teeth in the end. Give him no liberty in his youth, and wink not at his follies. Bow down his neck in his youth, and beat him on the sides while he is a child, lest he wax stubborn and be disobedient unto thee, and there shall be sorrow unto thy soul* (E 30[9-12]). But against its ferocious energy set the kindly, peaceable atmosphere of this exhortation in which Ben Sirach expands the fifth commandment on the relations of children to parents: *He that giveth glory to his father shall have length of days, and he that hearkeneth to the Lord shall bring rest to his mother. In word and deed honour thy father that a blessing may come upon thee from him: for the blessing of the father stablisheth the children's houses, but the curse of the mother rooteth out the foundations. . . . My son, help thy father in his old age, and grieve him not as long as he liveth. If he fail in understanding, have patience with him, and dishonour him not all the days of his life. For the relieving of thy father shall not be forgotten, and over against thy sins it shall be set to thy credit. In the day of thine*

Studies in Life from Jewish Proverbs

affliction it shall be remembered to thine advantage, to put away thine iniquities as the heat melteth hoar-frost (E. 3⁶⁻⁹, ¹²⁻¹⁵). Further, the severity of the Wise regarding children might seem less repellent if we appreciated more keenly the circumstances of their age. Probably their stern discipline has to be set against a background of disastrous slackness. How were children brought up in the Græco-Syrian cities? Were they sent forth untutored to join the mad dances of unbridled inclination? Was there in but too many Jewish, as well as Hellenic, homes appalling blindness to the need of control and moral training? Great allowance must be made for the Wise, if they were under the necessity of pointing a contrast. And who can deny the essential wisdom of their attitude? Who dare say that kindness does not lie in an excess of discipline rather than in an excess of indulgence? *Train up a child in the way he should go, and even when he is old he will not depart from it* (Pr 22⁶). As to the value which the Wise attached to the virtue of filial duty, if further evidence than the quotation just given from Ben Sirach is needed, it lies to hand in proverbs that condemn the deeds of unnatural children, who used violence to their parents (Pr. 19²⁶), or mocked and robbed them (Pr. 30¹⁷; 28²⁴). Listen to the indignation in this utterance: *Whoso curseth his father and mother, his lamp shall be put out in blackest darkness* (Pr. 20²⁰).

The servants of the household are less noticed in the proverbs than one would expect. Usually they were slaves, and the *status* to our mind suggests hardships and injustice. But the remarkable provisions laid down in the Hebrew Law regarding Hebrew slaves greatly alleviated their lot, preventing or mitigating cruelties which frequently befell the slaves of the Gentile nations. Few topics, in fact, more arrestingly demonstrate the superiority of the moral feeling of the Jews as compared with the Greeks or Romans than the treatment accorded to their respective slaves. In

The Ideal

ordinary circumstances the life of the Jewish slave was not unhappy, and to gain freedom might be disaster rather than benefit.[1] The trustworthy slave found satisfactory and sometimes honourable position in many Jewish households: he was in reality, though not in theory, a member of the home. On the other hand, among the Greeks and Romans the slave was regarded strictly as property, not necessarily to be treated as a human being. If a man chose to misuse or destroy his " property," so be it ! It was solely his affair. If he chose to wreak his anger at a certain cost to himself, no more need be said on the subject. Doubtless theory and practice did not always agree, and some Roman slaves were happy and well cared for, and some Jewish were miserable. But, generally speaking, it is true that the Jews were more humane to their servants than the Gentiles, although the evidence of the proverbs would not lead one to think so. Here, for instance, is a sufficiently sinister saying : *A servant will not be corrected by words, for though he understand he will not answer* (Pr. 29[19]). Similarly when Ben Sirach counsels a measure of restraint in dealing with a slave he does so on the Græco-Roman ground that he is part of one's possessions, and therefore not to be spent foolishly (E. 33[30, 31]); and he says bluntly and indeed brutally, *Fodder, a stick, and burdens for an ass ; bread and discipline, and work for a servant. Set thy servant to work, and thou shalt have rest: leave his hands idle, and he will seek liberty. Yoke and thong will bow the neck, and for an evil servant there are racks and tortures. Set him to work, as is fit for him ; and if he obey not, make his fetters heavy* (E. 33[24-28]). On the other side, however, may be set this proverb : *A servant that acteth wisely shall have rule over a son that doeth shamefully, and shall inherit among the brethren* (Pr. 17[2]), and Ben Sirach does something to redeem himself in these gentler sentiments, *Entreat not evil a servant*

[1] Cp *Luke* 16[3] (see Oesterley in *The Expositor* for April, 1903).

that worketh truly nor a hireling that giveth thee his life. Let thy soul love a wise servant; defraud him not of liberty (E. 7[20, 21]).

III.—IDEALS OF SOCIETY

The duties of men in general social relationships afforded a wide field for the application of wisdom. In expressing their views on these topics, the Sages said little that was original, much that was truly wise.

The perfect State will be one in which justice between man and man never faileth, and its operation must range from the highest to the lowest in the land. As for the great ones of the earth, the fateful consequences of their conduct is emphasised as follows: *As a roaring lion and a ranging bear, so is a wicked ruler over a poor people* (Pr. 28[15])—*By justice the king establisheth the land, but he that exacteth gifts overthroweth it* (Pr. 29[4]); and that the latter type of monarch or official was, alas! more than an evil dream is naïvely vouched for by the existence of a most unideal, if frank, intimation that *A gift in secret pacifieth anger, and a present in the purse strong wrath* (Pr. 21[14]). Princes are exhorted to temperance, "*It is not for kings, O Lemuel, it is not for kings to drink wine, nor for princes to say 'Where is strong drink?' lest they drink and forget the law, and pervert the judgement of the afflicted*" (Pr. 31[4, 5]); to justice, and consideration of the lowly, *The king that faithfully judgeth the poor, his throne shall be established for ever* (Pr. 29[14]); to kindness and truth, *Mercy and truth preserve the king, and he upholdeth his throne by mercy* (Pr. 20[28]). Two other sayings are worthy of mention; one a subtle proverb, *It is the glory of God to conceal a thing, but the glory of kings to search out a matter* (Pr. 25[2]); the other ominous, *The heaven for height, and the earth for depth, and the heart of kings is unsearchable* (Pr. 25[3]).

But this demand for right-dealing is extended through-

The Ideal

out the body politic: honesty was required in the courts of law from the witness (Pr. 24[28]) and from the judge (Pr 17[23]); from dealers in shop and market (Pr. 20[23]); and generally from all men, in a saying which is a significant and ringing echo of the Prophets' work in Israel: *To do justice and judgement is more acceptable to the Lord than sacrifice* (Pr. 21[3]).

Turning next to the disorders of society we find that the Wise set their face against the following offences. Land-grabbing, they declare, is a sin God will assuredly punish (Pr. 23[10, 11]), and so also oppression of the poor, *Rob not the poor because he is poor, nor crush the afflicted in the gate; for the Lord will plead their cause and despoil of life those that despoil them* (Pr. 22[22, 23]) Warnings are given against lawlessness: *Envy not thou the man of violence, and choose none of his ways; for the perverse are an abomination unto the Lord, but His friendship is with the upright* (Pr. 3[31, 32]); and in Pr. 1[11ff] there is an amusing description of outlaws enticing a novice to join them: "*Come with us, let us lay wait for blood . . . We shall fill our houses with spoil. Thou shalt cast thy lot amongst us; we will all have one purse*" Against drunkenness there is this effective saying: *Who hath woe? who hath sorrow? who hath quarrels? who hath complainings? who hath wounds without cause? who hath dimness of eyes? They that tarry long at the wine, that go to seek out mixed wine. Look not thou upon the wine when it is red, when it sparkles in the cup, when it goeth down smoothly. At the last it biteth like a serpent, and stingeth like an adder* (Pr. 23[29-31]). Still greater stress was laid on the peril of unchastity, and there are many earnest entreaties to shun the seductions of wicked women (cp. Pr. 5[1-14]; 6[20]-7[27]): *My son, attend to my wisdom, incline thine ear to my understanding, that thou mayest preserve discretion and thy lips keep knowledge. For the lips of a strange woman drop honey, and her mouth is smoother than*

Studies in Life from Jewish Proverbs

oil ; but her latter end is bitter as wormwood, sharp as a two-edged sword : her feet go down to death, and her steps take hold on Sheol. The spread of Hellenic civilisation in Palestine had increased luxury and sensuality, and in these matters the Wise doubtless were combating the most prominent vices of the age. Another common fault of town life which merited and received their vehement rebuke was malice against neighbours: to the portrait of the Slanderer already given (see p. 122) two proverbs may here be added: *Devise not evil against thy neighbour seeing he dwelleth securely beside thee* (Pr. 3^{29})—and this grand one, *Whoso diggeth a pit shall fall therein, and he that rolleth a stone, it shall return upon him* (Pr. 26^{27}).

Several interesting maxims of the Wise concerning Wealth and Poverty are kept for consideration in a subsequent chapter, and some have already been recorded, but the topic is one so intimately affecting the common weal that here also it must receive mention. These Wisdom proverbs are sometimes charged with exhibiting too mundane an attitude towards riches, so frankly and unreservedly do certain of them recognise the material advantages wealth confers. For the moment, however, we are not concerned with a general judgment but with noting ideals. Isolating therefore the nobler sayings, we find emphasis rightly laid on the broad distinction between just and unjust gains. For the former riches, which were the reward of diligence and shrewd but upright conduct, there is cordial approbation. Our deeper modern perplexities as to the proper distribution of wealth was of course beyond the Wise-men's ken ; it is enough that we find them clear on the issue presented to their day and generation: *The treasures of wickedness*, said they, *profit nothing* (Pr. 10^2)—*Better is the poor that walketh in his integrity than he that is perverse in his ways, though he be rich* (Pr. 28^6)—*Better is a little with righteousness than great revenues with injustice* (Pr. 16^8), and lastly the noble

The Ideal

passage (Pr. 30⁷⁻⁹, see p. 121) in praise of the Golden Mean will perhaps be remembered.

Further the Sages were stern in denunciation of greed and of indifference to the needs of the poor and defenceless: for instance, *He that augmenteth his substance by usury and interest gathereth for him that hath pity on the poor* (Pr. 28⁸)—*The Lord will root up the house of the proud, but he will establish the property of the widow* (Pr. 15²⁵); and correspondingly, they exalted the virtues of generosity and kindly help *He that giveth unto the poor shall not lack, but he that hideth his eyes shall have many a curse* (Pr. 28²⁷)—*Withhold not good from them to whom it is due, when it is in thy power to do it. Say not unto thy neighbour, "Go, and come again, and to-morrow I will give," when thou hast it by thee* (Pr. 3²⁷,²⁸).

The ideals of the Sages, so far as they are immediately visible in the proverbs, have now been given, at least in broad outline. It remains to sum up and to consider the result. Of the vices condemned, deeds of violence and sins of the flesh are prominent enough, but (and the fact is remarkable) almost equal stress is laid on the iniquity of many of the sins of the spirit. Thus, pride, jealousy, malice, revenge, contentiousness, and all forms of dishonesty, guile, and treachery are the way of the wicked; whereas humility, charity, peaceableness, purity of heart, and honest purpose mark the upright man. To be indolent, obstinate, and passionate in speech or action is characteristic of the fool intellectual and the fool ethical; whereas the sensible man is diligent, faithful to his friends, helpful to his neighbours, tactful and teachable. On the last point the Wise were urgent, and they deserve praise for their insight: that men have need to be apt to learn, not merely when they are young and ignorant, but after they have attained maturity and learnt much, is doctrine as important as it is unpopular. The frigid discipline advised by the

Studies in Life from Jewish Proverbs

Sages for the upbringing of children must be admitted to be harsh, but perhaps the conditions of the age almost dictated it, and at least it reflects the value that the Wise most rightly placed on learning young. Moreover, stern as their rule may seem, they did not deem it incompatible with the growth of affection and trust between fathers and sons. Of womanly virtue they held a high ideal, and the esteem felt for the good wife and wise mother was, for the ancient world, extraordinarily great. Ideal relations between master and servant were conceived in terms of fidelity, care for the interests of both parties, and possibly of friendship. In the perfect State there would be an upright government, riches acquired by just means only, and generous care to preserve the poor from suffering. There would be commercial honesty, thrift and industry; no slander, no impurity, no impiety, but only honourable and prudent conduct: in short, a peaceful, prosperous, kindly and contented society, devoted primarily to the pursuit neither of comfort nor of pleasure nor of riches, but of high Wisdom. Finally, as the climax, we must remember those exalted proverbs demanding the exercise of mercy, forgiveness, mutual help and love.

The standard of character the Wise thus set before men is open to adverse comment. It savours of salvation by merit. That therefore it falls below the Christian ideal, and below the majestic and penetrating conception of human possibilities that the great Hebrew Prophets urged, is undeniable. But such radical criticism may for the moment be put aside; later on we shall discuss what may be the relative values of the Wise-men's words and works. For the present all that is desirable is to consider certain surprising features which the reader may have noted in this outline of Good and Evil.

First, then, there are curious deficiencies in the list of the Virtues. Several qualities we admire are ignored or touched

The Ideal

rarely and with hesitation, as for example Courage. But, *with one exception*, these gaps in the Ideal are not so serious as might appear. The proverbs do not show all that was in their authors' minds and hearts. Altogether fallacious, as we shall see later, would be the notion that the prudence of the Wise was really pusillanimous, that they had in reality no place for courage in their conception of life, as they have little or no room for its mention in their proverbs. The valid inference from these absences is only that, as Toy says, " the Wise attached more importance to other qualities as effective forces in the struggle of life." But what can possibly be said concerning the apparent absence of Religion, the exception alluded to above ? That which one looked to find in the foreground of the picture—where is it ? Yet even in this point the plea just made might be repeated. The immediate object of the Wise was to commend certain ethical conduct as being, despite appearances, the right line to follow in order to command true success in the contingencies of daily life; and in pursuance of that task they could say a great many things without requiring to express their views on ritual worship or theological belief. Still, when the point at issue is a man's love for religion, to plead simply that he more or less ignored it in his teaching because other qualities seemed more effective in the struggle of life, would verily be a thin apology. The real reply to this serious charge is vastly stronger. It is the admission that our exposition of the Wise-men's thoughts has not been fair to them. One emphatic and reiterated proverb of theirs, which is evidently a key-proverb and interpretative of the general tenor of all their teaching, has not yet been given, and *it* is essentially religious :

THE FEAR OF THE LORD IS THE FOUNDATION OF WISDOM:
AND THE KNOWLEDGE OF THE HOLY ONE IS UNDERSTANDING (Pr. 9^{10}; 1^7).

Studies in Life from Jewish Proverbs

Consider the implication. The word "foundation" (usually rendered "beginning") in Hebrew unites the notions both of "beginning" and "best"; and "fear," of course, is to be interpreted religiously as "reverence" not as "terror." Such awe of God (say the Wise) is to be reckoned the commencement of Wisdom and also Wisdom's quintessence: it is both the root and the fruit of perfect living. Now Wisdom was the sublime source to which the Sages traced back even the simplest of their counsels, and the most practical of their observations on men and affairs; it was the creative sun, the derivative proverbs being, as it were, the rays by which its light is distributed over the whole of life. But now it appears that this sun and centre of all things itself was conceived as rising out of religious faith, for when the Sages considered this high Wisdom and asked what was *its* sum and substance, they answered, "The fear of the Lord," and, when they wondered what might be *its* origin, again they answered, "God." The fundamental importance of this one saying would therefore be obvious even if it stood alone as a solitary expression of faith. But other religious proverbs occur as we shall note in due course; for example, Ben Sirach's opening words, *All wisdom cometh from the Lord, and is ever with him* (E. 1^1), or this—*Trust in the Lord with all thy heart, and lean not on thine own understanding. In all thy ways acknowledge him, and he shall make plain thy path* (Pr. 3^{5,6}) Such sayings may not be numerous in comparison with the secular sayings, but there are enough of them to show that the great proverb quoted above is not an isolated sentiment of formal piety thrust into a mass of worldly-wisdom for appearance's sake. The soul of the Wise-men cannot accurately be gauged by deducting the few religious from the many non-religious proverbs, and drawing the inference that these men must have cared very little for God and overwhelmingly much for worldly prosperity. Human

The Ideal

nature guards its secrets from such cynical or mechanical treatment. Rather will it be true that when, as here, even one earnest plea is made for the love of God as the ultimate inspiration of conduct, *that* will give us the heart of the whole matter to which all else is subsidiary and only to be interpreted in and through the underlying religious faith. Matter-of-fact, prudential, moralisms might be far more numerous than they are in these Jewish proverbs, and still it would not follow that the Wise-men were devoid of religious feeling or fervour. Some doubtless were, but others assuredly were not, and *all* (save an occasional sceptic) would have stoutly maintained the view that their counsel was derived from the ultimate, fundamental doctrine of " the fear of the Lord."

The second obvious point of criticism is the indefiniteness apparent in this so-called Ideal of the Wise. Their ethic may justly be called redundant, or defective, or both ; and in truth their Utopia, even in its broad outline, does seem too confused and too fragmentary to provide any coherent scheme. Contrast the relatively clear-cut work of the Hellenic thinkers who, starting also from similar vague popular notions of ethics, correlated, combined, and sifted the material until, as in the Stoic and other philosophies, precisely formulated systems were elaborated. Was not the Jewish lack of method fatal to effective teaching ? No. The Wise did not, indeed could not, construct a strict unity out of their free-and-easy, uncorrelated aims. But they were not candidates for a degree in Moral Sciences, nor are their doctrines here exhibited as a satisfactory substitute for modern social philosophy. Their thinking, as a matter of fact, was definite enough to serve their day and generation. The position was not quite so serious as it may appear from a theoretical point of view. In reality, the Sages knew very well what they were aiming at, and had a reasonably

Studies in Life from Jewish Proverbs

clear idea of the type of character they wished to see developed in themselves and other men. Now it is fortunate that in the pages of *Ecclesiasticus* we possess not a little information about the thoughts, habits, and fortunes of its author, Jesus ben Sirach; for this man, though doubtless not a perfect embodiment of Wisdom, provides just what we most require at this point of our study—a historical figure, and an admirable and typical representative of his class. To envisage him will humanise our notion of the Wise-men and may give to their ideals a coherence which in the abstract they may seem to lack.

Jesus ben Sirach was a Jew of Jerusalem who lived about 250 to 180 B.C.; that is, well on in the period of Hellenic influence. By profession a scribe, he seems all his days to have been a man of earnest mind, naturally inclined to intellectual and literary pursuits. He was of good family, and presumably possessed of considerable means, to judge by his life-long leisure for study, the tone of his remarks on wealth, his easy and regular participation in social entertainment, and his foreign travels, which provided the one stirring episode in a placid career. From some remarks in his book we gather that his travels were undertaken whilst he was still a young man. Just when and where he journeyed is uncertain, but since he says that he came into touch with a foreign Court, in all probability he visited the great cities of Egypt and the Court of Alexandria. The important point is that his tour was not without excitement and real peril (E. 34^{12}, 51^{1ff}). Through some lying and malicious gossip he had the misfortune to incur royal displeasure, suffered imprisonment, and, in his own firm opinion, was for a time in gravest danger of losing his life. Such an experience is inevitably a severe test of any man's mettle, and is doubly sure to produce a deep impression on the mind of one so naturally unadventurous as Ben Sirach. His comments on the

The Ideal

matter are therefore a valuable clue to his character. He took the view that his travels, notwithstanding the danger, had been a great and lasting benefit, an experience in which anyone who aspired to be counted wise would do well to imitate him. It had proved worth all the hardship and anxiety—a fine broadening influence: *He that hath no experience knoweth few things, but he that hath travelled shall increase his skill. Many things,* he reflects, *have I seen in my wanderings* (E. 34^{10}). The other impression left by his adventures was the paramount value of Israel's Wisdom. In the hour of his danger he would have perished but for the principles of discreet and honest conduct in which Wisdom had instructed him. (E. 34^{12}).

He returned from abroad to settle for the rest of his days in belóved Jerusalem, where he became an honoured citizen, a man of considerable weight socially as well as intellectually, and a notable exponent of Wisdom, whose advice in the manifold affairs of daily life was sought and respected. There are grounds for thinking that for some years he may have conducted a regular school for instruction in the science of Wisdom. He was a thorough townsman, loving the busy life of his city, keenly observant of its varied occupations and appreciative of all opportunities of human intercourse. So far from thinking of him as a scholarly recluse, careless of all save his duties as a scribe or teacher, we have to picture a man who enjoyed dining out with his friends; no glutton, yet a frank connoisseur of food and wine. Feasting he considered a subject not to be trifled with, as is shown by the rules for polite behaviour, which he is careful in all seriousness to detail in his book. As for his faults, one suspects that in public he was inclined to be dictatorial and perhaps pompous, but he possessed a saving grace of humour. In his home, if we are to trust his own assertions, he must have been a strict disciplinarian.

Studies in Life from Jewish Proverbs

Many of his sayings are too worldly-wise to be commendable. Now and then he is cynical, and for the out-and-out fool he allows no hope: to essay teaching such an one is as futile as glueing a broken potsherd together (E. 22⁷); and again, *Seven days are the days of mourning for the dead, but for a fool all the days of his life* (E. 22¹²)! Still, Ben Sirach was no pessimist about humanity, and his judgments of men for the most part are kindly and hopeful.

The outstanding feature of his personality was his *breadth* of interest. "Whether it is upon the subject of behaviour at table, or concerning a man's treatment of a headstrong daughter, or about the need of keeping a guard over one's tongue, or concerning the folly of a fool, or the delights of a banquet, or whether he is dealing with self-control, borrowing, loose women, slander, diet, the miser, the spendthrift, the hypocrite, the parasite, keeping secrets, giving alms, standing surety, mourning for the dead, and a large variety of other topics—he has always something to say, which for sound and robust common-sense is of abiding value."[1]

Except that he puts the point in his own way, there is in matter or opinion little in Ben Sirach's book that could not be paralleled from the *Book of Proverbs*. But in manner an interesting difference is observable. *Ecclesiasticus* is far and away superior in point of literary charm. It has the merit of constant variety, and in places real grace of expression, for to a much greater degree than in the *Book of Proverbs* Ben Sirach has developed the brief unit-proverb into epigrams and sonnets, short essays, eulogies and longer odes; and although the unit-proverb is still frequent, it is no longer the sum and substance of the book. Thus by the skilful use of the more elaborate forms, the almost unrelieved disjointedness that detracts

---

[1] Oesterley, *Ecclesiasticus*, p. xviii.

The Ideal

so seriously from the pleasure of reading *Proverbs* is triumphantly overcome.

In criticism of Ben Sirach's ethical attainments, one is inclined to call attention to the juxtaposition of great and little matters which he perpetrates in his book: a feature also to be observed in *Proverbs*. Questions of fundamental moral law and trivialities of etiquette are astonishingly conjoined, apparently without his feeling the least sense of the absurdity. Thus he bids his pupil be ashamed " of unjust dealing before a partner and a friend, of theft in the place where he sojourns, and of falsifying an oath and a covenant, and of *leaning on the table with the elbow when at meat* " (E. 41[17-19]) ! Manners and morals, one is driven to suppose, had not been sufficiently differentiated in general opinion. Then also, just when our respect for Ben Sirach is quietly increasing, he is apt to dismay us by interjecting some most unideal observation, as when immediately after delivering a stinging censure on lying speech, he remarks (E. 20[29]) that gifts which *blind the eyes of the Wise, and are a muzzle on the mouth*, are an effective way of appeasing influential persons. Nevertheless, as one reads his book, the conviction deepens that Ben Sirach was sincere and earnest in his profession of morality, and such falls from grace as the proverb just quoted are probably due to his anxiety to give an honest representation of the facts of life. It has been said in his favour that he was no platitudinarian, by which, of course, is not meant that his book contains no platitudes, but only that in face of the supreme problems of human existence he did not cravenly blink the facts, but faced them and sought to do justice to them ; as for instance when, writing of death, he owns that to a healthy and prosperous man it is wholly a " bitter remembrance " (E. 41[1]).

From youth to his dying day this man loved and served Wisdom, and his volume is a storehouse of many noble

Studies in Life from Jewish Proverbs

and valuable thoughts. It may be charged against the authors of *Proverbs* that they paid scant regard to the peculiar national aspirations of their race. If so, Ben Sirach can be acquitted on that score. He had a thoroughly patriotic outlook, for he makes it quite clear that to his mind Judaism was the real home of Wisdom and the truly wise man is a loyal Jew obedient to the Law. His sense of the marvel of the world as a revelation of divine power, which he expresses in two chapters of considerable ability, shows that he was not without poetic feeling.[1] All his thinking rested on belief in a great and holy God, Source of all Wisdom, in whom he exhorts men to put their trust, from whom they must ever seek guidance.

A worthy citizen! Of whom does he remind us? Surely of such a man as was Horace, strolling on the Appian Way, pleased with himself and with his fortunes, much interested in the pageant of life, keenly observant both of the faults and the graces of his fellows, humorous, shrewd and kindly? Or of Chaucer, part courtier, part business man of London town, yet with a quick eye and swift sympathy for the deeper issues in the human drama? Or (to come nearer our own days) of Pepys, with his matter-of-fact ways, his sturdy, average morality, and his honest enjoyment of the good things of life? Or of Dr. Johnson, with his natural pomposity and his big, generous soul? Yes, of all these; but Ben Sirach had one great quality that perhaps none of these possessed to the same extent—a most earnest sense of duty in regard to his fellow men, a whole-hearted desire to give them the advantage of the lessons life had taught him.

Perhaps the reader is disappointed still. When the utmost has been said for these ideals, he may feel that there is no new insight into the mystery of things, and no irresistible appeal to conscience. But remember that even an

[1] E. 42, 43.

The Ideal

imperfect Cause and an inadequate Ideal, provided the fundamental aim be generous and sound, may be the source of real and lasting benefits to men, for life is such that the goal we fain would reach instantaneously must, as a matter of fact, be approached by small advances, which therefore ought not be despised. The Wise, it is true, were neither perfect Saints nor complete Philosophers, but our subject is the Humanism of the Jewish proverbs, and if even this Ben Sirach, model pupil of Wisdom, is not a wholly inspiring figure—is he not very human ? Moreover, the utmost has not yet been said on behalf of the Sages.

CHAPTER IX

The Exaltation of Wisdom

CONTINUING the criticism of the ideal or ideals of the last chapter, it may be said that the morality commended is not unusual nor markedly superior to that of other peoples. Do not many of these proverbs state the merest *a b c* of ethical sentiment, for which any civilised nation could produce a parallel in its proverbs ? The charge is not only true in a general way, it has special force in view of the circumstances of the fourth to the second centuries B.C. For there is evidence of a widespread tendency to sententious moralising in that period, and, had we so desired, this Jewish movement might have been considered only as part of a larger whole.[1] Among the Greeks, especially in Asia Minor, this was the age when several gnomic poets, such as Menander and Phocylides, won fame and popularity by their moral aphorisms, and indeed the Jewish proverbs have many opinions in common with contemporary Hellenic sayings. In Egypt also there was current a collection of ethical observations, the Precepts of Ptah-hotep and the Maxims of Aniy, so closely resembling the form and sentiment of the average Jewish proverb that it has been suggested that the Sages of Palestine were directly influenced by these Egyptian teachings. Certainly the resemblances are striking. These Egyptian books " inculcate the study of Wisdom, duty to parents and superiors, respect for property, the advantages of charitableness,

[1] See Skinner in the *Jewish Quarterly Review*, Jan., 1905, p. 258.

The Exaltation of Wisdom

peaceableness and content, of liberality, chastity, and sobriety, of truthfulness and justice; and they show the wickedness and folly of disobedience, strife, arrogance and pride, of slothfulness, interference, unchastity, and other vices." What then ? Is the idealism of the Jews decreased in value because other nations also had moral ambitions ? Judging from the facts of history, the elements of morality, and of commonsense, too, need constant iteration in all languages and all periods, not excluding the present. To discover that most of the Jewish proverbs are far from unique is no real loss, indeed the danger lies rather in the other direction. If it could be shown that these maxims were unlike those current elsewhere among men, the accusation would be serious, for then this volume must needs be written, not on the humanism, but on the unhumanism of a part of the Bible. The charge that the Jewish maxims are not unusual is to be admitted and—dismissed.

More disquieting would be the contention, which the number of self-regarding maxims readily suggests, that the general moral tone of these proverbs is not merely normal but actually low. There is no denying the unblushing utilitarianism that at times crops out. It is said: *I (Wisdom) walk in the paths of righteousness, in the midst of the paths of judgement, that I may cause those that love me to inherit substance and that I may fill their treasuries* (Pr. 8^{21})— *The reward of humility and the fear of the Lord is riches and honour and life* (Pr. 22^4). This sounds even more reprehensible than the famous definition of Christianity as " doing good for the sake of the kingdom of heaven." It seems suspiciously like doing good for the sake of the kingdoms of this earth! But, hear the defence. First it has already been urged that general judgments on the proverbs *as a whole* require most careful handling, if they are to be even moderately fair : let the utilitarian sage bear his own sin; his brother who said, " Love

Studies in Life from Jewish Proverbs

covereth all transgressions," ought not to be implicated in his fall. Secondly, there is the sensible, though not lofty, argument that since the Wise were dealing with men tempted to throw off even ordinary moral restraint in the burning desire to get all possible prosperity and enjoyment out of life, if they had pitched their key much higher it is very probable they would have received no hearing at all. Modern students of ethics are well aware that pleasure, however often it may accompany good conduct, cannot be made the motive for virtue. But the Wise were less sophisticated than ourselves, and it was therefore easy for them to make the mistake of expressing in too commercial a fashion their conviction that "honesty is the best policy"[1]; and even if they did sometimes over-emphasise the thought of external reward, we should remember that perhaps it was the only way to catch the ear of certain men and draw them back from the hot pursuit of Folly. The third point will be surprising to those who are not aware how late in Jewish history was the development of a worthy conception of immortality and the just judgment of the soul after death. Compared with the Christian, who starts from the belief that "God is not the God of the dead, but of the living," and that the consequences of good or evil conduct reach onwards beyond the grave, the Wise-men of Israel were cruelly handicapped in their consideration of the moral problem. Oesterley with justice pleads in extenuation of Ben Sirach's stress on the worldly advantages of Wisdom, "This is natural in a writer whose whole attention is concentrated on the present life, and who has nothing but the vaguest ideas about a life hereafter."[2] Fourthly, the Wise were not conscious of their utilitarianism. Of course it is bad to be utilitarian at all, but it is better to be so uninten-

[1] A proverb which does *not* come from the Bible, though many people have supposed it does.

[2] See further pp. 191f.

The Exaltation of Wisdom

tionally than deliberately. The ancients did not, could not, speak or write with that precise realisation of the implications of words, which often does, and certainly should, characterise a modern thinker. While therefore the Wise cannot be exonerated from blame in this respect, there is not a little to be said in mitigation of their offence.

But the last plea we have to advance on their behalf is the best; and indeed it is the main apology we wish to make for all their shortcomings—

A man's utterances are often an inadequate expression of his soul. Our final estimate ought to be based, not on the proverbs themselves, singly or collectively, but on what is behind them, the character of the speakers. The question is, Were these sayings just verbal piety and respectable commonplace, or were they, so to speak, waves borne on the swell of an advancing tide, having beneath and behind them the deep impulse of a live enthusiasm? What manner of men were the Sages at heart—mere talkers, seeking the mental satisfaction of turning a neat phrase and sunning themselves in popular esteem, or men genuinely concerned for the moral welfare of their fellows? One we have already considered and not found him altogether wanting. Much can be forgiven if only the majority of the Wise were like Ben Sirach, in earnest about their task. We ventured to describe him as a typical Wise-man, but what ground is there for that assertion?

Now this vital question is not an easy one to investigate and answer, since concerning the individual Sages, except Ben Sirach, no personal information has been transmitted, and we have therefore only their sayings from which to draw a conclusion. Even so the material is perhaps sufficient. Surely there is a valuable hint to be found in the "strict attention to business" of *Proverbs* as well as *Ecclesiasticus*; both of these books preach at us incessantly from their text "Wisdom." Why is it

Studies in Life from Jewish Proverbs

that every word they contain is directed to the end of moral improvement? Must there not have been a remarkable concentration on moral interests to account for the comparative absence of what one might describe as the neutral, non-moral observations on life, which are common in the proverbs of every other nation?[1] Fortunately however, there is one much stronger piece of evidence available. It has been explained that the abstract conception "Wisdom" represented the teaching of the Wise in epitome, and was the unification in thought of their manifold opinions. It follows that what they said, or left unsaid, about "Wisdom" furnishes an admirable test of their sincerity, revealing the presence or absence of enthusiasm for their work. Wisdom was the Cause they championed against Folly: it will be easy to tell whether they truly loved it. If they had been only clever people, content to parade their shrewdness, or comfortable upholders of law and order, proclaiming the maxims of respectability with a business eye to the security of their own possessions, then inevitably they would have betrayed themselves by giving an exposition of Wisdom coldly intellectual. But the opposite is what has happened, and the warmth and passion as well as the reverence, of their words in honour of Wisdom bear eloquent, unconscious testimony to the admiration and affection in which the Sages held their calling. Hear then the Praises of Wisdom—

Happy is the man that findeth Wisdom, and the man that getteth understanding; for the merchandise of it is better than silver, and the gain thereof than fine gold. She is more precious than rubies, and none of the things that thou canst desire are comparable unto her . . . (Pr. 3$^{13\text{-}15}$): surely a disconcerting verse for upholders of the supposed utilitarianism of the proverbs? Again, *How*

[1] *i.e.*, such proverbs as "A burnt child dreads the fire," or "He that is down need fear no fall."

The Exaltation of Wisdom

much better is it to get Wisdom than gold! Yea to get understanding is to be chosen rather than silver (Pr. 16^{16}, cp. 8^{10})—so much for the Sages' notion of comparative values. In chapter 9 of *Proverbs*, by a touch of fine imagination, Wisdom is daringly pictured as a noble Lady, bidding guests to her banquet. She is the counterpart of Madam Folly, who also gives a banquet and who thus invites a passer-by: *Stolen waters are sweet, and bread eaten in secret is pleasant,* (to which the Wise add in caustic comment as they see the foolish one enter: *But he knoweth not that the dead are there, that her guests are in the depth of Sheol,* Pr. 9^{17,18}). But, in contrast, Wisdom—*Wisdom hath builded her house, she hath hewn out her seven pillars: she hath killed her beasts, she hath made ready her wine, and furnished her table. She hath sent forth her maidens; on the highest parts of the city she crieth aloud, " Whoso is ignorant, let him turn in hither "; and to him that is void of understanding she speaketh, " Come, eat ye of my bread, and drink of the wine which I have made ready "* (Pr. 9$^{1-5}$). Ben Sirach knew that Wisdom was high, and he does not disguise that only by long, unwearying efforts can her favour be attained. But the reward, says he, outweighs the toil, and he bids men seek her: *At the first she will bring fear and dread upon a man and torment him with her discipline, until she can trust his soul and has tested him by her judgements* (E. 4^{17}; cp. E. 6$^{19-25}$). Nevertheless, he says, *Come unto her with all thy soul, and keep her ways with thy whole power. Search and seek, and she shall be made known unto thee, and when thou hast hold of her, let her not go. For in the end thou shalt find her to be rest, and she shall be changed for thee into gladness. Her fetters shall be to thee a covering of strength, and her chains a robe of glory* (E. 6$^{26-29}$).

Wisdom is the source of all right and noble conduct, the principle that in all things ought to regulate men's lives. Casting behind him the grim facts of Hellenistic courts, and

Studies in Life from Jewish Proverbs

perhaps of high society in Jerusalem also, one wise man, seeing in vision the world as it should be, put these glowing, optimistic words into the mouth of Wisdom: *By me kings reign, and princes decree justice. By me princes rule, and nobles, even all the judges of the earth* (Pr. 8:15,16).

But all these praises are slight compared with the thoughts inspired by the supreme conviction that Wisdom itself is derived from God and dwells in His Presence: "The Wisdom that illumines the lives of the good is a reflection of the full-orbed wisdom of God."[1] It is the ineffable counsel of the Almighty, the power by which He created heaven and earth (Pr. 3:19f), the principle through which the universe is still sustained. In face of this belief praise rose into exultation, and Wisdom was reverently but enthusiastically conceived as that which had been ordained of God from eternity to be His counsellor in the work of Creation and His daily delight:

Jehovah formed me first of His creation,
  Before all his works of old.
In the earliest ages was I fashioned,
  Even from the beginning, before the earth.
When there were no depths was I brought forth,
  When there were no fountains brimming with water.
Before the mountains were sunk in their bases,
  Before the hills was I brought forth;
Or ever He had made the earth and the fields,
  Or the first clods of the world.
When He established the heavens I was there,
  When he drew the circle over the abyss;
When He made firm the skies above,
  And set fast the fountains of the deep;
When He gave the sea its bounds,
  And fixed the foundations of the earth,

[1] Gordon, *Poets of the Old Testament*, p. 296.

The Exaltation of Wisdom

Then was I with Him as a foster-child,
  And daily was I His delight,
As I played continually before His eyes,
  Played o'er all the habitable world.
So now, my children, hearken unto me,
  Receive my instruction and be wise;
For happy is the man that heareth me,
  Happy are those that keep my ways,
Watching daily at my gates,
  And waiting at my gate-posts.
For he that findeth me findeth life,
  And winneth favour from Jehovah;
But he that misseth me wrongeth himself:
  All that hate me love death. (Pr. 8$^{22\text{-}36}$).[1]

In similar language Ben Sirach imagines Wisdom proclaiming her glory in the very presence of God Himself:

I came forth from the mouth of the Most High,
  And like a cloud I covered the earth;
I had my dwelling in the high places,
  And my throne was in the pillar of cloud;
I alone compassed the circuit of heaven
  And walked in the depth of the abysses,
In the waves of the sea and through all the earth;
  And in every people I got me a possession.
With all these I sought for a resting-place—
  " In whose lot shall I find a lodging ? "
Then the Creator of all commanded me,
  Even he that formed me, pitched my tent
And said, " In Jacob be thy dwelling,
  And in Israel thine inheritance."
In the beginning, before the world, He fashioned me,
  And to all eternity shall I fail not.

[1] Gordon's translation, *op. cit.*, p. 296.

Studies in Life from Jewish Proverbs

In the holy tabernacle I ministered before Him,
  And thus was I established in Zion;
Yea, in the beloved city He gave me resting-place,
  And in Jerusalem was my dominion (E. 24$^{3\text{-}11}$)[1].

Such words would have set the Greeks, as they set us, asking questions: " Is it implied that Wisdom is an entity distinct from God?"; "How far is it fair to see Greek influence in this apparent ascription of personality to Wisdom?" Both questions may be considered together. Too much stress cannot be laid on the firm hold which Monotheism had obtained in post-exilic Judaism; to the Jews of the Hellenic age the unity of God was a fundamental tenet. But the Jewish mind was as yet unphilosophical, not from lack of intelligence but from lack of inclination or initial suggestion. Hebrew thought started from the existence of God as an axiom, and was content to use the fact of conscience as the key to the interpretation of life, whereas Greek thought had naturally inclined towards making intellectual speculation the basis of its endeavour to attain through truth, morality, and beauty to the secret of life and the knowledge of God. Consequently many utterances that inevitably raise metaphysical questions in our minds, and would have philosophical meaning if spoken by a Greek, were put forward by the Jews most simply, without consideration of inherent intellectual problems. Of this character are the praises of Wisdom: although language is used that would fittingly be applied to a personal being, there was no intention to personify Wisdom as some kind of sub-divine Being other than God. The Wise

---

[1] Gordon, *op. cit.*, p. 298. Observe the touch of national sentiment which is characteristic of Ben Sirach. His view is that God intended good to every nation (not an easy doctrine to reach in face of the enormities of which some of the heathen nations surrounding Israel were capable), but, although God had offered wisdom to all, only Israel had responded to the offer and so received the divine gift.

The Exaltation of Wisdom

intended only to declare their fervent belief that the Wisdom they studied, loved, and trusted, was transcendently great, was *God's* Wisdom, was " from above." Wisdom in these proverbs was not consciously deemed to be more than an attribute of God, and phrases that seem to us to overstep the bounds and confer personality are to be regarded as an enthusiasm of the heart not implying metaphysical conclusions as to the ultimate nature of Deity.[1] This is the language not of philosophy but of affection and reverent esteem. From an early age there was a strong tendency in Hebrew thought towards clothing abstract and collective terms in the warm language of personal life, and the books of *Proverbs* and *Ecclesiasticus* may fairly be considered a natural development of pure Hebrew tradition.[2] And yet there are " signs of the times " about them. The description of Wisdom we are discussing would read strangely in pre-exilic Hebrew books; and so the question of Greek influence may still be pressed. In the opinion of the present writer the influence, if any, is confined to a slight unintentional colouring. Seeing that the Wise stood out against the pressure and menace of unscrupulous, secular Hellenism, and that they lived at a period when Greek intellectual prowess had not yet brought its full weight to bear on Palestinian, or at least on Judæan, thought, it is a reasonable conjecture that any trace of new philosophy in the proverbs has been introduced unwittingly and unwillingly. The general soundness of this opinion becomes vividly apparent, if the two passages quoted above are compared with the eulogy given in a Jewish work of considerably later date, the *Wisdom of Solomon*. There Wisdom, Artificer of all things, is described as

---

[1] See the discussion in Abelson, *The Immanence of God in Rabbinical Literature*, pp. 199ff.

[2] Cp. G. A. Smith, *Modern Criticism and the Preaching of the Old Testament*, p. 288.

Studies in Life from Jewish Proverbs

A spirit, quick of understanding, holy,
Only-begotten, manifold, subtle, mobile,
Pure, undefiled, clean,
Inviolable, loving the good . . .
For Wisdom is more mobile than any motion,
Yea, she pervadeth and penetrateth all things
By reason of her pureness;
For she is a breath of the power of God,
And a pure effulgence of the Almighty.

(*Wisdom of Solomon,* 7[22ff]).

and in one verse (*W.S.* 9[4]) Wisdom is actually called *She that sitteth beside Thee on Thy throne*, astonishing words from a Jew. The atmosphere of Hellenic philosophy being here unmistakable, the contrast between the language of this passage and the restrained phraseology of *Proverbs* and *Ecclesiasticus* is accordingly significant.

As the *Book of Job* is treated in another volume of this series, the reference to it must here be brief, but a chapter on the Exaltation of Wisdom must not close without some mention of the wonderful poem in that Book, where also confession is made of the sublimity of Wisdom, but it is insisted that Wisdom dwells far beyond the reach of mortals, unknown and unknowable, save to the inscrutable Deity who wills not to reveal its secrets unto suffering man. Each section of this great passage begins with the haunting question, *But Wisdom—whence cometh it, and where is the place of understanding?* We quote the last stanza only.

But Wisdom—whence cometh it,
  And where is the place of understanding?
It is hid from the eyes of all creatures,
  And concealed from the fowls of the air.
Abaddon and Death acknowledge:
  " But a rumour thereof have we heard."

The Exaltation of Wisdom

God alone hath perceived the way to it,
He knoweth the place thereof—
Even He that made weights for the wind
And meted the waters by measure,
When He made a law for the rain,
And a way for the flash of the thunders.
Then did He see it and mark it:
He established and searched it out (Job 28$^{20\text{-}27}$).[1]

"The Humanism of the Bible"—who would ask finer acknowledgment of one aspect of life, its profound mystery; who could fail to hear in those grand but desolate words the pathos of our mortal ignorance voicing its immortal longing? Happier than this poet, and more in accord with ordinary human experience, were the Wise-men of *Proverbs;* for theirs was the faith that, though Wisdom might dwell in the innermost light of God's presence, the boon of its guidance was not wholly denied to men. They praised its exceeding great glory, acknowledging its transcendence, yet quietly rejoicing in the measure of knowledge they were conscious of receiving:

> *Wisdom is the principal thing,*
> *Therefore get Wisdom:*
> *Yea! with all that thou hast gotten*
> *Get understanding* (Pr. 4^7).

---

[1] Gordon's translation, *op. cit.*, p. 304.

CHAPTER X

The Hill "Difficulty"

THE Wise had not found the last secrets of Wisdom. There were ranges of human nature beyond their imagining, there were paths to salvation not visible from the highroad of respectability. Perhaps they suspected as much in moments when the sublimity of Wisdom towered over them. But usually no doubt they felt convinced that, given an unquestioning acceptance of their precepts, this world would be made perfect. Better it would have been, but that is all. Perfection is higher than climbing humanity believes, and short cuts to the summit prove delusive. Mechanical obedience to rules and regulations for our conduct will certainly not suffice, for character fails to ripen in that dry soil. So to reverence the past as to accept its thoughts as finished standards, requiring from us only the repetition of the lips and not the re-affirmation or re-statement of heart and intellect, is to exclude the possibility of progress; and that, racially, is the unpardonable sin. Tradition, an invaluable servant, is a fatal master. God means us to own no ultimate authority save His eternal and ever-present Spirit. There was room in the world for many a Ben Sirach, but there was even more room for men like St. Peter and St. Paul, who could break free from conventional standards of morality, and penetrate further into the exceeding great and precious promises of God.

Moreover it would have been disastrous for the Wise themselves, had the world accepted their way of life as indis-

The Hill "Difficulty"

putable truth. Think what would have happened to their characters, already inclined to superiority, if with one accord men had bowed down to their every word and received their maxims as beyond the breath of criticism. The point of course, is not one that the Sages would have appreciated. Few men can resist the impression (and those few must be cold-blooded, unenthusiastic souls) that all would be well, provided their lightest word was law. What a truly delightful world, where one's judgments met only with reverent and grateful admiration! Yet were God to give us the desire of our hearts, we might construct a universe excellent according to our standard, and be left ourselves the only insufferable persons in it. "Sweet are the uses of adversity."

There was, however, little danger of the Wise being spoilt by approbation. They may have had a sufficiently good conceit of themselves, but they cannot possibly have been ignorant that many of their neighbours held them in very different esteem; and whenever a Wise-man in old Jerusalem put his heart into the effort to guide his brethren into the path of understanding he can have been under few, if any, delusions regarding the obstacles in the way. In the last two chapters we have been picturing life as the Wise desired it to be, not as they actually found it. Our next duty is to descend from these heights to the plain where opposition waited to test what stuff the Wise-men's dreams were made of. Not without courage, not without patience, were they able to keep these ideals in their hearts.

The discouragements they suffered are written large across the face of the literature. Consider first the reception accorded to their teaching. All the Jews were not lovers of Understanding, nor was Jerusalem a State wherein the dictates of celestial Wisdom ruled with unquestioned sway. No doubt the note of confidence which pervades *Proverbs* and *Ecclesiasticus* implies that many people

Studies in Life from Jewish Proverbs

respected the Wise-men's dignity and paid deference to their speeches. But the presence of outspoken hostility is not a whit less clear. They did not preach unchallenged at the entry of the Gates. On the contrary the number and severity of the proverbs denouncing " scorners " show that the irreverent were a vigorous section of the population. We have to bear in mind that the Gateway was open to all-comers, and *Psalm* 1¹ (*Blessed is the man that sitteth not in the assembly of the scornful*) supplies a hint that the scoffer (and his friends) may have had an inconvenient habit of claiming his own corner of the ground, and that not infrequently it pleased him to be merry at the Wise-man's expense, now pretending he could not, or would not, hear the sermon (*A scorner heareth not rebuke*, Pr. 13¹), now deriding the doctrine (*I have called and ye have refused, I have stretched out my hand and no man regarded: Ye have set at nought all my counsel and would have none of my reproof*, Pr. 1²⁴ᶠ); now encouraging others to make vexatious interruptions (*Cast out the scorner, and contention shall go out*, Pr. 22¹⁰). Sage-baiting seems to have been a joke that waxed not stale with repetition: "*How long*," asks one Wise man pathetically, "*how long will scorners delight in their scorning*" (Pr. 1²²)? *He that reproveth a scorner getteth himself insult* (Pr. 9⁷)—behold a sage by the street-corner, wise in words but by no means so sharp in repartee, shaking a puzzled head and wondering what the laughter had been about and why his audience had so speedily melted away.

Besides these cynical persons—the scorners or intentional fools—there were fools-by-birth, whether dull-witted or coarse-natured or both, " Simpletons," to whom the Wise were perhaps less charitable than is meet. But then " suffering fools gladly " belongs to the apostolic ethic; and it vexed the Wise to think how much breath they had wasted in seeking to teach these folk. Glorious Wisdom stirred no enthusiasm in their obtuse souls, and the

The Hill "Difficulty"

shafts of morality seldom discovered a joint in the armour of their self-content. Wherefore, concerning these also went up the cry, "*How long, ye simpletons, will ye love simplicity*" (Pr. 1^{22})? And when we read that *the sluggard is wiser in his own conceit then seven men that can render a reason* (Pr.26^{16}), who can fail to see a baffled Sage turning wearily and disgustedly away? Towards the dull-witted is due mercy and patience; but oh! those self-satisfied, petty persons, ignorant of their ignorance, into whose mental darkness no new illuminating thought can penetrate. These were the prime objects of the Wise-men's indignation—and legitimately; for in all ages they have been the curse of society, the mainstay of old abuses, rocks which have to be blasted from the path of progress. Of your charity, then, bear in mind that the Wise did not lecture picked pupils only, but faced the contradictions and stupidities of the highway, and endured the disappointment of seeing men hostile or indifferent to their teaching.

But the point will bear further consideration. Two types of opponents may be distinguished. First, the actively hostile, whose manner of life was in violent contradiction to the Wise-men's principles, men who must often have hated them for their moralising efforts. In the mirror of the sayings we observe the immoral, the cruel, the violent, plotters of mischief against their neighbours, whose deeds were evil, whose words scorched like a fire (Pr. 16^{27}); dishonest dealers and pitiless usurers, who robbed the poor and crushed the defenceless (Pr. 22^{22}); men who lured others into wickedness; bloodthirsty men, thieves, cut-throats, and reckless outlaws (Pr. 1^{11f}). Against these Wisdom, for all its exaltation, must often have seemed powerless. Secondly, there was the mass of the indifferent, who, being neither very good nor very bad, did not think Wisdom mattered very much or that it was any special concern of theirs: a type with abundant representatives to-day.

Studies in Life from Jewish Proverbs

Why will they not comprehend that it is to them, almost more than to any others, that Wisdom is crying aloud; and that their co-operation is desperately needed for the advancement of mankind? Why do they saunter so carelessly down the streets of life, sometimes to fall into sore disaster from which a little Wisdom, had they sought it, would have saved them? Why do they always pass " the preacher for next Sunday " without a second thought? Ah! these are they that require a full church and good music and a first-rate sermon. But if *they* attended, the churches would be full and the choirs strong; and sermons have a way of winning home when men are out not for oratory, but to seek the truth of God.

Certainly the Wise were not ignorant of the problem of the inattentive. Something of disappointment and perplexity lies behind the reiterated appeals of the *Book of Proverbs*: *Hear, O my son, and receive my sayings . . . My son, let them not depart from thine eyes . . . Hear, my son, the instruction of a father, and attend to know, for I give you good doctrine*. Granted that the exhortation tended to become a set phrase, and that " my son " was often spoken to an eager pupil or an attentive class in the Wise-man's house, it was also used in the market place, and for one man that stopped and responded how many passed by unheeding? *Doth not Wisdom cry and Understanding put forth her voice? In the streets she takes her stand; beside the gates, at the portal of the city, at the entrance of the gates she cries aloud* (Pr. 8^{1-3})—frequently, we may suspect, with small result. See, yonder is Alexander ben Simeon, young, confident and well-to-do, proud to think that his parents have called him by the name of the great Greek conqueror. He comes strolling through the bazaar to the gate of the city. There two voices accost him. One, that of his friend Aristobulus: " Greeting, Alexander! Hast heard news of the boxing? 'Tis said that Aristonicus is beaten

The Hill "Difficulty"

in the Olympic *pankcration*. 'By whom?' By Cleitomachus of Thebes.[1] But I swear it cannot have been by fair means. How sayest thou?" The other voice was that of Judah the Wise, who, perceiving the two young men in talk, approached them hopefully and earnestly, though of course with all necessary dignity. "A wise son," said he, "maketh a glad father, but a foolish son is a heaviness to his mother. Now, therefore, my sons, hearken unto me, for blessed are they that keep my ways. Treasures of wickedness profit nothing, but righteousness . . ." Unfortunately the last words were not heard by Alexander and Aristobulus. They were already some distance off, hunting for the man who had spread the rumour of the downfall of Egyptian athletics.

But others besides the young could be deaf to good counsel. Jerusalem had many confident citizens of middle life, into whose soul the cares of the world and the deceitfulness of riches and the lusts of other things had entered, choking the Word: *the rich man's wealth is his strong city, and as an high wall in his imagination* (Pr. 18[11]), said the Wise with a sigh. There is one proverb that suggests where the most grievous personal disappointment of the Wise lay: namely, in those, whether boy or man, who said "I go, Sir; but went not": *Cease, my son, to hear instruction, only to err from the words of knowledge* (Pr. 19[27]). Surely there was sorrow in the heart of him who uttered those words of warning?

In the next place consider the hindrances that the general conditions of the age placed in the path of morality. These also are not difficult to perceive. The moral corruption of the luxurious Hellenic cities may have been perfectly obvious and the danger unmistakably clear, but dazzling opportunities, political, social, and commercial,

[1] At Olympia in the year 212 B.C. Aristonicus was the *protégé* of King Ptolemy, and champion of the Egyptian gymnasia.

Studies in Life from Jewish Proverbs

also lay waiting there for the young and ambitious Jew. Is it to be wondered if many a lad was ready to make a bid for fortune, and let his morality take its chance ? Important families of Jerusalem, with a handsome son who might perhaps win favour at the foreign courts or shekels in their markets, will have had little love for old-fashioned, moralistic Wiseacres, who forsooth were stupid enough to oppose " the onward march of progress."

One passage (Pr. 1^{10-19}), addressed to " my son," urges him not to take up highway robbery as a career : *If they say,* " *Let us lay wait for blood, let us lurk privily for the innocent without cause* " . . . *consent not thou,* but there cannot have been much outlet for promising youths in that direction; it is perhaps a formal rather than a serious warning. Much more prominent were the sensual temptations to which prosperous persons were exposed, temptation to indulge in gluttonous feasting and drunken revelry. Such vices were alluring to an extent unknown to us who live in an age when society is no longer slave-ridden, when the wealthy can have as many duties to occupy their energies as the poor, and when it is no longer gentlemanly to be drunk. You cannot make a drunken man wise until you have sobered him. But the evils of intoxication, though real enough, were less serious in old Jerusalem than in modern cities, and in wine the Wise saw an enemy only where pronounced abuse was present. Complete abstinence is unmooted, and even temperance is demanded in very temperate terms. Ben Sirach bestows an encomium on wine taken in moderation. *Wine,* says he, *is as good as life to men, if thou drink it in its measure. What life is there to a man that is without wine ? And it hath been created to make men glad. Wine drunk in season and to satisfy is joy of heart and gladness of soul* (E. 31^{27}). He observes its quarrelsome tendencies, but thinks it necessary only to counsel tact ! *Rebuke not thy neighbour at a banquet of*

The Hill "Difficulty"

wine, neither set him at nought in his mirth. Speak not unto him a word of reproach, and press him not then for repayment of a debt (E. 31³¹). In like manner *Proverbs* 31⁶,⁷ is not suitable as a text for a Temperance address, even if (which is doubtful) it be partly metaphorical: *Give strong drink unto him that is ready to perish, and wine unto the bitter in soul: let him drink and forget his poverty and remember his misery no more.* Here's a stick to beat the teetotallers withal! How one can imagine some foolish persons discovering that even a text is worth picking up (if it will serve to throw at an opponent), and pouncing gleefully upon these sayings. "Foolish persons"? Yes, "foolish"; for the effects of alcohol in the development of modern society have been, and are, calamitous to the material as well as the spiritual progress of the race. Moreover, even the Wise were insistent in denunciation of *excessive* drinking. Said Ben Sirach, *Wine drunk largely is bitterness of soul with provocation and wrath.*[1] *Drunkenness increaseth the rage of a fool unto his hurt; it diminisheth strength and addeth wounds* (E. 31²⁹,³⁰; cp. Pr. 20¹, 23²⁹ff, quoted pp. 138, 232). There is no possible doubt what their attitude would have been towards the facts of the modern Drink Question. Had they seen one thousandth part of the moral and material losses consequent upon drunkenness and heavy drinking in the great European or American cities, the book of their proverbs would have been replete with commands and entreaties for reform.

In respect of the relations of the sexes, the *morale* of the post-exilic Jewish state was high. Monogamy was the custom, and the virtuous wife received a degree of honour unequalled in the old Oriental world. There are, however, in the proverbs frequent warnings against adultery; but, as the Hebrews were more outspoken than ourselves on such

[1] The Hebrew text seems to have read, "Headache, shame and disgrace are the effect of wine drunk in provocation and wrath."

Studies in Life from Jewish Proverbs

matters, it may be that the prominence of the subject points not so much to the prevalence of the offence as to the indignation with which it was regarded. Yet it must be borne in mind that the crowded city life of the period increased temptations to that sin. More serious socially was the evil of venal women. Schechter[1] is of opinion that the repeated denunciations of " strange women " exaggerate the low state of morality in Jerusalem, but, with all reasonable allowance for rhetoric, it is certain that the peril was never absent from the streets of Jerusalem, and in the brilliant cities of Egypt and Syria, so close at hand, licence walked unrestrained and unrebuked. The Wise knew only too well how powerful and deadly a foe this evil could prove to their hopes for men.[2]

The arch-enemy, not only of Idealism, but of the mildest proposals for reform has ever been the selfish individual. Turn to the proverbs, many of which have already been quoted, about rich men, about money-lenders, false-witnesses, slanderers, oppressive rulers and unjust judges; and it becomes easy to realise how strong was the opposition confronting the preachers of Wisdom.[3]

Finally, recollect the gulf between a reform in words and its translation into fact. With all our political machinery designed to yield better legislation, how difficult it is to give effect to the will of the wiser and nobler members of the community. Ancient society found it incalculably harder to redress its wrongs. Grievances were not always stifled; they might be aired in moderation and provided the charge was vague. But, short of revolution, how was it possible to bring adequate pressure to bear on the guilty, strongly entrenched in their high offices by birth and wealth and

[1] *Judaism* (second series), p. 57.

[2] Cp. Pr. 2$^{16-19}$; E. 9$^{3-9}$, 19^2, 41^{20}; and refs. on p. 153.

[3] See especially chaps. vii., viii., and xviii.

The Hill "Difficulty"

autocratic might? These and similar considerations will suggest the external difficulties of the life in which the Wise were placed.

To the " fightings without," however, must next be added a tale of " fears within." The Old Testament writers were not unconscious of the intellectual problems of religion. It is true that they do not debate, or often doubt, the *existence* of God. But the question of the Being of God is, in a sense, academic; the question of His character and relation to men is vital; and this problem the Jews felt as acutely and faced as honestly as any modern men can do. Many of them had encountered realities of experience sterner than most modernists have known—at least until 1914. Some of the Sages, no doubt, were unspeculative persons, content with traditional beliefs. But others there were not blind to any of the poignant elements of life. All may have assumed God as a fact, but some realised that only if God be just and holy and merciful, was the ground of morality solid beneath their feet. Men who maintained that in the fear of the Lord and honourable conduct is found the key to a successful career, could not ignore the fact that in reality the wicked were frequently prosperous and the good subject to misfortune, injustice, pain, and bitter hardships. How could such things be in the world of a righteous God? Not until the post-exilic period was it vividly realised by a number of Jewish thinkers how obdurate these facts are to an optimistic interpretation of life, and how they menace not only belief in a gracious God, but also the whole structure of morality. In many of the later Psalms, and in portions of the Wisdom literature, to which the *Book of Proverbs* belongs, the stringency of the problem is clearly recognised, and the struggle for faith grows corespondingly severe. Men cried to God to sustain their trust despite the awful enigmas of suffering and wrong. They wrestled agonisingly with the facts, turning now to

Studies in Life from Jewish Proverbs

one, now to another, explanation, if in any wise hope in God might be preserved.

Our consideration of the great subject must here be confined to considering the proverbs of the period. From these it appears that the rank and file of the Wise-men either did not feel the problem in its acutest form or failed to reach those heights of spiritual insight that some of the Jews attained. In the proverbs a variety of sensible but unsatisfactory arguments are put forward. One method of defence was to challenge or deny the reality of the facts alleged: *There shall no mischief happen to the righteous, but the wicked shall be filled with evil* (Pr. 12^{21})—*Say not thou, "I will recompense evil." Wait on the Lord, and he shall save thee* (Pr. 20^{22})—*The Lord is far from the wicked but he heareth the prayer of the righteous* (Pr. 15^{29})—*The Lord will not suffer the soul of the righteous to famish, and he thrusteth away the desire of the wicked* (Pr. 10^3). No one capable of sympathy with human perplexity will dismiss such assertions as merely stupid. Pathetically insufficient they may be, but these are the words of men convinced that somehow their instinct for God and the moral life is sound; and there is grandeur in the unyielding defiance. Another favourite reply was to insist on the solid rewards of virtue or to maintain that in the end it *is* honesty that pays best: *The wicked earneth deceitful wages, but he that soweth righteousness hath a sure reward* (Pr. 11^{18})—*He that soweth iniquity shall reap calamity* (Pr. 22^8). The Wise liked also to dwell on the fear of retribution which is likely to haunt the evil-doer: *His own iniquities shall take the wicked, and he shall be holden in the cords of his sin* (Pr. 5^{22}), a retort to the power of which many a villain, dogged by the thought of exposure, could bear witness. After all, there generally is *human* justice to be considered, although the *divine* seem far away. Sometimes The Wise had recourse to the suggestion that *the fear of the Lord prolongeth life, but the years of the wicked shall be*

The Hill "Difficulty"

shortened (Pr. 10²⁷). Some, more daringly, declared that the agony of a single day or hour might redress the balance; thus Ben Sirach: *It is an easy thing in the sight of the Lord to reward a man in the day of his death according to his ways. The affliction of an hour causeth forgetfulness of delight, and in the last end of a man is the revelation of his deeds. Call no man blessed before his death*[1]*; and* (yet another suggestion) *a man shall be known in his children* (E. 11²⁶⁻²⁸). This further possibility that Justice, if nowhere manifest in a man's own life, will certainly appear in the fortunes of his descendants, is emphasised also in several Psalms and in passages of the *Book of Job* (*e.g., Job* 5⁴), and apparently was more satisfying to the Jews than it would be to ourselves. A new argument, too vague to be consoling, is hinted in Pr. 16⁴, where it is declared that *God hath made everything for its own end, even the wicked for the day of trouble.*

These answers, of course, do not cut deep enough, and their inadequacy reflects adversely on the value of the Wise-men's judgments of life. But three important points must be noted in extenuation. First, the best that Israel's Wisdom had to say on the sore problem was not said in the proverbs to which we are here limiting attention. If anyone desires to know how unflinchingly certain Wise-men and other Jews could face the facts and uphold their faith, he must turn to the *Book of Job*, to the *Psalms*, to *Daniel* and the daring aspirations of Apocalyptic writers. Secondly, there was as yet among the Jews no active belief in the continuance of personal consciousness after physical death, and thus the moral problem raised by

[1] This maxim was familiar among the Greeks, and is quoted by Æschylus, Sophocles, Euripides and other writers. Tradition ascribed its origin to Solon, the statesman of early Athens, who was reckoned one of the seven Sages of Greece. Its occurrence in *Ecclesiasticus* is an interesting illustration of the cosmopolitan aspect of the Wisdom movement.

Studies in Life from Jewish Proverbs

the suffering of good men was immensely harder for them than it is for ourselves. The Hebrews from earliest times had believed vaguely that a phantom-like continuation of individuality awaited good and bad alike in the underworld of *Sheol*; but that existence was not reckoned to be " life " in any real sense; certainly it was not thought that a man could receive the reward of his merits in *Sheol*, the land of shades. *Sheol* offered no solution, or even alleviation, of the moral enigma confronting the Wise. If there was to be a Divine vindication of morality, in their opinion it must needs be shown on earth, either in the lifetime of the sufferer himself or in that of his children. In the period we are considering, reason and intuition were already pointing the Jewish thinkers to a higher doctrine of human immortality; but no traces of the great liberating conception have made their appearance in the proverbs.[1] The attitude of the Wise towards death may be grasped from Ben Sirach's words: *When a man is dead he shall inherit creeping things and beasts and worms* (E. 10[11])—*Thanksgiving perisheth from the dead, as from one that is not; he that is in life shall praise the Lord* (E. 17[28]). Death to Ben Sirach is a great silencing fact, not a mystery provoking thought. Sometimes he speaks of it very quietly: *All things that are of the earth turn to the earth again, and all things that are of the waters return to the sea* (E. 40[11]), and he bids men fear it not, seeing that death comes to us all: *Fear not the sentence of death. Remember them that have been before thee and that come after. This is the sentence from the Lord over all flesh, and why doest thou refuse when it is the good pleasure of the Most High? Whether thou livest ten or a hundred or a thousand years, there is no inquisition of life in the*

---

[1] Pr. 14[32], *The righteous hath hope in his death* . . . comes nearest to the idea of immortality; but the accuracy of the Hebrew text is doubtful. Pr. 15[24] and 23[17,18] are to be understood as referring to the character of the good man's life on earth (see Toy's notes on these passages).

The Hill " Difficulty "

grave (E. 41 3,4). The same unquestioning acquiescence appears in the helpless commonplace of the following: *O death, how bitter is the remembrance of thee to a man that is at peace in his possessions, unto the man that is at ease and hath prosperity in all things, and that still hath strength to enjoy luxury. O death, acceptable is thy sentence to a man that is needy and that faileth in strength, that is in extreme old age and is distracted about all things, and is perverse and hath lost patience* (E. 41 [1,2]); and still more grimly in his unconsciously brutal counsel to beware of long sorrow for the dead: *My son, let thy tears fall over the dead, and as one that suffereth grievously begin lamentation, and wind up his body according to his due, and neglect not his burial. Make bitter weeping and passionate wailing, and let thy mourning be according to his desert, for one day or two, lest thou be evil spoken of; and so be comforted for thy sorrow. For of sorrow cometh death, and sorrow of heart will bow down the strength. Set not thy heart upon him, forget him, remembering thine own last end. Remember him not, for there is no returning again: him thou shalt not profit, and thou wilt hurt thyself* (E. 38 [168]).

This great difference of outlook would of itself incline one to a lenient judgment on the imperfections of the proverbs. But thirdly, and chiefly, remember that the Wise-men lived in a world that knew not Jesus, a world in which the supreme moral fact had not yet appeared. Therefore they lacked what we possess—the assurance that nothing, tribulation or anguish or persecution, or famine, nakedness, peril or sword, can sunder the spirit of Man from the love of Him whom to know is life eternal. To them it was not possible, as it is for us, to confront the reality of evil with the greater reality of good, to answer the mystery of present suffering with the deeper mystery of the peace of Christ.

Lastly, the noblest of the proverbs has been kept in reserve till now. Said one of the Sages, perceiving that suffering (be it justly or unjustly incurred) is at least an efficient teacher: *My son, despise not the chastening of the Lord, neither be weary at his reproof. For whom the Lord loveth he reproveth, and paineth the son in whom he delighteth* (Pr. 3^{11,12}). The author of *Hebrews* 12, writing to men enduring great distress but with the fact of Christ before them, thought fit to quote those words; and we also will do well to ponder them. It is reasonable to believe that hardships (which judged from certain aspects often are unjust), even such terrible hardships as men sometimes endure, are inevitable in a world where moral personality is in the making: not otherwise could God Himself make man " in His own image "; not otherwise could even He create beings who should learn to seek the Truth, and to will the Good, in freedom. It is easy to see that courage, to take one instance, cannot be disciplined in sham fight, but only in the hazard of real risks. So also, it may be, all other fruits of the Spirit will grow for men nowhere save on the rugged slopes of the hill called " Difficulty." The Wise, therefore, despite their perplexities, were not pessimistic. But, though they resolutely drove out despair, they knew depression: *Even in laughter the heart may be sorrowful, and the end of mirth be heaviness* (Pr. 14^{13}), and *A faithful man who can find?* (Pr. 20^6)? To at least one of the Sages God seemed far distant, silent and inscrutable. Thus Pr. 30$^{1-4}$—*The Words of Agur, . . . I have wearied myself, O God, I have wearied myself, and am consumed, I surely am more foolish than other men, and no wisdom have I acquired to give me knowledge of the Holy One. Who hath ascended up into heaven and descended? . . . What is his name and his son's name, if thou knowest?* The sturdy rebuke that immediately follows, (Pr. 30$^{5-6}$)—*Every word of God is tried. He is a shield to them that trust in Him. Add not thou unto His words, lest He reprove thee, and thou be found a liar*, is the sentiment of another and a happier man than Agur.

The Hill "Difficulty"

Such was the world in which the Wise had to labour and to think. How like our own! How sobering in the discipline it imposes on the idealist! To one who reads without consideration of the back-ground the sententiousness of these Jewish proverbs may soon prove irksome. But the fault becomes bearable, and the Wise grow very human, when we recognise that for all their bold words, they were not always confident of their creed, and that to many an earnest man among them the preaching of morality must at times have seemed a weary and a fruitless task.

CHAPTER XI

Harvest

WE have seen the Wise at work, breaking up the hard ground, ploughing the field and scattering the seed. Came ever their toil to harvest? And since the world is the field, to what place in the wide world, what point of time in the world's long story, ought our search to be directed? "They that sow in tears," said a brave man long ago, " shall reap in joy; though he goeth on his way weeping bearing forth the seed, he shall come again rejoicing bringing his sheaves with him,"—and his words encourage us to search for effects of the Wise-men's teaching in the immediate history of their times. No matter how often the Psalmist's expectation has gone unfulfilled, something in us cries assent to his daring, and we shall therefore follow his guidance; nor shall we look in vain. But one knows that the proverb Jesus quoted to His disciples, *One soweth and another reapeth*, is more often true to the facts of life; and therefore, following its warning, we must be prepared also to seek traces of the Wise-men's influence in times and places unforeseen by them

So wide a range of human history thus opens for consideration that the task we are attempting in this chapter is necessarily difficult. It is still further complicated by the problem of analysis. For example, to say bluntly that in the modern determination to remedy existing evils in our social organisation the Christian Church may see the harvest of its labours is ultimately true, but it is not the whole truth, and because there is so much more to be said on the matter

Harvest

the statement might be challenged as actually untrue by those whose thoughts leap at once to the chequered official record of the Church in the last few centuries. But the opposition with which such cut-and-dry assertions are received often requires only a more careful analysis for its removal. Quite certainly, despite the antagonism of certain professed Christians, the penetrative influence of the regular preaching and teaching of Christianity, especially during the last generation or so, has done more towards rousing and enlightening the national conscience regarding social conditions than can easily be measured; but the social movement of to-day also owes much to the rise of ambitions that naturally accompany the increase of wealth, to scientific invention, to popular education, and to other factors that might be mentioned. The progress of mankind is the product of many influences that have worked together for good, and the ethical and intellectual condition of a people at any given period is like a garment woven from many threads but without seam. Analysis of history is desirable; but to attempt an analysis so subtle that we can say, "Just so much is due to this influence from the past, so much to that," is always difficult, if not impossible. In part of what follows we must be content to describe certain events and circumstances concerning which we make no greater (but also no less) a claim than that the Wise were a *contributory* cause, their words and their example having co-operated with the work of others in producing the result described.

Where then, may it be said, that the seed they sowed took root and ripened? One general answer may be given instantly—Wherever the Bible has been known and read: a result immeasurably exceeding the utmost expectations of the Wise. Who among them ever hoped that their proverbs would receive a place in a Book destined to exercise pre-eminent moral and spiritual force throughout

Studies in Life from Jewish Proverbs

the world, and that through all these centuries the best part of their wisdom, wit, and idealism would be known and esteemed in a myriad Gentile homes?

For closer consideration three themes may profitably be singled out; the first being that of immediate Jewish history in Palestine, by which is meant the critical centuries 350 to 150 B.C. This topic will first be discussed generally, and then attention will be concentrated on certain events during the years 200 to 150 B.C., when the struggle between Judaism and Hellenism came to a climax and was decided.

I

(a) Less than justice is done to the Wise in the picture of post-exilic Judaism usually presented to students. They are not wholly ignored, but their value as a formative influence in the community of Jerusalem and Judæa, we venture to think, has been insufficiently appreciated. For this misjudgment there are several plain reasons which will prove to be well worth examining.

In the first place, the absence of theological fervour in the proverbs, their matter-of-fact standpoint, and the doubtful propriety of certain sayings have been disappointing and even disconcerting to many readers of the Bible. Judged too hastily by the superficial features of their writings, the Wise have been dismissed either as altogether wanting or, at best, as of small moral and religious importance. But how serious an error that method of rough-and-ready judgment may induce, can readily be imagined. It is much as if some future historian, attempting to estimate the value of Christianity to this generation, had to derive his opinion from a survey of the volumes of sermons published, many of which he might be inclined to criticise on the ground that they were concerned with the inculcation of commonplace moral duties. There is far more behind such a book as *Proverbs* than can appear in it. The Wise have been

Harvest

considered too much from the literary point of view, too little from the human.

But, secondly, it is not surprising that the attractive, "human" aspect has been overlooked or underestimated. We miss the warmth of personal history in the proverbs. One's interest is stirred so much more deeply by persons than by things or even ideas; and the proverbs are so coldly impersonal that only close scrutiny, such as we have here attempted, reveals the Wise as men. They *may* often have been pompous, self-satisfied folk, but it cannot be denied that in their writings they were anything but self-advertising, saying many things about Wisdom and next to nothing about themselves.

Even more serious for their repute than this praiseworthy self-reticence is, thirdly, the fact that the Wise soon vanish from the surface of Jewish affairs, apparently as completely as the prophets. But again appearance is misleading, and the explanation that can be found for this fact deserves to be set forth at some length, because it is likely to help us further in the understanding of our subject. Commencing perhaps as early as the latter part of the fifth century, B.C., there developed in the loyal Jewish community, alongside of the elaborate worship of the Temple, a custom of meeting together for purposes of religious exhortation and prayer, and, above all, for study of the great Law which was increasingly felt to be the strength and heart of Judaism. At these meetings, or *Synagogues*, the delivery of a moral discourse would be appropriate, perhaps was formally arranged, and the speaker selected for this purpose must often have been one of those known as the Wise. But commendation and exposition of the Law was even more in place on these occasions, and this duty would naturally be entrusted to one of those who were making the exact interpretation of the Law a life-long interest and indeed a profession; that is, to one of those who are familiar to us

Studies in Life from Jewish Proverbs

by the title "Scribe." Now it is easy to see that the functions of the Wise and of the Scribes were not far sundered, and these "synagogue" meetings must have done much to promote and hasten the approximation of the two classes.[1] Indeed the process of fusion can be watched in the pages of Ben Sirach's book. From it we learn that Ben Sirach, prominent as a Wise-man, was himself professionally a Scribe, and he praises that occupation as the best of all careers, the one most suitable for a disciple of Wisdom (E. *Prologue* and 39^{1-3}). What more was needed than that the Sages should recognise in the Law of Moses the mysterious Wisdom which they served? And we find this very identification expressly made by Ben Sirach, who declares (in reference to certain wonders of Wisdom he has set forth in previous verses) that *All these things are the book of the covenant of the most high God, even the Law which Moses commanded us* (E. 24^{23}; cp. 15^1, 19^{20}, etc.). What happened is clear. From about the beginning of the second century B.C. the functions of moral exhortation—the special sphere of the Wise, at least in public—were discharged by persons who were Scribes; henceforth, to put it briefly, the Wise were mostly Scribes, and the Scribes were mostly Wise. The disappearance of the Wise-men is thus explained; seated in Moses' seat, they have passed out of our sight and so out of mind; or, if dimly recognised by us in their new character, they have been involved in the Scribes' not wholly merited disfavour.[2]

In the fourth place, the Wise have also suffered unduly from the overwhelming prestige customarily assigned to the

---

[1] "The influence of the synagogue as a religious factor, even in the times of Ben Sirach, was felt more deeply than the scarcity of references to it in the contemporary literature would lead us to believe", Schechter, *Judaism* [Second Series], p. 65; cp. J. Abrahams, *Studies in Pharisaism and the Gospels*, pp. 1ff.

[2] The reader familiar with the Gospels should guard against the notion that the Scribes were always guilty of the worst qualities that

Harvest

Law in post-exilic times. Many scholars have so sat in its shadow that they seem to lose sight of all other elements in the situation, nay! even to have forgotten the sunny side of the Law itself. Jerusalem is sometimes pictured as a city of ecclesiastical lawyers, and the Jews as a congregation clustered round a book of rules ; an exaggeration and misconception that might never have gained favour, had the mass of spiritual exposition and reflection embodied in early Rabbinical literature been more accessible to Christian students. It is a question of proportion. Without denying that the Law had become the rallying-point of distinctive Judaism, and was destined to obtain a paramount place in Jewish life and thought, we have to insist that it held no monopoly of influence in the period before 150 B.C., when the Wise were still distinctively the Wise. Jewish legalism may already have become an important fact in the national consciousness, but plenty of room remained for Jewish humanism; We would insist that whilst the Law had one great rival—the spirit of indifference to all its teaching which the growth of Hellenic fashions favoured—it had also coadjutors. There were other spiritual influences at work, moulding the standards and ideals of the Jews ; one of these was the study and appreciation of the writings of the great Prophets of Israel, whence before long came the high aspirations of the Apocalyptic school of thinkers ; and another was the example and teaching of the Wise. Consider the point in view of the normal qualities of human nature. What impresses ordinary folk? How do they learn new knowledge? Men are impressed by worth and dignity in their teachers; the Easterns in particular paying

---

legalism is apt to foster. A class ought not to be equated with its less worthy representatives, unless we are willing, for example, to condemn the first Christians for the sins of certain orders in the Mediæval Church, or to saddle the eager pioneers of the Reformation with the shortcomings of their followers in the eighteenth century.

Studies in Life from Jewish Proverbs

even undue deference to age and prosperity. And most men learn by small degrees: as Isaiah put it, they need to be taught *precept upon precept, line upon line, here a little, and there a little*. Is not that exactly what the Wise were best fitted to give them—precept upon precept? Here were some of the most honourable and prosperous citizens of the day, not keeping their Wisdom jealously to themselves, but counting it their serious duty to impart the secrets of success; now teaching chosen pupils; now mingling in the open with all sorts and types of men (Did not Wisdom cry aloud and utter her voice in the broad places, and cry her message in the chief place of concourse, even at the entering in of the gates, cp. Pr. 1^{20f}, 8$^{1-3}$?); everywhere upholding reverence towards God and a standard of morality, if not perfect, at least far superior to average attainments. Day in, day out, the social and personal idealism, and the wholesome vigorous commonsense of these proverbs were being instilled into the ears of the people by teachers whose prosperous respectability alone was enough to gain them popular attention. Must it not be that all this had effect, and great effect, on the Jewish community? The Law no doubt enlisted the prime devotion of the pious, the prophets appealed most to the enthusiast, but the Wise must have had the ear of the ordinary folk—that is, of the majority of men.

(*b*) Detailed proof of the conclusion thus drawn from general considerations is of course not available. There is, however, one direction in which immediate evidence of the Wisemen's influence may be sought, namely in the issue of the struggle between Judaism and Hellenism. To this end let us briefly pass in review certain events of the years 200 to 150 B.C. It will already be clear to the reader how slight was the chance of the older Jewish habits persisting in face of the full tide of new life and thought, which was steadily smoothing them away as waves will melt sand-

Harvest

castles on the shore. By the end of the third century the infection of Hellenism was rife, not only in the upper classes, but in all grades of Jewish society; "even in the very strongholds of Judaism it modified the organisation of the State, the laws, public affairs, art, science and industry, affecting even the ordinary things of life and the common associations of the people."[1] Black as was the outlook for Judaism at this date, it was soon to grow much worse. Early in the second century the leading families of Jerusalem had become thoroughly Hellenic in their point of view, and, worst of all, in 174 B.C. the office of the High Priesthood fell by intrigue into the grasp of an unscrupulous man, Joshua or (to use the Greek name which he adopted and preferred) Jason. This Jason, to curry favour with the Syrian king, set to work to complete the transformation of Jerusalem into a Grecian city. Accordingly a gymnasium was now built, and so popular was the High Priest's policy, so forgotten the old-fashioned sentiment, that even the Priests were found willing to participate actively in the competitions of the public athletic games. The unholy zeal of the more ardent Hellenists, however, crystallised into definite shape such opposition as still existed. A body of men, convinced upholders of strict Judaism, now drew together and became known as *Hasidim*, *i.e.*, "The Conscientious" or "The Faithful"; but their ranks were recruited largely from the poorer classes, they lacked intellectual prestige, and no doubt their opposition to Hellenism in some respects had the weakness of mere unreasoning conservatism. The party did not seem fitted either to grow in numbers or to continue through many years, and with its passing the old Jewish piety bade fair to perish finally.

But at this stage occurred one of the most astonishing *dénouements* in history. In 175 B.C. Antiochus IV

[1] See the article *Hasideans and Hellenism* (*Jewish Encyclopædia*, Vol. VI.).

Studies in Life from Jewish Proverbs

Epiphanes began to reign over the Syrian dominions: a remarkable but dangerous man, eccentric to the verge of insanity; inordinately vain, yet endowed with great ability, energy, and ambition. Soon after his accession certain tumults took place in Jerusalem. The rioting was directed against Syrian authority, but did not amount to anything which could fairly be construed as rebellion, being in fact mere faction-fighting. None the less Antiochus, whose exchequer happened to be in sore straits for money, made the occurrence a pretext, first, for plundering the Temple of its treasures and, two years later, for inflicting on the Jews a cruel punishment. Entering the city in 168 B.C. he razed its walls, and desecrated the Temple in an abominable fashion, sacrificing swine on the altar and converting it into a sanctuary for Hellenic worship. Still more important, however, was his resolve once and for all to stamp out any obscurantists among the Jews who might presume any longer to follow their ancestral customs and oppose the Greek culture. Then began throughout the Jewish province a fierce persecution. In all towns and villages men and women were sought out and slain—whosoever was found guilty of practising Jewish observances, or possessed a copy of the Jewish Law, or refused to offer worship at a heathen shrine. The position of the loyal Jews soon became desperate. The threat of torture and death was stamping out relentlessly the last flicker of resistance. Many of the *Hasidim*, refusing to make the great surrender, died for their faith, and the small companies who escaped to the deserts for refuge, though steadfast in determination to resist, were in despair, feeling that Jehovah had forsaken His people utterly. A famous passage in I Maccabees (2$^{29\text{-}38}$) relates how one thousand of them, men, women and children, pursued into the wilderness by the Syrian troops, were overtaken on a Sabbath day, and how (rather than violate the laws of the Sabbath by fighting)

Harvest

they sought neither to escape their enemies by flight nor yet to defend themselves, but stood and met death in heroic silence.

Such was the condition of affairs when suddenly a change came over the character of the Jewish resistance. A certain Mattathias, a priest of the village *Modein*, with his five sons (one of whom was the famous *Judas*, afterwards surnamed *Maccabeus*), indignant at what was taking place, and convinced of the futility of such passive martyrdom as had led to the massacre just mentioned, struck a blow for freedom, and began to organise active opposition. The *Hasidim* fell in with the new policy, and men rallied to the support of Mattathias and his sons. It was as if the latent patriotism of the Jews had waited only for a spark to kindle it, had required only action on lines of sufficient common sense to offer a faint chance of success in combating Antiochus. The new army that sprang dramatically into being was fortunate in its commander. Under the brilliant leadership of Judas Maccabeus surprising victories were gained, and after vicissitudes of fortune which it is not in point here to record, there emerged a Jewish State, free from the tyranny of Syria, and eager to preserve the essence of that moral monotheistic faith which had been Israel's one unique glory.

But whence this astonishing revival? The *Hasidim* were none too numerous, and if, as is entirely probable, a large proportion of their men were advanced in years, they can hardly have been the most efficient portion of the Maccabean armies from a military point of view. Victories in war are won by young, vigorous men, and the swift triumph of the Maccabees implies the adhesion to their cause of numbers of young Jews from within and without Jerusalem; and that again is explicable only by the presence in the nation of a strong undercurrent of respect for the older, distinctive Judaism. Things were not quite so

Studies in Life from Jewish Proverbs

desperate as they had seemed. Hellenism had progressed far; but it had not eaten out the heart of the people. Obviously if all the young Jews had been convinced Hellenists, content to follow the lead of the high-priestly party to any lengths and wholly contemptuous of Israel's former piety, they would have looked on with indifference, or even approval, while the last remnants of the puritanical *Hasidim* and the villagers of Modein were being blotted out. But from that attitude they had evidently been saved, and it is fair to acknowledge that the Wise must have done much to achieve that consummation. Their broadminded outlook, their sensible but genuine piety, their solid worth of character, their shrewd yet earnest and at times enthusiastic teaching, all had helped effectively to maintain regard for the old-fashioned interpretation of life that rested on " the fear of the Lord." With the example of the Wise-men before them, there must have been many who, though they felt that Hellenism was wonderful, yet knew in their soul that Judaism also was great and wise. So soon therefore as the vileness of a bloody and remorseless persecution clarified the moral issue and compelled a choice, men were found who could make the right resolve to fight for their liberty and their fathers' God. The result of the Maccabean conflict was a real decision; the tide had turned, and the losing battle was not lost. Hellenic thought and method would in days to come mould and modify the Jewish people in many ways, but its strangle-hold on the vital point of Jewish religion was loosened, never to be renewed. The spiritual genius of Judaism could breathe again. Henceforth, to quote a memorable saying of Wellhausen, " in a period when all nationalities and all bonds of religion and national customs were being broken up in the seeming cosmos and real chaos of the Græco-Roman Empire, the Jews stood out like a rock in the midst of the ocean. When the natural conditions of independent nationality all

Harvest

failed them, they nevertheless artificially maintained it with an energy truly marvellous, and thereby preserved for themselves, and for the whole world, an eternal good."

II

The second field in which one may reasonably look for signs of the Wise-men's labours is of course subsequent Jewish history, the question being, " Did the teaching of the Wise slip out of sight and memory when the crisis we have described was ended, and when the professors of Wisdom became the Scribes and were more and more absorbed in purely scribal interests, or did it escape oblivion and continue a living influence in the life of the Jews ? " The ground that must furnish an answer to our question is chiefly the presence or absence of references to these proverbs, or of imitations and echoes of them, in the later Jewish literature. To begin with, however, there is one clear, independent proof of the esteem in which at any rate the *Book of Proverbs* came to be held, and that is its inclusion in the Hebrew Bible. This fact alone is irrefutable and sufficient testimony that the thoughts of the Wise never ceased to influence the minds and characters of loyal Jews. So much for *Proverbs*, but what of *Ecclesiasticus?* It also was far from being forgotten. Though it failed to secure a place in the Hebrew Canon, it was included in the Septuagint[1], the Bible of the Greek-speaking Jews of Egypt. The Talmud in one ultra-orthodox passage forbids quotations to be made from Ben Sirach's book, but actually there are quotations from it in the Talmud itself! In fact, a vast number of references might be adduced from the whole range of Jewish literature testifying both to the popularity of these two great treasuries of the Sages' sayings, and to the steady appreciation of proverbs old and new, which the Jews displayed.

[1] Commonly referred to by the abbreviation LXX.

Studies in Life from Jewish Proverbs

To set forth proof of this assertion even in barest outline would involve technicalities that might be wearisome. We give therefore but two or three points in illustration. Perhaps the most interesting, and for Gentile readers the most accessible, source of evidence is a work of the first and second century A.D., a compendium of the ethical ideas and ideals of certain famous Jewish teachers, bearing the title *Pirke Aboth*, that is *The Sayings of the Fathers*.[1] Throughout this treatise the influence of the Wisdom writings is clearly indicated by the sententious style that characterises the several *Sayings*, as well as by the numerous direct references to *Proverbs*. A few quotations will bring this out, and at the same time illustrate the high ideals, curiously but often very attractively expressed, of which the book is full:—

Ben Zoma said, "*Who is mighty? He who subdues his nature, for it is written 'He that is slow to anger is better than the mighty'* (Pr. 16³²)."[2]

Antigonous of Soko used to say, "*Be not like servants who work for their Lord with a view to receiving recompense, but be as slaves that minister without seeking for reward, and let the fear of heaven be upon you.*"[3]

Rabbi Chananiah said—something that might have averted the European war, and made Germany a blessing instead of a curse, had her rulers and thinkers accepted his deep counsel!—*Whenever in any man his fear of sin comes before his wisdom his wisdom endures, but whensoever a man's wisdom comes before his fear of sin his wisdom doth not endure.*"[4]

Rabbi Judah ben Thema said, "*Be bold as a leopard, and swift as an eagle, and fleet as a hart, and strong as a lion to do the will of thy Father which is in heaven.*"[5]

---

[1] See Dr. Taylor's edition (Cambridge, 1877).   [2] *Aboth*, iv. 2.

[3] *Aboth*, i. 3.   [4] *Aboth* ii. 13.   [5] *Aboth* v. 30.

Harvest

And there was Rabbi Samuel the Little, who chose for his life's motto just one verse of *Proverbs* (24^{17}), and added thereto no word in comment: "*Rejoice not when thine enemy falleth, and let not thine heart be glad when he stumbleth*"[1]

So the topic might be pursued, and from *Midrash* and *Talmud* might be drawn examples in plenty, both references to the ancient proverbs and quotations of new ones— words of wit and humour, of prudence and fine idealism— applied to all manner of human intercourse, and witnessing abundantly that in Israel Wisdom was still known of her children. Space must be found for just these three observations on married life:

> *Whose wife dies in his lifetime, the world becomes dark for him* (C. 55)[2].

> *He who loves his wife as himself and honours her more than himself . . it is of him the Scripture saith "Thou shalt know that thy tent is in peace"* (C. 55).

And, lastly, this gentle and subtle saying:—

> *If thy wife be short, bend down and whisper to her* (C. 55).

If Wisdom is an influence at all, it is always an intimate influence working in homes and individual consciences as well as in street and market-place, so that besides noting the frequent mention of proverbs in the literature, consideration should also be paid to the vigour of Jewish morality in the Christian era. Perhaps the simplest and most human point at which to test the matter briefly will be the ethic of the Jewish home. Dispossessed of their native land and

---

[1] *Aboth* iv. 26.

[2] N.B.—C.55=Cohen, *Ancient Jewish Proverbs*, No. 55. Quotations of these later Rabbinical Jewish proverbs will be given in this manner, as a reference to Mr. Cohen's handbook is likely to be of more use to readers than a citation of original Rabbinic sources.

Studies in Life from Jewish Proverbs

scattered to a thousand different cities, the Jews were compelled to work out their own salvation under great and increasing difficulties.[1] *God*, says a significant Talmudic comment, *dwells in a pure and loving home;* and no one, aware of the evils that were rampant in the decaying paganism of the Græco-Roman Empire and persisted, still powerful though not unrebuked, in the slowly developing society of nominally Christian Europe, would deny that the isolated and often harassed communities of the Jews did their utmost to make that noble saying a reality, maintaining with amazing courage and pertinacity a splendid ideal of family and communal existence. A discussion of the topic in the *Jewish Encyclopædia* concludes with the following affirmation: "Throughout these centuries of persecution and migration the moral atmosphere of the Jewish home was rarely contaminated, and it became a bulwark of moral and social strength, impregnable by reason of the religious spirit which permeated it." And in elucidation of what

[1] Jew and Christian, too often ignorant of the virtues each possesses, are painfully conscious of one another's defects. Better knowledge of history would do much to relieve or lessen mutual prejudices. How seldom do Christians realise that some of the less amiable qualities found in certain classes of modern Jews (Are there no objectionable Gentiles?) are the logical result of regulations decreed by our mediæval Christian forefathers. For example, the Jews were once as catholic as any other nation in the arts and industries they followed for a livelihood, until legal restrictions were multiplied against them. "Even in Spain," writes Mr. Abrahams, "Jews were forbidden to act as physicians, as bakers or millers; they were prohibited from selling brass, wine, flour, oil or butter in the markets; no Jew might be a smith, carpenter, tailor, shoemaker, currier or clothier for Christians . . . he might neither employ nor be employed by Christians in any profession or trade whatsoever. . . . In other parts of England these restrictions were far more rigidly enforced than in Spain. In England money-lending was absolutely the only profession open to the Jews. On the Continent Jews were taxed when they entered a market and taxed when they left it; they were only permitted to enter the market place at inconvenient hours, *and the Church ended by leaving the Jews nothing to trade in but money and second-hand goods, allowing them as a choice of commodities in which to deal new gold or old iron.*" (*Jewish Life in the Middle Ages.* p. 241).

Harvest

was involved in the persecution referred to let this one grim statement speak: From the sixteenth century, and earlier, regulations were enforced compelling the Jews of numerous large cities to reside in certain confined areas, "ghettos." Nevertheless the dreadful overcrowding to which this led resulted in no serious moral evils: "The purity of the Jewish home-life was a constant antidote to the poisonous suggestions of life in slums, and it was even able to resist the terrible squalor and unhealthiness which prevailed in the miserable and infamous Roman ghetto, where at one time as many as 10,000 inhabitants were herded into a space less than a square kilometre. In the poorer streets of this ghetto several families occupied one and the same room. The sufferings of the Jews in that hell upon earth were not diminished by the yearly overflowing of the Tiber which made the Roman ghetto a dismal and a plague-stricken swamp."[1]

Of course many things worked together to sustain the morality of the Jewish people—the long-suffering of the Psalmists, the golden promises of the mighty Prophets, and the strength of the ancient Law. But surely also that store of homely, yet stirring and challenging, proverbs which the Wise-men had created, may claim a real share in the magnificent result? And if, quite rightly, it be insisted that the Law, with its fascination of hallowed customs and manifold spiritual suggestions, played the all-important part, then in reply we may still enter the plea that, as Ben Sirach had felt and said, for the Jew the Law was Wisdom and Wisdom had become the Law.

III

In the third place, the words of the Wise were given an honoured place in the mind of the Lord Jesus Christ. To some that may be an unexpected statement. It is well-

[1] Abrahams, *Jewish Life in the Middle Ages*, p. 68.

Studies in Life from Jewish Proverbs

known that Jesus was intimately familiar with the doctrine of the Prophets, and many have perceived how conscious He was of all that is admirable in the Law, the spiritual essence of which He fulfilled. But, though His interest in the Wise is seldom noted, it is no less true that He had considered deeply and sympathetically the idea of the Divine Wisdom, and was familiar with the famous proverbs that sought to apply its guidance alike to the greatest and the least of our affairs. Just how often a memory of Wisdom is traceable in the recorded words of Jesus cannot be determined with certainty. *Verbatim* allusions are rare, perhaps because the ideas of the Wise and their more memorable sayings had become so familiar in our Lord's time as to be common ground between hearer and teacher, so that often it was only the point made by the Wise that was hinted at, or caught up and given some new turn and emphasis. But echoes from the thoughts and images of the proverbs are so frequent in the Gospels that together they furnish ample evidence of His having known and valued the ancient treasury of Wisdom. The evidence is, of course, cumulative, and its strength must not be judged by the following few illustrations.[1]

No fewer than seven of the eight Beatitudes (*Matt.* 5¹ff) recall proverbs of the Wise; what had been, as it were, a seed of thought in the proverb finding ripe expression in the Beatitude. For instance, *Blessed are the poor* (*i.e.*, humble) *in spirit, for theirs is the kingdom of heaven*, said Jesus—*Better*, said the Wise, *is it to be of a lowly spirit with the poor, than to divide the spoil with the proud* (Pr. 16¹⁹). With Jesus' condemnation of mischievous talk, *Every idle word that men shall speak they shall give account thereof in the day of judgement; for by thy words shalt thou be justified*,

---

[1] The argument is worked out at greater length by C. F. Kent, (*Wise Men of Israel*, pp. 176ff), in an essay to which this brief review of the theme is much indebted. See also p. 268.

Harvest

and by thy words thou shalt be condemned (*Matt.* 12^{36,37}), compare Pr. 18 ^{20,21} *Death and life are in the power of the tongue; and they that love it shall eat the fruit thereof* (also Pr. 13^2, 15^4, 21^{23}, etc.). With the teaching, *Lay not up for yourselves treasures upon the earth . . . but in heaven*, compare Pr. 11^{4,28}, 15^{16}, 16^8, etc. *Give us this day our daily bread* seems to echo Pr. 30^8: *Give me neither poverty nor riches; feed me with the bread that is needful for me.* In the command for generous dealing, *Give to him that asketh thee, and from him that would borrow of thee turn not away* (*Matt.* 5^{42}), there is perhaps a precise reminiscence of Pr. 3^{28}: *Say not unto thy neighbour, "Go and come again," when thou hast it with thee* (cp. also Pr. 19^{17} with *Matt.* 25^{40}); and again when Jesus encouraged His disciples saying *Be not anxious how or what ye shall speak . . . For it is not ye that speak but the spirit of your Father which speaketh in you* (Matt. 10^{19,20}), perhaps the very words of Pr. 16^1 were in His memory: *The plans of the heart belong to man, but the answer of the tongue is from the Lord?*

Some of the immortal images in our Lord's parables may have been painted from the thought suggested by a proverb. In the parable of *Luke* 14$^{7-11}$, the command not to seek the highest seats at the banquet may originate in the saying of Pr. 25^6 as much as in the concrete examples of the failing which contemporary life no doubt afforded. So also the famous parable of the two houses, one built on rock, the other on sand, perhaps goes back to the seed-thought in Pr. 12 ^{7}: *The wicked are overthrown and are not, but the house of the righteous shall stand;* and the proverb *Boast not thyself of to-morrow, for thou knowest not what a day will bring forth*, Pr. 27^1, might be text for Christ's parable of the rich man and his barns (*Luke* 12$^{16-21}$). Again when Jesus, speaking of the kingdom of heaven, likens it to a marriage feast (*Matt.* 22$^{1-14}$; etc.) and elsewhere compares it in its infinite value to a hidden precious pearl, there are

Studies in Life from Jewish Proverbs

details in the language used which suggest that the picture of Wisdom's banquet (Pr. 9¹⁻⁵), and the proverbs on the incomparable worth of Wisdom were not far distant from His mind.

More important than even the certain or possible verbal reminiscences of the proverbs is the resemblance between the manner of Jesus' teaching and the manner of the Wise. Like them, He also taught in the streets, seeking the people where they were most easily to be found; and though His words were infinite in depth of insight and spiritual grandeur, He was wont to clothe them in simple language—now quoting a telling proverb, *Physician, heal thyself*, now kindling imagination by a familiar but graphic metaphor or comparison that went home to the heart, and challenged the conscience, and was comprehensible to learned and unlearned equally. Like the Wise, He spoke constantly on those simple but supreme issues which concern every man that cometh into the world; and His highest doctrine was often cast, like the lessons of ancient Wisdom, in brief sentences that refused to be forgotten: *Blessed are the pure in heart, for they shall see God—He that findeth his life shall lose it, and he that loseth his life for My sake shall find it*. Many readers will realise that the deepest thing concerning the relation between Jesus Christ and Wisdom has not yet been referred to, but that we deliberately reserve. Enough has been said for the present purpose.

Who in face of all these facts would dare to maintain that the Wise-men toiled to no purpose. Their love's labour was not lost. In the issue of the struggle with Helleinsm and the revival of the Jewish national consciousness with its unique moral and religious features, some of them witnessed a result such as their teaching, whether they were fully conscious of the fact or not, had tended to achieve.

But also there came gradually in later generations, and in lands of which they had not so much as heard, a rich reward

Harvest

of which the end is not yet in sight. Could they but have foreseen even a small corner of this ultimate harvest field, how completely depression would have vanished, and all mistrust of God's dealings with faithful men been lifted from their minds! Their proverbs were laid on the foundation of a religious and ethical idealism, and if some have proved to be only wood, hay and stubble, others were gold, silver and costly stones, and these have obtained a place in the temple of eternal Truth. Doubtless the imperfections of the Wise were great and their failures and disappointments many, but all the time they were building far better than they knew. Is it not always so with every courageous effort after righteousness, every honest search for the kingdom of the living God?

CHAPTER XII

Values

OUR fathers required no volumes on the Humanism of the Bible. They felt themselves close-linked with its heroes; Patriarchs, Judges, Warriors, Kings, and Prophets were their kith and kin, not in blood, but in the nearer relationship of human experience. Saul, in his pride, his jealousy and desolate death, stood in warning beside them; David, pattern of faith and fortitude in adversity, was at their right hand, so that in their distresses men would take courage, remembering that David also had cried unto the Lord and been delivered. But the perspective of the years has ceased to be foreshortened, and between our generation and the old world of the Bible a great gulf now seems fixed. Nevertheless our fathers were right, and we are wrong. Saul and David and the men of the Bible are not separated from us by 3,000 years, nor yet by one year, for difference of race and custom are trivialities compared with the fundamental conditions of life and the unalterable principles of character. Our predecessors may have made too light of the differences, but that is a small fault compared with the modern tendency to ignore the resemblances: not to ask " What do these men and these events say to us concerning the eternal things we share with them? " is to miss the one thing needful.

To illustrate the argument, recollect that skeleton of dates, *William the Conqueror* 1066. . . . which not so long ago did duty in our schools for the record of the glory of England. What could have been more ineffective

Values

for revealing the soul of history? Now-a-days, the tale is better told but, even so, be the events narrated never so graphically, unless they are conceived in relation to ourselves we are little benefited. To use the famous simile of the prophet, bone may come to its bone, and sinews be upon them, and flesh come up and skin cover them above, until the very semblance of men rises before our eyes; but there will be no breath in them. Only when it is realised how out of the living past has grown the living present, only then enters the breath of God into the men of old and they live and stand up upon their feet, an exceeding great army— to our aid in the shaping of what is to be. History is profitable in so far as its significance for the present is understood.[1] Thus, with fine insight, the Jews perceived that even their majestic Law would be of no avail if it were heard only as the recital of words delivered long ago at Sinai, and accordingly the exhortation ascribed to Moses in the *Book of Deuteronomy* comes to its climax in this deep saying: *The commandment is not too hard for thee, neither is it far off. It is not in heaven, that thou shouldest say " Who shall go up for us to heaven, and bring it down unto us, and make us hear it, that we may do it?"*. . . *But the Word is very nigh thee, in thy mouth and in thy heart, that thou mayest do it.*[2]

And so also in like manner this account of the history behind the Jewish proverbs has not been told in order to evoke for a brief moment nerveless phantoms of the Wise in ancient Israel, but with the hope that a voice would be heard saying even of this Word " It is very nigh thee, in thy mouth, and in thy heart, that thou mayest do it." What is the significance *for us* of these men and their experiences?

Consider some of the features of this Movement, if so precise a term may for convenience be applied to the easy,

[1] Cp. Marvin, *The Living Past*, pp. 2, 3.   [2] Deut. 30[11-14].

Studies in Life from Jewish Proverbs

natural, teaching of Wisdom. In the first place observe the thorough and effective contact established by the teachers of Wisdom with the people they sought to reach. One of the main problems confronting Christianity is the severance of the potential influence of its Churches from the life of the people; verily Mahomet sits waiting for the mountain. What then? Ought the Churches to be abandoned, and men go a-worshipping in the market-place? "Impractical—at the best it would soon lose its effect—the experiment has been made, with sadly limited results": a thousand valid objections! But the problem must not be dismissed so lightly with a bare consideration of its obvious difficulties, for the issues at stake are too serious; the bulk of the population live perilously free from the stimulus of any Ideal, whether self-sought or impressed from without by the teaching of others. Seeing then that the Wise succeeded where we have missed the mark, their ways must at least deserve a scrutiny; here is a method by which the poor were preached to, and religion stood daily in the streets and morals in the market-place; here is idealism put in language the unlearned could both comprehend and recollect. Indeed the proverb was wonderfully suited to their needs, for even its riddles were easily solved, not darkening counsel but devised only to awaken curiosity and so assist the slow and simple mind. Of course a slavish imitation of the Wise-men's procedure is out of the question in modern circumstances, but slavish imitation is not suggested. Said Sir Joshua Reynolds when urging the students of the Royal Academy to the study of the Old Masters, "The more extensive your acquaintance is with the works of those who have excelled, the more extensive will be your powers of *invention*." There is a force of idealism latent in almost all men, but it requires to be brought to the surface, examined, criticised and judiciously directed to the attainment of practical objects; otherwise the greater

Values

part of its potential energy will never be brought into action; and in this easy-going land of ours there is more than normal scope for increased discipline of the mind. We can afford to think much harder than we have ever yet done without losing the virtue of humorous, tolerant good-nature. As Mr. Clutton Brock has said recently, " The fact that some thinking is bad is not a reason why we should not think at all. The Germans have been encouraged by their bad thinking to exercise certain virtues perversely and to bad ends, but still to exercise them in a manner which has astonished the world; while we have been little encouraged by thinking, good or bad, to exercise any virtues."[1] There is ample room for more *outspoken* interest in the ends and principles of human life, more earnest and stringent consideration of the problems of social organisation—provided our discussions be undertaken, not in the spirit of silly contention, mere bolstering up of unconsidered prejudice, but in a sincerity that will be both more critical and yet more humbly eager, for truth's sake, to learn one from another. For it is not division of opinion, or even real conflict of interest that prevents and retards reform, so much as the dead weight of ignorance, of indifference and of paltry pride in argument—the very sins which in the past were the prime cause of the evils that call for remedy.

No less than the ancient Hebrews we moderns stand in need of the exhortation to let Wisdom *enter into our hearts and knowledge be pleasant unto our souls* (cp. Pr. 2^{10}). Neither with all our heart, nor even with all our mind, far less with all our soul, have we yet sought her whose *ways are ways of pleasantness, and all her paths are peace* (Pr. 3^{17}); nor have we understood sufficiently that *she is a tree of life to all that lay hold on her, and happy is every one that retaineth her* (Pr. 3^{18}). Says a later Jewish proverb,

[1] *The Ultimate Belief*, p. 2.

Studies in Life from Jewish Proverbs

Lackest thou Wisdom, what hast thou acquired? Hast acquired Wisdom, what lackest thou? (C. 93.)

Secondly, the constant intimate contact that the Wise maintained with the actualities of men's ordinary experience was beneficial not only to the taught but to the teachers. It kept the Wise in touch with work-a-day problems (the most difficult of tasks for the idealistic thinker), and so helped to make their toil productive. It taught them how to bring Heavenly Wisdom down from the right hand of God that she might dwell with men, and make their homes pure and loving, and their business just, and their pleasures clean. And herein is a thought of no little encouragement for preachers and teachers in these days of not overcrowded Churches. Somehow it seems that personal contact is invaluable in the moral and spiritual education of man. That is why the leading article, with its scores of thousands of readers, may sometimes have less effect than a good sermon heard by a few hundred. The Press addresses us from an Olympian but distant Fleet Street, thundering at us—but in cold print; whereas the parson and the teacher, if he is a true man, somewhere and to some few is a neighbour and a friend. However excellent the Manual of Ethics, it will not serve to influence the lives of many. The Son of Man, it seems, must come eating and drinking and teaching in our streets.

In the next place, this Movement is an interesting and important example of independent as opposed to systematic instruction, illustrating both the weaknesses as well as the strength of pronounced individualism, and supporting the opinion that, if only one safeguard be present, the advantages of individualism outweigh its dangers. Teachers less restricted than the Wise it is difficult to imagine. Each was free to develop his own opinions on the nature of life and the principles of success and failure, even to the point of open agnosticism. What prevents

Values

such licence from becoming chaos? The reply indicated by the Wisdom Movement is that freedom, even extreme freedom, of judgment in matters of conduct and faith will not result in chaos provided there is an underlying unity of aim. All the Wise were lovers of Wisdom. They conceived their theme in different fashions, but they had all the same intention—to teach and to practise Wisdom and not Folly; hence, despite the diversity in their proverbs, the shifting standpoints, the variety of ethical standards, even the contradictions of advice, their teaching was ultimately effective. If we had had space to consider their work in relation to other movements in the intellectual life of that period, both in Palestine and also in the wider world, it would have been easy to show that the immaturities in the Wise-men's thoughts, the uncertainties of their faith and ethic (the very points on which the cynical would pounce as evidence of failure) on a wider and wiser survey of the facts were in reality co-operating influences, clearing the way for a deeper, fuller, faith. Truth is eternal, but men's apprehension of it is progressive; and it should be insisted that, given the presence of one fundamental purpose so that an ultimate unity of spirit must necessarily exist, divergence of opinion, even on matters of high importance, does not indicate weakness or indecision or decay, but rather is a sign of vitality and hope. The reason for this is obvious. Final statements can be made only with regard to the conceptions of the abstract sciences, such as mathematics, or to the judgments we can sometimes pass on lost causes; and on the other hand power to perceive the imperfection of present attainment has ever been, and still is, the prime condition of human progress: "God," said John Robinson, minister of the Pilgrim Fathers, "has yet more truth to break forth out of His Word."

The bearing on modern Christianity is not far to seek. A doctor recently remarked to the present writer

Studies in Life from Jewish Proverbs

that one had only to enter the several Churches of a certain town to discover that Christians were now in hopeless confusion, ignorant as to what they did or did not believe, and that if the professed followers of the faith could not state their doctrine coherently, others might well be excused from attempting the task of ascertaining what Christianity now meant. The argument is not unusual, but it is profoundly mistaken. It might have been retorted that divergencies of medical opinion (and many patients will bear witness that they are neither slight nor few) are no indication whatever of the essential unsoundness of the science of medicine, but rather the guarantee of its advance into more accurate knowledge. Moreover had the critic been in actual touch with the feeling and activities of the Churches in question, he would have recognised that the points of disagreement, though important, were not upon the vital question of faith in God and general attitude towards life ; so that whilst he personally might still have been unable to accept Christian belief, he could not possibly have formulated such an indictment as appears above. The real peril of Christian theology has not been vagueness, but the Hellenic tendency to essay the definition of all things to the last *iota*. But from the perils inherent in that attitude Christianity has been delivered by the passionate instinct of mankind for truth, and by the reforming energy of great individuals ; and will be delivered, so long as the Church has faith in the guiding Spirit of God.

There is value in the Wise-men's witness to the intimate relation between faith and morality. The religion of Israel in its higher development is magnificent in its clear recognition that the claim of God upon man is absolute, complete and not partial—if there be one God, Creator of heaven and earth, then certainly He besets us behind and before and lays His hand upon us—and that the love of God and the love of our fellow-men must be indissolubly related, faith

Values

being the inspiration of morality, and moral action the necessary outcome of faith. With these sublime beliefs, proclaimed by Prophets and Psalmists, the Wise were in accord : they also in their more homely fashion recognised the universality of the Divine claim, and its operation in the realm of moral duty. Perhaps those thoughts may seem to some readers only elementary and obvious ideas on spiritual things. But they ought to be regarded not as elementary (and therefore of small account) but as fundamental and vital conceptions. Every student of comparative religion would testify how great and terrible a gulf in human life was crossed when first a Hebrew Prophet conceived the thought that God desireth mercy and not sacrifice, not ceremonial worship but *philanthropy* (in the true sense of the word), and how glorious a hope for the future of religion then dawned upon our race. Moreover the fact remains that, even if to many these thoughts of God and the nature of His service may be no novelty, even if they have grasped the idea in its full significance and are conscious of its exact bearing on manifold contemporary affairs, there is still room for its reaffirmation. Said a soldier in France, after a discussion about Christianity to which he had listened intently and with some surprise, " But, as I understand it, religion is all talk about heaven. What's it got to do with morality ? " Religion *has* got to do with morality, and morality, like the demand for truth and the instinct for the beautiful, penetrates life through and through to its least details. Christianity is not a bargain with the Deity entailing magical immunity from hardship in this life and special privileges in the next. It is such an attitude of the essential personality as should wholly determine our activities in each and every aspect life can present to us, both now and hereafter. The scope of religion is as wide as our interests ; and what could serve more happily to remind us of that fact than these Jewish

Studies in Life from Jewish Proverbs

proverbs which, beginning with the fear of God, range from kings to labourers, from merry men to broken hearts, from dreams of perfect justice to cynical observations on the uses and advantages of bribes? Wisdom is indeed ubiquitous: *Divers weights and false balances are an abomination unto the Lord*, say the Wise in the busy mart; and then in the hour of leisure and of plenty *It is not good to eat much honey*—and all this in the name of transcendent Wisdom, *whose fruit is better than gold, yea, than fine gold;* Wisdom that was *set up from everlasting, from the beginning, or ever the earth was.*

Incidentally we have also to note how thoroughly these proverbs, by reason of the range of interest of which we have just been speaking, and by the sensible attitude they endeavour to preserve, illustrate the Humanism of the Bible; for surely the most ungenerous of critics would not accuse them of being unpractical or absorbed in supra-mundane matters. The point has already been emphasised, and therefore we will not dwell upon it again, except to remark its importance as one instance of a general principle: that Idealism to be effective must needs grow out of the soil of commonsense. There is a degree beyond which existing facts must not be disregarded. For example, men have not mastered the art of flight by ignoring gravitation, but by having studied its laws and conquered the difficulties they present. In the admirable words of a friend of the writer, " Christian opinion is peculiarly liable to the danger of running counter to the average common sense in the midst of which it finds itself; that is a natural alternative to simply falling into line with current common sense views. . . . Thought that has its head in the clouds must have its feet planted firmly in sound common sense, if its heart is to be in the right place. . . . No one can think of Jesus as the devotee of a faddist cult. He entered wholeheartedly into the common joys and sorrows and into the

Values

common interests of the people : their wedding-feasts and their mourning for dead friends and their longing for freedom from the Roman yoke. . . . *He entered by the open door of common sense, and led out the spirit of man into a larger life than it had ever conceived.*"[1] Omitting the superlative " ever," these words in italics are wonderfully apposite in reference to the genius of the Wisdom Movement in Israel.

There is value for us in the confidence which the Wise-men showed in their attitude towards life. They, like ourselves, lived in an age when all things were being put to trial, and doubt and perplexity were rife. They were aware that even their instinctive fundamental ideas were under challenge, aware that the path they followed was unfinished ; and yet, as the general tone of the proverbs indicates, they lived with firmness and decision, and therefore achieved much. They were wise indeed in that they perceived the issue between good and evil to be clear enough for a man to choose which of the twain he will pursue. Having chosen, these men did not content themselves with expressing a timorous hope that the moralistic view of life might ultimately be proved correct ; they did battle for righteousness, valiantly and practically. So with ourselves. Stringent and systematic application of the test of reason is a most necessary attitude to preserve, but it is not a whit less necessary, despite our uncertainty regarding ultimate problems of existence, early in life to form a definite idea whither we wish to direct our steps. To do so is the only highway to an effective life. Nor is it unreasonable to demand from men that much resolution, for Good and Evil do present themselves quite distinctly as alternative routes. Of course, all the coward in us and all the sluggard prompts a protest for delay : we see a hundred reasons for postponing judgment, or for arranging a compromise

[1] Professor D. K. Picken, in the *Australasian Intercollegian Magazine, Dec.,* 1916.

Studies in Life from Jewish Proverbs

between the claimants; " our philosophy is unsettled; we have neither proved God to our complete satisfaction, nor has He clearly justified His ways to us: so that surely it is not reasonable to insist that we make choice (and therefore, we take it, the subsidiary matter of our unwillingness need not arise)—let us drift a little longer through these puzzling mists." Nothing but a bold decision for Wisdom or for Folly ever clears those mists away. To shirk the challenge (as some do all their lives) is easy and at first may seem the natural course to adopt, but it entails a heavy penalty. It deprives us of any firm criterion of judgment, and we must needs go fumbling with the golden opportunities which come but return not. Take then the Wise for an example. Uncertainty they felt, but uncertainty did not paralyse their power, because they met perplexities in the open field of action. From us, as from them, many secrets of creation are concealed; but some things are certainly evil and some are pure and good. A blessing and a curse are set before us, and the difference between them is in no way obscure. We ought to choose the blessing; and then, in faith that the Good is really and ultimately the True, act vigorously in support of our belief. Wisdom we know and Folly we know; Christ we have seen and the fruits of wickedness: in the name of sanity how much clearer need the issue be?

Passing from the methods and manner of the Movement, it is encouraging to turn for a moment to the thought of its success. When we measure the might of the forces making against Wisdom, the numbers and influence of those bent on pleasure or on riches with scant regard, or none at all, for nobler possibilities in life, it is wonderful that the ideals of the Wise should have become known to vast numbers of men in alien lands, and that, enshrined in the Bible, their influence should still remain unexhausted. Had the memory of them continued in honour only for a century

Values

or two and been restricted to the limits of the Jewish communities, even that would have been a result exceeding what had once seemed probable. For Hellenism was a monstrous flood apparently capable of sweeping away far larger obstacles than all Judaism combined—priests, prophets, and Wise-men—could raise against its onset. But Wisdom and Law and Prophets survived the deluge, quite unharmed and indeed strengthened by the trial they had undergone. Why was it so? How comes it to pass that the Wise after all do not toil in vain; that the Crucified conquers; that St. Paul, who in his lifetime can establish no more than a few struggling Churches, eventually commands the intellect of Greece and subdues the power of Rome? Surely because, in the words of yet another great passage in the Hebrew Scriptures, Elisha's vision in beleaguered Dothan was no mirage in the eyes of a famine-haunted man, but truth of truth, and the mountains of Reality which compass the City of Human Faith are full of the chariots of the Lord of Hosts. Christianity is not dying, nor is the Church doomed, nor is the work of idealists in this generation of no avail. Rather he is blind that imagines so, blind to the armies that in the soul of Man do battle for the one eternal God.

Such are some of the reflections prompted by the history of the Wisdom Movement. We come now to what those unacquainted with the events we have been describing may have imagined to be the only, as it is the most obvious and perhaps the most important, gift the Jewish Sages have left for our inheriting—the proverbs themselves, considered apart from their origin or use in relation to any particular historical events. Not all the sayings are of value in themselves, for some are trivial and some are obsolete, some have been said better, and a few were better left unsaid. But there remain many having permanent interest, and many that speak deep and undying truth, truth which we, no

Studies in Life from Jewish Proverbs

less than our fathers, have need to learn, and which those who come after us will have to learn or suffer loss. Had we chosen to use such proverbs as texts whereon to build discussion, illustration or enforcement of their thoughts and counsels, they are enough to fill not one but many volumes of this size. For stirring subjects would open up on every side. How shrewd, for example, are these Jewish maxims in their insistence that principle should precede practice, that success in life is won not by experiment unguided by fixed purpose but by the early adoption of certain great principles which our experiences will continually test and interpret, clarify and confirm! How sensible in their demand for the use of unsparing criticism —both the discipline of self-imposed criticism, and the humility that will receive, and, if necessary, assent to the reproof of others! How true the instinct which taught them to feel that real Wisdom is not merely an intellectual affair; so that they bid men seek not learning but rather the power to use it for right purposes, not knowledge of fact so much as the understanding mind. It is of profound importance in life this distinction between intelligence and knowledge. As the late Lord Cromer remarked to one of his friends soon after the outbreak of the European war, " I believe that Germany will live in history as the supreme example of the failure to distinguish Wisdom from Learning." It is Wisdom that the Jewish Sages preached. And how wise they were in the emphasis they lay on the necessity of application in the difficult task of awakening and cultivating the dormant powers of the mind.[1] Above all, how more than wise how humane, are they in depicting Wisdom in lovely colours, not as cold and repellent, but as warm and welcoming, an infinitely desirable, compassionate

---

[1] " I know no teachers who lay more stress upon the cultivation of the mental power of attention," G. A. Smith, in *Modern Criticism and the Preaching of the Old Testament*, ch. VIII.

Values

Friend of Humanity! How much we have still to learn from them in that respect, we who are not yet wholly delivered from an age that of set purpose hid the fascinating light of knowledge under a bushel of dull and unimaginative discipline, making education seem a thing to be endured—till we grew up—and depicting Morality as an All-seeing Eye, unblinkingly on the watch for our misdemeanours, a sort of inescapable Super-Spy! And again, treating the proverbs from this general point of view, what inexhaustible variety of themes would be at our disposal—education, commerce, responsibility, virtue and vice, hardships, luxury, marriage and friendship, idleness and diligence; in fact we might talk " of shoes and ships and sealing-wax, of cabbages and kings "; an *embarras de richesses*.

The remaining pages of this volume will be given to a review of certain of the Jewish proverbs, grouped under several topics. The principle on which these topics and the proverbs used in their illustration have been selected is chiefly the avoidance of repetition, so far as has proved reasonably convenient. Obviously, many most suitable subjects, such as the personal virtues, and many sayings that might fittingly be quoted in exposition of the themes actually chosen for the following pages, have already been utilised in our account of the Wisdom Movement. These then, with a few exceptions, will not be reproduced again, partly because there is little need to draw upon them, the stock of Jewish proverbs being far from exhausted, but mainly because it is to be hoped that their wit and wisdom for ourselves and for all men did not pass unnoticed and unconsidered in the historical setting. The sins of omission of which the following pages are guilty are patent even to the author. If they rouse the reader into making a better selection for himself, good and again good.

Studies in Life from Jewish Proverbs

To preserve a thread of connection with what precedes, we may commence by reviewing first *Nature* and then *Humour* in the Jewish sayings, both of which subjects have not only a certain general interest, but will help further to show how the proverbs can contribute to our realisation of the Humanism of the Bible.

CHAPTER XIII

Nature in the Proverbs

In comparison with the Greeks and those peoples who have inherited something of the Grecian genius for form and colour in the world, it may fairly be said that the Hebrews were inartistic. When, however, they are charged with being " unresponsive to Nature," or " lacking the artistic sense," it is time to protest. For the Hebrews were not unobservant of Nature or unsympathetic, and the writers of the Old Testament make many allusions to the scenes and processes of the visible world, and they recognise its beauties and its marvels. The artist's proper quarrel with the Hebrews is that very seldom did they see Nature in and for itself, but almost always through the medium of its relationship to the mental or physical interests of Man—how far does Nature threaten or encourage his faith and aspirations? what does it teach him? The Psalmist does not tell you " what a glorious night it is " or that " the sunset is magnificent "; he says that *the heavens declare the glory of God, and the firmament sheweth His handiwork*. We are bidden to lift our eyes to the hills, not to perceive the lights and shadows on their slopes, but because thence we may look to see the advent of our hope. Let us set two famous passages in contrast, the first from Greek literature, the second from the New Testament. In one of Pindar's jewelled Odes, the poet—singing the praises of Iamos, a mortal born of the god Poseidon and a human mother—first paints in rich and glowing words a picture of the infant hero laid in a cradle among the rushes, " his soft body

Studies in Life from Jewish Proverbs

bedewed with light from the yellow and purple colours of the pansies," and then goes on to show him, now grown to manhood and tasting the first fresh glory of his youth, " going down to the midst of the Alphæus stream, there to invoke the regard of his divine progenitor and to beseech of him the favour of a hero's task—$\nu\upsilon\kappa\tau\grave{o}s$, $\dot{\upsilon}\pi\alpha\acute{\iota}\theta\rho\iota o s$, *by night under the open sky*."[1] No one who has ever felt the magic of a star-filled night can miss the art that makes the passage culminate in those two words. Now compare this from the New Testament, of course in reference to the literary question only:—. . . " So when he had dipped the sop, he taketh and giveth it to Judas, the son of Simon Iscariot. And after the sop, then entered Satan into him. Jesus therefore saith to him, That thou doest, do quickly. Now no man at the table knew for what intent he spake this unto him. For some thought, because Judas had the bag, that Jesus said unto him, Buy what things we have need of for the feast, or that he should give something to the poor. He then having received the sop went out straightway: *and it was night*."[2] Here also is art, the highest art—it needed the darkness to cover Judas and make possible his sin—but the art is unconscious. The words are given only as a detail of fact, an indication of time, added without a thought of their effect on our emotions. The writer of the Gospel is altogether absorbed in the agonising human interest of the scene.

No expectation therefore should be entertained that Nature in the Jewish proverbs will be presented with unusual beauty or close observation. Nothing very wonderful is remarked of the world outside the little world of man, and the allusions almost always are made in relation to human hopes and fears and habits. But Nature has not been expelled from the proverbs; she crops out now and then, and, if we bear in mind this warning against undue hopes,

[1] Pindar, *Olympian* VI., 54ff.   [2] St. John, 13[26].

Nature in the Proverbs

the subject seems worth a brief examination. Well then, the following proverbs are assembled solely on account of their references to natural phenomena. That is the one and only pretext for their collocation. Some perchance may say that the excuse is insufficient—but they forget that "a touch of Nature makes the whole world kin."

Since tradition saith of Solomon that "he spake of trees from the cedar that is in Lebanon even unto the hyssop that springeth out of the wall; he spake also of beasts and of fowl and of creeping things and of fishes," we can see where we ought to make a start.

We begin with the *trees*. The *trees* however will disappoint us. Wisdom, we are baldly told, *is a tree of life to them that lay hold upon her* (Pr. 3^{18}), and it is said (Pr. 27^{18}) *Whoso keepeth the fig tree shall eat the fruit thereof.* Even if we get so far as to spy a little fruit upon a tree, and imagine that we have it safely gathered, lo! and behold! it rolls out of our fingers. For the famous proverb,

> *Like apples of gold in baskets of silver,*
> *So is a word spoken in season* (Pr. 25^{11}),

is pretty but elusive, the truth being that the vague phrasing of the English Version is due to nobody knowing what the Hebrew really means! The best passage is this from Ben Sirach, *As the flower of roses in the time of new fruits, as lilies at the waterspring, as the shoot of Lebanon in time of summer, . . . as an olive tree budding forth fruit, and as an oleaster with branches full of sap* (E. $50^{8\text{-}10}$).

Here are the *birds* in proverbs:

In vain is the net spread in the eyes of any bird (Pr. 1^{17}).

> *As a bird that wandereth from its nest*
> *So is a man that wandereth from his home* (Pr. 27^8).

Birds resort unto their like,
And truth will return to them that practise it (E. 27^9).

Studies in Life from Jewish Proverbs

The eye that mocketh at a father,
And despiseth an aged mother,
The ravens of the brook shall pick it out,
And the young eagles shall eat it (Pr. 30^{17}).

The *beasts* may be divided into the wild creatures untamed by man, and the domestic animals. Some of the latter are to be seen wandering most naturally through this picture of the wise farmer:

Be thou diligent to know the state of thy flocks,
And look well to thy herds;
For riches endure not for ever,
Nor wealth to all generations.
When the hay is carried and the tender grass springeth,
When the grass of the mountains is gathered,
Then the lambs will supply thee with clothing
And the goats yield the price of a field,
And give milk enough for thy household,
Enough for the maintenance of thy maidens (Pr. 27$^{23\text{-}27}$).

For the *horse* see Pr. 26^3, E. 30^8 and 33^6; of the *dog*, whom we shall meet again in the next chapter, there is a famous saying in *Eccles.* 9^4, *Better a living dog than a dead lion.*

Among the *wild animals*, the lion (Pr. 30^{30}) and the bear enjoy the most fearsome reputation according to the proverbs—*The king's wrath is as the roaring of the lion* (Pr. 19^{12})—*As a roaring lion and a ranging bear, so is a wicked ruler over a poor people* (Pr. 28^{15}). But there are worse things than either—*Let a bear robbed of her whelps meet a man rather than a fool in his folly* (Pr. 17^{12})—*I will rather dwell with a lion and a dragon than keep house with a wicked woman* (E. 25^{16}). The references to *conies*, *locusts*, and *lizards* in Pr. 30$^{26\text{f}}$ may be remembered (see p. 47). *Wine*, said the Wise, *goeth down smoothly, but* (was there gout, or worse, in those days?) *at the last it biteth like a serpent,*

Nature in the Proverbs

and stingeth like an adder (Pr. 23^{32}), and the *serpent's* elusive track across the rock is mentioned in Pr. 30^{19}. Perhaps these references to snakes should have been placed at the head of a paragraph on *creeping things*. However that may be, one of the creeping things, being " exceeding wise " (Pr. 30^{24}), received an immortality in *Proverbs* :

> *Go to the ant, thou sluggard,*
> *Consider her ways and be wise* . . . (Pr. 6^6).

Cannot one see a Sage in some leisure hour, bending down to watch the busy energetic little creature hurrying about its toil ? And then—" Aha ! " said he, " behold a proper scourge for lazy bones " !

The one reference to *fishes* makes one wonder whether the days of yore, like our own times, had their sea-serpent season. Says Ben Sirach,

They that sail on the sea tell of the danger thereof,
And when we hear it with our ears we marvel.
Therein be also those strange and wondrous works,
Variety of all that hath life, the race of sea-monsters (E. 43^{24,25}).

The proverbs may lack something as a text-book for young scientists ; yet here is the very essence of the fact of gravitation observed and duly noted : *He that casteth a stone on high casteth it on his own head* (E. 27^{25}).

Two or three features in what one may call civilised Nature, are worth recording here, although Man played the chief part in their appearing :—

A glimpse of a battlemented town :

> *A wise man scaleth the citadel of the mighty,*
> *And bringeth down its strong confidence* (Pr. 21^{22}).

Of great ships on the sea :

> *She is like the merchant ships,*
> *She bringeth her food from afar* (Pr. 31^{14}).

Studies in Life from Jewish Proverbs

Of a prosperous dwelling-place:

Through Wisdom is an house builded
And by understanding it is established,
And by knowledge are the chambers furnished,
With all precious and pleasant riches (Pr. 24^{3,4}).

Curiously enough, no reference to sun, moon or stars occurs in *Proverbs*[1], but there are several allusions in *Ecclesiasticus*, especially in one remarkable chapter of really poetic appreciation, which tells first of the wonder and the blazing intolerable heat of the sun (E. 43$^{1-5}$), and then celebrates the glories of moon and stars and rainbow—*the moon increasing wonderfully in her changing, a beacon for the hosts on high, shineth forth in the firmament of heaven. The beauty of heaven is the glory of the stars, an array giving light in the highest heights of the Lord: at the word of the Holy One they stand in due order and sleep not in their watches. Look upon the rainbow and praise him that made it; exceeding beautiful in the brightness thereof. It compasseth the heaven round about with a circle of glory; the hands of the Most High have constructed it* (E. 43$^{8-12}$). Again in a panegyric on the virtues of Simon, the son of Onias, the high-priest "great among his brethren, and the glory of his people,"[2] Ben Sirach says that, when the people gathered round him as he came forth out of the sanctuary, he was glorious

As the morning star from between the clouds;
  As the moon at the full;
As the sun shining forth upon the Temple of the Most High;
And as the rainbow giving light in clouds of glory (E. 50^{6,7}).

The elements and seasons, in one way or another, are referred to not infrequently. For instance, Pr. 25^{13}, *As the*

[1] The *moon* once (Pr. 7^{20}) but merely in indication of time.

[2] He was gratefully remembered for his work in strengthening the defences of Jerusalem and executing repairs to the Temple about 190 B.C.

Nature in the Proverbs

coolness of snow in time of harvest, so is a faithful messenger to them that send him[1]*:* a proverb we might appreciate more fully if either we had to go harvesting under an eastern sun or if His Majesty's postal system were suddenly abolished.

> *As clouds and wind without rain,*
> *So is he that boasts of gifts ungiven* (Pr. 25^{14}).

—how tantalising to see the precious moisture far overhead and drifting hopelessly out of reach, in a land where rain was desperately needed!

One passage from the poetical chapter of *Ecclesiasticus* mentioned above has something of the Grecian charm, combining as it does grace of expression with precise observation of Nature. Save in the spring-song of *Canticles*, in one or two *Psalms* and in some exquisite chapters (*e.g.*, chapters 28 and 38) of *Job*, it has few, if any, rivals in ancient Jewish literature. Mark the skilful transition from the raging of the tempest to the stillness of the snows :—

> *By His mighty power Jehovah maketh strong the clouds,*
> *And the hailstones are broken small:*
> *At His appearing the mountains shake,*
> *And at His will the south wind rages,*
> *And the northern storm and the whirlwind;*
> *The voice of His thunder maketh the earth to travail.*
>   *Like birds flying down He sprinkleth the snow,*
> *And as the lighting of the locust is the falling down thereof:*
> *The eye will marvel at its white loveliness,*
> *The heart be astonished at the raining of it.*
> *So also the hoar-frost He spreads on the earth as salt,*
> *And maketh the shrubs to gleam like sapphires* (E. 43$^{15-19}$).[2]

---

[1] For allusions to the heat and thirst of the reapers, cp. *Ruth* 2$^{7-9, 14}$, and 2 Kings 4$^{18, 19}$.

[2] The Greek text is no less effective—*And when the frost is congealed it is as points of thorns,* but it is only a misreading of the Hebrew.

Studies in Life from Jewish Proverbs

Some of the simplest allusions to natural phenomena are among the most memorable of these "Nature" proverbs perhaps because it happens that the clear and simple image from the world without is linked to some equally clear and simple, yet poignant, experience of human life:—

> *As cold waters to a thirsty soul,
> So is good news from a far country* (Pr. 25^{25}).

*As in water face answereth to face,
So answereth the heart of man to man* (Pr. 27^{19}).

*As the sparrow in her wandering, as the swallow in her flying,
So the curse that is causeless alighteth not* (Pr. 26^2).

Dreams give wings to fools (E. 34^1).

*The path of the righteous is like the light of dawn,
Shining more and more unto the perfect day* (Pr. 4^{18}).

CHAPTER XIV

Humour in the Proverbs

DISCRETION counsels the suppression of this chapter. Justice insists that it shall be written, for the Hebrews, on the evidence of the Scriptures, have been accused of lacking humour; a much more serious offence than being inartistic. Humour, divine gift, is no merely ornamental or superfluous quality we can easily afford to do without, but is the active antagonist of many deadly sins. From inordinate ambitions and peacock vanity humour is a strong deliverer. If only Germany could have laughed at herself now and then these past thirty years! Of course the mere fact that the accusation has been levelled against the Hebrews is nothing serious, for the same charge has actually been made against the Scotch; but whilst the Scot is well able to take care of his own reputation, few have been concerned to defend the Hebrew on this score.

The Bible is on the whole a solemn book, but remember the nature of its subjects. British humour is plentiful enough; but you will seek it in the pages of *Punch* rather than in our volumes of jurisprudence or in official histories or in impassioned orations urging the redress of wrongs, or in *The Book of Common Prayer*, or in the hymnaries. It is not fair to expect that Hebrew humour will show itself to full advantage in the Scriptures. However, the least promising material has a way of supplying against its will one form of humour—the unintentional; we can all quote some examples from the hymn-book. Of this *unconscious* humour, the Bible has its share. Many no doubt will

Studies in Life from Jewish Proverbs

recall that stricken Assyrian army of whom it is naïvely said in the Authorised Version that "when they arose early in the morning, behold, they were all dead corpses." So in the proverbs there are numerous sayings which to us are provocative of a laugh or a smile, or at least bring to memory certain amusing incidents of life, but which probably were uttered by their authors without a thought of anything comical in the words. Thus, the following, *There is one that toileth and laboureth and maketh haste, and is so much the more behind* (E. 11^{11}), may be meant as a solemn inculcation of the doctrine "More haste, less speed," but *we* conjure up a vision of our fussy friend and see the fun in it. Again the remark (Pr. 26^{17}), *He that passeth by and vexeth himself with strife not belonging to him is like one that taketh a dog by the ears* (and then finds he dare not let go!), is to us amusing but to its author may have seemed merely a shrewd or apt comparison; and yet in this instance we may suspect the Sage also had a smile for the impulsive man's predicament. Is the humour of this unconscious: *Houses and riches are an inheritance from fathers, but a prudent wife is from the Lord* (Pr. 19^{14})? Far be it from a prudent man to say.

The question of Hebrew humour, however, goes much deeper. Doubtless there is a philosophy of laughter, and an ideal humour, possibly a standard joke to which all other jokes imperfectly conform; but what the definition of this perfect humour may be who dare yet say? At present the nations have each their own opinion and the divergencies are great. We must ask of the Hebrew no more than Hebraic humour, and it does not necessarily follow that his notion of fun will coincide with ours or even nearly resemble it. Was he humorous in an Eastern way?—nothing more can reasonably be required.

What then was the way of humour in the Semitic East? Fortunately life in Palestine has altered so little that

Humour in the Proverbs

modern observation can help us to an answer. "The first appearance of an Eastern", writes Dr. Kelman[1], "is grave and solemn, with an element of contempt in it rather trying to the stranger. The Eastern does not understand chaff, his wildest outbreak of humour reaching no further than those solemn and laboured puns of which he has always been so fond. . . . Perhaps it is due to the ever-present remembrance of danger that the Eastern—especially if he be an Arab—so often assumes a show of superiority and bullying swagger, which seem to the uninitiated quite impervious to any thought of fun. *But the mask is easily laid aside*, and the gravest and most contemptuous Syrian will suddenly collapse into harsh laughter or forget himself in childish interest. Their notion of entertainment differs so much from ours that Eastern " festivities " may appear to us only wearisome or even ridiculous. On one occasion we arrived at our tents to find a 'poet' or improvisator, waiting for us. The minstrel seated himself on the ground, while we formed a wide circle round him, and the camp-servants stood behind. From a cloth-bag he produced an instrument which bore close resemblance to a domestic shovel, much the worse for wear and perforated with little irregular holes as if it had been shot. He began to play, and sang a selection which soon conquered any levity that may have greeted his beginning. He had but a few tunes and they all ended in the Minor *doh si lah*, the *lah* being prolonged, diminuendo and tremolo, in a long wail that had a sob in it. While the wail was dying away his head was thrown forward and his face uplifted, the upper lip quivering rapidly and the eyes rolling from side to side. Then just as he seemed to have reached silence, came a quick spasmodic outburst, very loud and clear, with vigorous accompaniment, which in its turn died off in the same long wail. All this must be imagined with a wonderful sunset of gold in a sky of

[1] "The Holy Land," pp. 209ff.

Studies in Life from Jewish Proverbs

indigo and grey, against which the figure of the Arab sat in dark silhouette." A pleasure so ludicrously sad would certainly seem to imply a lack of humour in those who can enjoy it; but—"the minstrel whom we have described was quite open for joking when he had emerged from his ecstasy. . . . Often at night there is singing among the servants of the camp and outbursts of hilarity can be heard. . . . When a fantazia (to celebrate the gift of a fatted sheep) was held there was no possibility of mistake as to the mirth." Thus there is good reason to mistrust appearances. And certainly it is inherently improbable that the Hebrews should have been devoid of humour; for, as Dr. Kelman goes on to insist, " the East is full of provocatives to mirth. Take the one instance of the camel. Much has been written about him from many points of view, but justice has never been done to the camel as a humorous animal. Yet he is the most humorous of all the inhabitants of the East. Beside him, with his sardonic pleasantry, the monkey is a mountebank and the donkey but a solemn little ass. He has been described as 'the tall, simple, smiling camel'; but on closer acquaintance he turns out to be hardly as simple as he might be taken for, and if he smiles, he is generally smiling at you. The camels you meet in Syria are carrying barley with the air of kings and regarding their human companions with, at best, a contemptuous tolerance." Dr. Kelman in conclusion comments on, and cites examples of the camel's unsanctified capacity for conduct bearing a horrible resemblance to that abomination of human invention—the practical joke.

To sum up. Eastern humour is by no means non-existent, but being often deliberately concealed or restrained in the presence of strangers and being of a different temper from our own, it may easily fail to be observed by Western eyes. Generally speaking, it is apt to be of the most awkward Order of the Camel's Hump, tending to other

Humour in the Proverbs

people's disadvantage, fond of personalities, often coarse because primitive, and, it may be, cruel. This being so, it will now readily be understood that the Bible held for its contemporaries much more wit than we are wont to perceive in it. Thus to many a Hebrew the incidents of Jacob's clever, and none too scrupulous, dealings narrated in *Genesis* would seem not only edifying but also extremely amusing. From this point of view such a saying as (Pr. 17^{12}) *Let a bear robbed of her whelps meet a man rather than a fool in his folly* is a merry jest; other examples from the proverbs will be given below.

But however plentiful this fierce and bitter kind of fun, the sting of the original accusation is not drawn. After all, our conviction remains deep-rooted that there is only one real humour—our humour; and no other brand is genuine. What men miss, and complain of missing, is that fine impartial sense of the ludicrous which is just as ready to see the disproportionate in ourselves as in others. The humour we demand is that kindly, tolerant, variety which can laugh at our own folly with profit and enjoyment, and at our neighbour's without malice. But is even this best of all humour absent from the Bible? Rare it may be; absent altogether it is not, and with a certain triumph we venture to claim its presence in not a few of the Wise-men's sayings, to which may be added an occasional proverb from the Rabbinic literature.

Beginning, however, with examples of the dry or caustic type of wit, camel-humour, let us take some of the sayings on Woman to illustrate the point. Doubtless the ladies had a great deal to say in reply, but with the customary meanness of man their remarks have been suppressed by the Sages:

As a jewel of gold in a swine's snout,
So is a fair woman without discretion (Pr. 11^{22}).

Studies in Life from Jewish Proverbs

*It is better to dwell in the corner of the roof
Than in a wide house with a fractious woman* (Pr. 25^{24}; cp. 21^9)

A continual dropping in a very rainy day and a contentious woman are alike (Pr. 27^{15}).

One saying there is on this topic, which comes nearer to our thought of humour, its bitterness being forgotten in the quaintness of the simile employed:

*As the going up a sandy way is to the feet of the aged,
So is a wife full of words to a quiet man* (E. 25^{20}).

Some of the characters pictured in Chapter VII. lent themselves to sarcasm, particularly the Sluggard, and the Fool; but, if certain of the proverbs about them may seem too heavy-handed, touched with the camel brand of humour, others surely come near to being " the real thing." Of the Sluggard the remark, *He that is slack in his work is brother of him that is a destroyer* (Pr. 18^9) is true, undeniably true, but a trifle icy in its wit. More amusing and much more genial were these sayings, which we may repeat from Chapter VII.: *The sluggard saith, " There is a lion in the way; a lion is in the streets"* (Pr. 26^{13})—*The sluggard burieth his hand in the dish, it wearieth him to bring it again to his mouth* (Pr. 26^{15})—and, above all, the Sluggard's Anthem, *Yet a little sleep, a little slumber, a little folding of the hands to sleep* (Pr. 24^{33}). Of the Fool, some observations are almost savage, such as Pr. 17^{12} (quoted above), and this—*Though thou bray a fool in a mortar . . . yet will his folly not depart from him* (Pr. 27^{22}). The following are more subtle and on the whole more kind: *The legs of the lame hang loose, so doth a story in the mouth of fools* (Pr. 26^7)—*The eyes of a fool are in the ends of the earth* (Pr. 17^{24})—*He that discourseth to a fool is as one discoursing to him that slumbereth; at the end of it he will say, " What is it? "* (E. 22^8). But the Fool and Mr. Lazybones were ever an easy target: it needed

Humour in the Proverbs

a prettier wit to slay the Self-Advertiser with a word, but does not this saying despatch him neatly, *It is not good to eat much honey; so for men to search out their own glory is not glory* (Pr. 25^{27})?

Here is a pleasing pair of contrasts—to the disadvantage respectively of a would-be " silent Solomon," and of a Chatterbox:

There is that keepeth silence, for he hath no answer to make;
And there is that keepeth silence as knowing his time (E. 20^6).
There is that keepeth silence and is found wise;
And there is that is hated for his much talk (E. 20^5).

In conclusion we give some proverbs that seem to the present writer still more clearly to come within the category of modern humour, whether by reason of their sly shrewdness or some droll comparison, or even a frank intention to rouse our sense of fun:

He that pleadeth his cause first seemeth just, but his neighbour cometh and searcheth him out (Pr. 18^{17}).

Better is he that is lightly esteemed and hath a servant, than he that makes a fine show and lacketh bread (Pr. 12^9).

There is that buyeth much for a little and payeth for it again sevenfold (E. 20^{12}).

In the city my Name, out of the city my Dress (C. 265).

Sixty runners may run, but they will not overtake the man who has breakfasted early (C. 86);

Thy friend hath a friend, and thy friend's friend hath a friend (C. 258)—a canny hint on Gossip.

Confidence in an unfaithful man in time of trouble is like a broken tooth or a foot out of joint (Pr. 25^{19}).

If one person tell thee thou hast ass's ears, take no notice;
Should two tell thee so, procure a saddle for thyself (C. 191).

Studies in Life from Jewish Proverbs

If our predecessors were angels, we are human ; if they were human, we are asses (C. 141) !

As for this last observation, it may have been well enough once upon a time, but of course one would not dream of asserting it now-a-days—as regards the present generation it would be, yes, altogether inappropriate. Well, let us not dispute the matter. Ancient and modern, East and West, we can all unite to enjoy the honest fun and good counsel of Ben Sirach's advice (E. 19^{10}) to that distracted individual the man with a secret :

Hast thou heard a word ? Let it die with thee. Be of good courage, it will not burst thee !

CHAPTER XV

From Wisdom's Treasury

WISDOM EXALTETH HER SONS, AND TAKETH HOLD ON THEM THAT LOVE HER:
HE THAT LOVETH HER LOVETH LIFE.
AND THEY THAT SEEK HER EARLY SHALL BE FILLED WITH GLADNESS:
HE THAT HOLDETH HER FAST SHALL INHERIT GLORY (E. 4[11,12]).

But Wisdom will brook nothing less than the full purport of those words—a diligent search, a genuine love, and an unrelaxing grasp—in exchange for her high rewards. And though it is better to find her late than not at all, as a rule it is true that only the life she has entered early is likely to know great happiness. Yet Wisdom makes no mystery of her treasures, nor hides them willingly.

Here are some of her most precious truths.

How simply told! How hard to make our very own!

As iron sharpeneth iron,
So man sharpeneth man.[1]

Faithful are the wounds of a friend.[2]

Who is ignorant of it? As Bacon says in his essay on Friendship, "There is no such flatterer as is a man's self; and there is no such remedy against flattery as the liberty of a friend." And yet how rarely, in actual experience,

---
[1] Pr. 27[17]   [2] Pr. 27[6].

Studies in Life from Jewish Proverbs

have men the grace to appreciate, or tolerate, even the kindliest of their critics.

* * * * *

A soft answer turneth away wrath.[1]

Have you tested the matter yet?

He whose spirit is without restraint is like a city that is broken down and hath no wall.[2]

* * * * *

Seest thou a man wise in his own conceit?
There is more hope of a fool than of him.[3]

Pride goeth before destruction,
And a haughty spirit before a fall.[4]

* * * * *

The wicked flee when no man pursueth.[5]

If a righteous man fall seven times, he riseth up again;
But the wicked are overthrown by calamity.[6]

* * * * *

He that despiseth small things shall fall by little and little.[7]

Be not wise in thine own eyes;
Fear the Lord and depart from evil.[8]

* * * * *

Hope deferred maketh the heart sick;
But a wish fulfilled is a tree of life.[9]

Woe unto fearful hearts and to faint hands,
And to the sinner that goeth two ways!
Woe to the faint heart, for it believeth not;
Therefore shall it not be defended.
Woe unto you that have lost your patience!
What will ye do when the Lord shall visit you?[10]

* * * * *

[1] Pr. 15^1; cp. 16^{32}. [2] Pr. 25^{28}; [3] Pr. 26^{12}. [4] Pr. 16^{18}
[5] Pr. 28^1, cp. Shakespeare's "Conscience does make cowards of us all."
[6] Pr. 24^{16}. [7] E. 19^1. [8] Pr. 3^7. [9] Pr. 13^{10}. [10] E. 2$^{12-14}$.

From Wisdom's Treasury

There is no wisdom nor understanding,
Nor counsel against the Lord:
The horse is prepared for the day of battle,
But the victory is of the Lord.[1]

> *Truth stands:*
> *Falsehood does not stand.*[2]

*   *   *   *   *

This is a very long chapter;
Think on these things.

---

[1] Pr. 21$^{30, 31}$.   [2] C. 78.

CHAPTER XVI

The Body Politic

THE art of hurling texts dies out of fashion, is almost dead, perhaps because it yielded the delight of victory so seldom, but for deeper reasons also. It was ever a game at which two could play; the Scriptures proving so rich a quarry that your skilled antagonist would quote you text for text. Both Socialist and Individualist have found therein ammunition in plenty for their long quarrel, by reason of the disconcerting manner in which the Bible preaches both doctrines and gives its sanction to neither. Thus it never so much as questions the propriety of individual ownership, yet on the other hand continually and with awe-inspiring vehemence it is found denouncing the wickedness of individual owners and the wrongs arising from their sins and negligences. So for the unreflecting text-hunter confusion was apt to grow worse confounded. The existence of this *impasse*, which in reality pointed only to an error in method, has helped to create the notion, characteristic of the present time, that the Bible having failed to settle the difficulty, we ought to consider our problems entirely without its aid. So completely are we now supposed to be the sole arbiters of our conduct that, even if the Bible had been found to enjoin (or forbid) explicitly and beyond all possibility of doubt certain socialistic measures, it would in no way follow that what may have been right in Jerusalem long ago is right now, or what was wrong then wrong now. Up to a point this attitude is sound: not to consider our duties

The Body Politic

for ourselves, as if our ancestors or any external authority could rightly determine them for us without our active consent, is to fall into a sin that, however innocently committed, sooner or later benumbs the conscience and, if historical experience has any lesson whatsoever to teach, paralyses social progress.

But the legitimate distrust which the modernist feels for mere text-hunting can be, and often is, pushed too far. To construe it as a mandate contemptuously to ignore the thinking and ideals of the past is to be guilty of as foolish a blunder as ever was involved in the old method of determining an issue by proof-texts; for the relation between even the Old Testament and the social affairs of any modern community is far too valuable to be disregarded with impunity; and on these three grounds at least. *First*, the experiences of the Israelitish people constitute incomparably the most amazing national career the world has witnessed; and the story of their fortunes testifies for all time that one nation, situated in no secluded and sheltered corner of the globe, but occupying a little land encircled by vast and jealous Empires and covered time and again by the surge of successive civilisations, prolonged its life and in all essential respects maintained its identity, not by bread alone, but by words that proceeded out of the mouth of God. For, undeniably, Israel has preserved its continuity not merely through the stormy fourteen hundred years of which the Biblical records tell, but subsequently throughout the Christian era, in virtue of distinctive moral and religious qualities; and whatever view a man may hold regarding the truth of religion and the validity of morals, no serious student of human affairs can afford to overlook their practical effect in the history of the Jews. *Secondly*, in the course of that history (limiting our attention to the Old Testament literature) there appeared certain great personalities, in particular the true prophets, whose insight

Studies in Life from Jewish Proverbs

into the problems of society, whose enthusiasm for the welfare of men, and whose burning invective against all forms of injustice and oppression, ought to be familiar to every man who feels within him the sense of social obligation. The example of the Prophets of Israel and also, though less brilliantly, of her Psalmists, her Law-makers and her Wise-men, is a magnificent incentive to duty, quickening the conscience, stimulating one's resolution under difficulties, and encouraging to good hope. *In the third place*, the record of these men's thoughts frequently deserves our *intellectual* consideration. Modern industrialism has created unsolved problems of organisation and production, upon which it would be idle to contend that the conditions of life in the Judæan highlands offer valuable comment; but since modern commerce, for all its marvellous development of wealth and resources, has signally failed to remove the vast inequalities between man and man, indeed has only accentuated them and made the contrast still more bitter for the unskilled, the weakly, and the unfortunate, it follows that from the standpoint of human happiness the social problem is in its essence unchanged: the poor, in fact, are still with us, with their great virtues and also their shortcomings, their pathetic lack of opportunity, and often their failure to profit when they might, and above all, with their capacity for joy and sorrow and aspiration, which things they share with the richest in the land. No wonder that he who reads the Old Testament with intelligence and sympathy will constantly feel its words on the social needs of men not merely pricking his conscience but holding and challenging the intellect—how wealth is made, how rightly used, how kept, how lost; what it feels like to be poor; of the duties of him that hath to him that hath not; by what things a city is preserved, and of the power we each possess to make or unmake one another's joy in life.

The Body Politic

On these and kindred subjects the Jewish proverbs have a vast deal to say that is worthy of attention, but an outline of their comments and pleadings has been given in the description of the Wise-men's ideals (Chap. VIII.). It may be hoped that the foregoing remarks will help to make more clear the bearing on present social duty of the teaching there related in reference to a distant past. Here then follow only a few considerations which will suggest how the subject might be developed, and will at the same time give opportunity for the quotation of some fine proverbs not mentioned in Chapter VIII.

1. In dealing with the perplexities of organised society, we moderns possess the advantage of high and increasing skill in the use of classification, so that we are able to envisage our problems in abstract terms, analysing the population into reasonably exact groups, and considering the inter-relations of " classes " and the reconciliation of class interests one with another. This attempt, crude though it still may be, to employ scientific method in the treatment of humanity is all to the good; but if one thing more is forgotten, our best-laid schemes somehow refuse to work or are apt to work amiss. For—" the ' masses ' and ' the poor ' whom it is ' our ' duty to keep are neither sycophants nor toadies nor sponges nor are all of them at the last gasp. They resent the control of their destinies by classes or persons who profess to know what is good for them. They will never become the passive instruments of anybody's social theory. They will trust themselves only to those who love them. Individualists and socialists take note! Experts and doctrinaires, be warned in time ! "[1] Now the Jewish proverbs, not of set purpose but by sound instinct, subtly and insistently remind us how personal all social questions ultimately prove to be. They think and speak with the individual in the foreground of the mind. They

[1] L. P. Jacks, *From the Human End*, p. 16.

Studies in Life from Jewish Proverbs

prefer the concrete to the abstract, with how great advantage! Contrast the effect of these two passages; the occasional, abstract type, *Water will quench a flaming fire, and almsgiving will make atonement for sin* (E. 3³⁰), with the much more frequent personal presentation: *Incline thine ear to a poor man, and answer him with peaceable words gently. Deliver him that is wronged from the hand of him that wronged him* (E. 4⁸,⁹). We discuss "Capital and Labour"; but the Jewish proverb says (Pr. 22²; cp. 29¹³)

> *The rich and the poor dwell together,*
> *The Lord God made them both;*

and how deep the proverb goes, how swiftly it strikes home and excites the imagination. *Rich and poor together*, yes, in a sense—united within one city's bounds; and yet how far apart they dwell from one another. How tragically far apart! But are they so greatly sundered as at first thought one imagines? In the things that matter ultimately— their manhood, womanhood; their tears and laughter; their loves; their sinning and repenting; their strength and health; their death and immortality? Perhaps there is just one meeting-place where rich and poor unite and stand absolutely equal; but it is there where earth and heaven fade away—the great white throne of God.

Mark how the sense of the individual man, with whom eventually all our plans to remedy the mischiefs in the body politic must come to terms, permeates the following proverbs:—

> *A good man leaveth an inheritance to his children's children;*
> *But the wealth of the sinner is laid up for the righteous*
> (Pr. 13²²).

(No pious platitude this, but a keen-sighted observation of fact. It is seldom indeed that wealth is handed down through many generations, except in a morally "good"

The Body Politic

family ; and on the other hand the sinner's undisciplined children can usually be depended on to make ducks and drakes of their inheritance).

Whoso stoppeth his ears at the cry of the poor,
He also shall cry, and shall not be heard (Pr. 21¹³).

There is that scattereth and increaseth yet more ;
And there is that withholdeth that which is meet,
and it tendeth only to want (Pr. 11²⁴).

Hast given the poor to eat and drink, accompany them on their way (C. 208).

In the recognition of personal faults as the bane of society :

He that covereth a transgression seeketh love,
But he that harpeth on a matter separateth chief friends.
(Pr. 17⁹).

For the drunkard and the glutton shall come to poverty,
And drowsiness shall clothe a man with rags (Pr. 23²¹).

These few maxims might be multiplied with ease, but they are sufficient for our purpose. Is it not clear how profoundly humanistic are these Jewish proverbs in their outlook on social affairs ? Except our science be tempered by the same redeeming grace, we shall succeed on paper but fail in fact.

2. The Jewish proverbs throw out a challenge to the present age in the demand they make for commercial honesty and consideration of the general welfare of the community. This claim is put forward in a variety of ways, and there is no mistaking its earnestness ; as in the famous saying, *A false balance is an abomination unto the Lord, and a just weight is His delight* (Pr. 11¹), a maxim reiterated in similar language in Pr. 20¹⁰,²³. Again it is said, *The getting of treasures by a lying tongue is a vapour driven to and fro : they that seek them seek death* (Pr. 21⁶)—*Better is the poor*

Studies in Life from Jewish Proverbs

that walketh in his integrity than he that is crooked in his ways though he be rich (Pr. 28⁶); and memorably—*Better is a little with righteousness than great revenues with injustice* (Pr. 16⁸); to which add this startlingly modern protest against the food-profiteer, *He that withholdeth corn, the people shall curse him; but blessing shall be upon the head of him that selleth it* (Pr. 11²⁶). "Ah! but the times have changed, and the complications and stringency of modern business often render the employment of perfectly honest methods impractical. In those byegone days a man of industry and ability had perhaps little temptation to double-dealing, or at least was not compelled to follow the tricks of the trade in order to squeeze out a livelihood." But no! that shortcut out of the difficulty is barred. Ben Sirach puts the matter bluntly: *A merchant*, says he, *shall hardly keep himself from wrong-doing, and a huckster shall not be acquitted of sin* (E. 26²⁹). "Well, then, have the proverbs any remedy to suggest? It is easy for the purist to *talk*. No one wishes to deny the courage of him who maintains a life-long protest against sharp practice, and we grant you the desirability of the protest; we can even admit the success of one here and there who has undertaken it. But it may seem doubtful if such unbending rectitude could be carried out generally; and at any rate, as matters stand, there must be thousands of well-meaning men who to keep themselves and their families from want and hunger must bow themselves slightly in the modern house of Rimmon "—so may a plea for a reasonable latitude be advanced.

What solution do the proverbs offer for the stern facts of present-day commerce? None; but that is no reason why we, following the spirit of their teaching, should not strive to find a remedy for our more complex problems, especially since the line along which progress can be made is surely not difficult to discover. The root of the matter is in the fact that whilst commercial dishonesty may benefit

The Body Politic

(in a material sense only) certain persons, it can only do so at the expense of the many, so that its elimination would necessarily conduce to the general welfare of organised society. Meantime it is hard for the individual to kick against the pricks of a system far greater than he, but it does not follow that the *community* of individuals is unable to fight the giant and slay him. Though the present situation is such that the guilt of the individual is lessened (it is of course still real), the guilt of the community in tolerating such a condition of affairs is the more increased. For union is immense strength. It is the imperative duty of modern man by collective action (which may require eventually to become world-wide) to check, diminish and abolish those evil and improvident conditions which now impose such pressure upon the integrity of individuals. A herculean task! What then? The resources of civilised man are already vast, and they increase with marvellous rapidity. We stand at the beginnings of organised achievement; yet already magnificent opportunities for the betterment of human life lie within our reach, and wait only the consent of mind and conscience for their realisation. False weights have continued, despite the Jewish proverb, these twenty centuries and more; it does not follow that they need continue to the twenty-first.

3. Much of the injustice and degradation still prevalent in our civilised society would be brought to an end by the force of public opinion, were it not for wide-spread ignorance of the facts. Sometimes the ignorance is wilful blindness and no true ignorance; men refuse to look or listen; but as a rule it is due to mere lack of interest and unimaginative carelessness. No decent man or woman could desire the appalling facts of child-labour in the mines and factories of this country during the first half of the last century, or, for the matter of that, the facts of sweated industries at the present day; but many respectable people wished not to

Studies in Life from Jewish Proverbs

know and vastly many more troubled not themselves to know, and so the horrible and disastrous iniquities went on year by year. Time and again the frank uncompromising proverbs of the Jews set us an example by their bold recognition of evil. They proclaim it for what it is, not mincing words but denouncing wickedness outspokenly and vehemently. A hundred illustrations could be taken from the maxims already quoted. Here, from sayings not yet mentioned, are three vigorous assaults on the hypocrite, the oppressor, and the morally perverted.

There is a generation that are pure in their own eyes, and yet are not washed from their filthiness. . . . There is a generation whose teeth are swords and their mouths armed with knives, to devour the poor from off the earth, and the needy from among men (Pr. 30^{12,14}).

As one that killeth a son before his father's eyes,
So is he that bringeth a sacrifice from the goods of the poor.
The bread of the needy is the life of the poor;
He that depriveth him thereof is a man of blood.
As one that slayeth his neighbour is he that taketh away his living;
And as a shedder of blood is he that depriveth a hireling of his hire (E. 34$^{20\text{-}22}$).

He that saith unto the wicked "*Thou art righteous," peoples shall curse him and nations shall abhor him* (Pr. 24^{24}).

4. OF RICHES AND THE DECEITFULNESS THEREOF

Weary not thyself to be rich. . . . For riches certainly make themselves wings, like an eagle that flieth toward heaven (Pr. 23 ^{4,5}).

" Believe not much them that seem to despise riches; for they despise them that despair of them. . . . Be not penny-wise; riches have wings, and sometimes they fly

The Body Politic

away of themselves, sometimes they must be set flying to bring in more "[1]

A good name is to be chosen rather than great riches (Pr. 22¹).

" I cannot call riches better than the baggage of virtue. The Roman word is better, *impedimenta*. For as the baggage is to an army so is riches to virtue. It cannot be spared nor left behind, but it hindereth the march; yea and the care of it sometimes loseth or disturbeth the victory. Of great riches there is no real use except it be in the distribution; the rest is but conceit."

His riches are the ransom of a man's life, but the poor heareth no threatenings (Pr. 13⁸).

" But then you will say, they may be of use to buy men out of dangers or troubles. As Solomon saith, ' Riches are as a stronghold, in the imagination of the rich man.'[2] But this is excellently expressed, that it is in imagination, and not always in fact. For certainly great riches have sold more men than they have bought out."

Wealth gotten in haste shall be diminished, but he that gathereth slowly shall have increase (Pr. 13¹¹).

" Seek not proud riches, but such as thou mayest get justly, use soberly, distribute cheerfully, and leave contentedly."

Health and a good constitution are better than all gold, and a good spirit than wealth without measure (E. 30¹⁵).

Riches profit not in the day of wrath, but righteousness delivereth from death (Pr. 11⁴)—

whereat the shallow-minded may smile if it please them.

5. " Most gracious God, we humbly beseech Thee, as for this Kingdom in general, so especially for the High Court of

[1] Bacon, *Essay on Riches*. [2] Bacon is referring to Pr. 18¹¹.

Studies in Life from Jewish Proverbs

Parliament: that Thou wouldest be pleased to direct and prosper all their consultations to the advancement of Thy glory, the good of Thy Church, the safety, honour, and welfare of our Sovereign and his Dominions; that all things may be so ordered and settled by their endeavours, upon the best and surest foundations, that peace and happiness, truth and justice, religion and piety, may be established among us for all generations."

How the Jewish proverbs would endeavour to give effect to the prayer for good government has been told already (p. 152), and it may be remembered that their teaching was described as a demand for a reign of justice extending from the highest to the lowest in the land. But that was an inadequate description. Examine more carefully what they say, and it will appear that the Jewish proverbs ask for more than bare justice; they enjoin mercy, they plead for honour, kindness, generosity, and affection between man and man; in a word they plead for *humanity* as the supreme solvent of human need. And are they not profoundly and rebukingly right therein? Justice may be the stones of the great building, but Love is the cement without which the fabric will not cohere. The stability of society depends on the good-will of well-intentioned men—*By the blessing of the upright the city is exalted, and it is overthrown by the mouth of the wicked* (Pr. 11^{11}).

6. One other arresting feature concerning the relations of rich and poor. The poorer classes of Jerusalem must have had many faults, but the Wise were very gentle towards them; scarcely ever do they reproach the poor *directly* for their shortcomings. On the other hand they have no mercy for the sins of those in high places, their instinct seeming to be that the root of evil in the State is in the neglect of opportunity on the part of those who possess the means for well-doing: and this is the more significant

The Body Politic

and conscience-searching in that the speakers of these proverbs were themselves, as a rule, members of the " fortunate " classes. " The poor, forsooth, are thieves ! " Are they ? Then, why ? *If a ruler hearkeneth to falsehood, all his servants are wicked* (Pr. 29^{12}). " The poor are disloyal and jealous of their betters ! " Are they ? *The king that faithfully judgeth the poor, his throne shall be established for ever* (Pr. 29^{14}).

7. In conclusion, a few memorable proverbs that will repay consideration. Here is an ambiguous maxim—from one point of view a platitude, from another a deep saying :

Sovereignty is transferred from nation to nation
Because of iniquity, violence and greed of gold (E. 10^8).

Does it mean that greed and evil ambitions incite nations to war, to conquest, and so to the acquisition of new territories ? If so, we are none the better for the information. Yes, but sometimes the " transference " takes place the other way, and not as the covetous folk desire it should. There have been peoples whose blind lust for power overreached itself, to meet with disaster and condign punishment. Concerning them too might it be said, though with a different accent to our words, " Sovereignty is transferred from nation to nation, because of iniquities, violence and greed of gold."

There is no ambiguity, and no indecision, in these fine sentiments, which are none the less admirable, because they do not tell us how to reach the Golden Age :

When the righteous prosper the city rejoices ;
And when the wicked perish there are shouts of joy (Pr. 11^{10}).

Righteousness exalteth a nation,
Whereas sin is a shame to any people (Pr. 14^{34}).

Studies in Life from Jewish Proverbs

But of all that the Jewish proverbs have to say on the duties of our interrelated lives, this is the best in that it *does* show the gateway to the Golden Age, and allows no man to pass by unchallenged,

> *If thou wilt lift the load I will lift it too ;*
> *But if thou wilt not lift it, I will not* (C. 257).

CHAPTER XVII

A Chapter of Good Advice

SUPPOSE A LECTURE (subject, GOOD ADVICE) to be given in THE LARGE LECTURE HALL, to-night, by the Venerable Rabbi Wiseman. We go, but with mixed feelings, assuring ourselves we do not care a straw for his advice, but we have nothing much better to do, the man has a reputation, and we wonder whether the hall will really be full to hear him. Somewhat to our surprise, the hall does fill rapidly, is full! Extraordinary how a well-known name will draw: doubtless the man has got a " following " in every town, prepared to drink in every word he says. But that will not altogether account for it; there must also be a big number here to-night who have come, like ourselves, out of mere curiosity. We wait the great man's arrival with impatience, uncomfortably conscious that we are meant to be edified, expectant that we shall be merely bored. (A lecture of " Good advice," forsooth. As if we haven't a right to our own opinions, and are not competent to advise ourselves: it will take him all his time to impress us!) The Rabbi arrives, to the usual clap-clapping of his admirers in the hall. . . . We are a little surprised at his appearance—a strong face, but his best friends would not call him handsome. At the same time, to give him his due, one could not call him *pompous*. . . . Why doesn't the Chairman stop talking? Who wants to listen to him? Seeing that we are " in for it," let's hear what the speaker has to say, and so get it over—

Studies in Life from Jewish Proverbs

At last the Rabbi rises, and proves wiser than we have expected; wise enough to be also wily. He begins with a touch of humour; we smile, are caught off our guard, and for a few moments (it was all he needed) he has captured our attention.

Here is the thread of his remarks:

Commend not a man for his beauty,
And abhor not a man for an ugly appearance.[1]

Be willing to listen to every godly discourse,
And let not the proverbs of understanding escape thee.
If thou seest a man of Wisdom get thee betimes unto him,
And let thy foot wear out the steps of his doors.[2]

But, *Let thy foot be seldom in thy neighbour's house,*
Lest he be weary of thee and hate thee.[3]

Answer not a fool according to his folly,
Lest thou be like unto him.[4]

He that giveth answer before he heareth,
It is folly and shame unto him.[5]

Learn before thou speak; and have a care of thy health,
Or ever thou be sick.[6]

Prepare thy work without and make it ready for thee in the field; and afterwards build thine house.[7]

Hast spoiled thy work? Take a needle and sew.[8]

Boast not thyself of to-morrow;
For thou knowest not what a day may bring forth.[9]

---

[1] E. 11^2. [2] E. 6^{35,36}. [3] Pr. 25^{17}. [4] Pr. 26^4. [5] Pr. 18^{13}.
[6] E. 18^{19}; cp. *First learn, then form opinions* (C. 217).
[7] Pr. 24^{27}. [8] C. 181. [9] Pr. 27^1.

A Chapter of Good Advice

Change not a friend for the sake of profit,
 Neither a true brother for the gold of Ophir.[1]

Laugh not a man to scorn when he is in the bitterness
of his soul ; for there is one who humbleth and exalteth.[2]

Reproach not a man when he turneth from sin ;
 Remember we are all worthy of punishment.
Dishonour not a man in his old age ;
 For some of us also are waxing old.
Rejoice not over one that is dead ;
 Remember that we die all.[3]

Do no evil, so shall no evil overtake thee ;
 Depart from wrong, and it shall turn aside from thee.
My son, sow not the furrows of unrighteousness,
 And thou shalt not reap it sevenfold.[4]

Be not thou envious of evil men, neither desire to be with them, for their heart studieth oppression and their lips talk of mischief.[5]

Let not thine heart envy sinners, but be thou in the fear of the Lord all the day long ; for surely there is a reward and thy hope shall not be cut off.[6]

Say not thou, " It is through the Lord that I fell away : for that which He hateth He made not." Say not thou, " It is He that caused me to err, for He hath no need of a sinful man."[7]

Say not, He will look upon the multitude of my gifts, and when I offer to the Most High God He will accept it.[8]

[1] E. 7^{18}.   [2] E. 7^{11}.   [3] E. 8^{5-7}.   [4] E. 7^{1-3}.
[5] Pr. 24^1.   [6] Pr. 23^{17}.   [7] E. $15^{11,12}$.   [8] E. 7^9.

Studies in Life from Jewish Proverbs

Keep thy heart with all vigilance,
For that is the way to life.[1]

Be not faint-hearted in thy prayer,
And neglect not to give alms.[2]

Commit thy ways unto the Lord,
And thy purposes shall be established.[3]

A brief lecture, but none the worse for that. Much Wisdom in small compass. Depart, as you must, whether touched or ostensibly indifferent. However that may be, whatever your feelings now, you cannot forget all his words; some of them are fastened in the memory. One day you may act upon them and discover that they were wise indeed, and then you will want yourself to move a vote of thanks to the lecturer.

---

[1] Pr. 4^{23}. [2] E. 7^{10}. [3] Pr. 16^{5}.

CHAPTER XVIII

Conduct

THIS chapter will prove less ambitious than its title suggests. As the remarks made a few pages back, on *The Body Politic* were meant to be taken in conjunction with what was said in Chapter VIII. regarding social and family conduct, so here also only a few reflections will be given in summary, or in supplement of the Wise-men's ideal of personal character. It is perhaps as well that it seems superfluous to recapitulate the various attributes that the proverbs say are to be chosen or eschewed by the perfect man; for when the Vices have been assembled they form a dismal and depressing crowd, and when the Virtues are lined up over against them, they are a celestial host but they glitter on high beyond a modest man's attainment. Moreover the art of noble living is best practised not by those who go spelling out the details, as if the Virtues were meant to be acquired singly or the Vices attacked and conquered one by one, but by those who from sound instinct or a wisely-trained intelligence have mastered a few great thoughts and assented to follow their guidance in the maze of life. It is the purpose of these pages to touch only on certain of these controlling facts, principles, or ideals of conduct. The task before us is therefore neither intricate nor long. It is simple, yet (for all its simplicity) serious.

There is one quality that is not so much a part of character as the very soil out of which it grows—*Honesty of purpose;* if absent or only fitfully present, moral growth

Studies in Life from Jewish Proverbs

is either stunted or cut off; if present, then a multitude of imperfections are found pardonable. Wise therefore is the Jewish proverb that says of *Deceitfulness*, using a realistic metaphor more eloquent than many words, *Bread of falsehood is sweet to a man, but afterwards his mouth shall be filled with gravel* (Pr. 20[17]). Over against it set this strong simple plea for *Sincerity: Strive for the truth, unto death, and the Lord God shall fight for thee* (E. 4[28]); and then consider the implication in the contrast of those maxims—that Evil is first sweet then bitter, and Good first painful then joyous. Sometimes those propositions are visibly, demonstrably, true in their entirety; sometimes the second part of them to be credited requires faith in the spiritual nature of man. But of the first part there can be no question; 'tis a matter of universal experience—moral victories at the first are difficult, moral defeats easy, *The way of sinners is smooth without stones, but at the end thereof is the pit of Hades* (E. 21[10]), a glissade to the precipice and over; *facilis descensus Averno*.

Setting aside for the moment the influence of religious belief on conduct (the next chapter will have something to say upon the point), it would seem that there is one outstanding quality to which the Jewish proverbs recur again and again, as if to tell us that here is the supreme secret. That quality may be called *Receptivity*, but it has many aspects for which other titles might more fittingly be used: it is the willing mind, the open eye and the hearing ear; in youth it is zeal to learn, in manhood more often the grace to profit by mistake. So from teachableness it is wont to pass into penitence, the recognition of error and imperfection—not passive penitence, however, but the active desire to improve—and then from this virile penitence it should rise into that disposition of Charity or Love towards others, which is the highest virtue, without which a man may have many talents and yet profit nothing. Let us

Conduct

trace the sequence in the proverbs, commencing with the desire for knowledge:

> *The fear of the Lord is the chief part of knowledge,*
> *But the foolish despise wisdom and instruction.*
> *My son, hear the instruction of thy father,*
> *And forsake not the teaching of thy mother;*
> *For they shall be a chaplet of grace unto thy head*
> *And ornaments round thy neck* (Pr. 17-9).

> *Yea, if thou cry after discernment,*
> *And lift up thy voice for understanding;*
> *If thou seek her as silver*
> *And search for her as hid treasures* . . .
> *Then shalt thou understand righteousness and judgement,*
> *And equity, yea, every good path* (Pr. 2³,⁴,⁹).

To him that is willing to learn, the proverbs promise rich and wonderful reward, and the New Testament repeats the promise:

> *God scorneth the scorners,*
> *But He giveth grace to the lowly* (Pr. 3³⁴).[1]

> *If thou desire wisdom, keep the commandments,*
> *And the Lord shall give it unto thee freely* (E. 1²⁶).[2]

Thus far the subject is familiar. Twice already reference has been made to this virtue of Learning-Ever. Impenitently we bring it up again, seeing that the Jewish proverbs are most urgent on the matter and also that men to-day stand in no small need of the counsel. For all its vaunted liberty of thought, our age is by no means patient of personal criticism, doubtless because owing to the swift and amazing

---

[1] Cp. *James* 4⁶; 1 *Peter* 5⁵.

[2] A verse which, as Oesterley observes, affords an interesting combination of the doctrines of Grace and Free-will; cp. *John* 7¹⁷.

Studies in Life from Jewish Proverbs

increase in control of material resources it has been peculiarly successful in certain directions (not, however, the most important); and the success has made us vain. To know a little about the universe (and we know no more) is a very dangerous thing.

But observe how from the initial grace of an eager, receptive attitude towards life, other virtues naturally appear. Frankly and patiently to recognise one's errors is to increase in wisdom, to learn before it is too late, to see the pitfalls one has narrowly escaped, and so to be humbled, to feel the sense of a great forgiveness vouchsafed to the simple-hearted, and accordingly to be grateful and to be happy:

He that covereth his transgressions shall not prosper:
But whoso confesseth and forsaketh them shall obtain mercy.
Happy is the man that feareth alway:
But he that hardeneth his heart shall fall into calamity
(Pr. 28[13, 14]).

This experience, if at all intense, has a profound effect on character; he that knows he has been forgiven much will love much, and his gratitude towards the Giver of all mercy will spontaneously show itself in mercy towards other men. Others will wrong him and disappoint him often, but, remembering his own imperfections, he will want to judge them gently and never to despair of helping them; to him it seems as if " they know not what they do." But this is the very disposition required of us in the prayer " Forgive us our trespasses, as we forgive them that trespass against us," and the question must surely be rising in the reader's mind, What relation can possibly be discovered between these high thoughts and the Jewish proverbs? This surprisingly intimate relation—that whilst the manifestation of perfect forgiveness in Christ's own Person made His Prayer a new power in the world, the thought in this petition was not new; it goes back to these words of Ben Sirach, *He*

Conduct

that taketh vengeance on his neighbour will meet vengeance from the Lord, and his sins will surely be confirmed. Forgive thy neighbour the hurt that he hath done thee, and then shall thy sins be pardoned when thou prayest (E. 28 [1, 2]) ! Who dares withhold his approval from the condition in the abstract ? If we are Christians at all, our conscience must welcome its eternal justice, recognising that we can ask no greater mercy to be extended us by God. And so we are wont to repeat the Prayer willingly without reservations or misgivings . . . just until the day come when " our neighbour " has gotten him a name and we lie dazed and bleeding from the hurt that he hath dealt us. *That* is the moment for which these words were spoken—*Let not mercy and truth forsake thee, bind them upon thy neck* (Pr. 3³). Know that—*By mercy and truth iniquity is purged away, and by the fear of the Lord men depart from evil* (Pr. 16⁶). By the time a man has schooled himself to put those exhortations into practice, he will be in no danger of treating forgiveness lightly : true forgiveness is conditioned by the Moral Law, is no futile shutting-of-the-eyes to uneradicated sin, and may therefore call for faithfulness unto death and necessitate the greatest sacrifice earth knows, even the Cross of Christ.

And with the thought let us return to that saying of Ben Sirach, *Strive for the truth unto death.* " The Truth " is here to be interpreted in the fullest sense of the term ; it means Righteousness or Justice ; it denotes sincerity in things great and small, in thought word and deed. The proverb then may serve as a reminder of the uncompromisingly stern and perilous element in human experience. Until three years ago many men had no lively sense of that aspect of things. The sinister possibilities were not absent, but often they were fallaciously concealed. When a man catches the same train to town day after day and his outward circumstances are uneventful and regular as some

Studies in Life from Jewish Proverbs

slow-moving stream, he may easily be deluded into thinking that his inner, spiritual self is likewise pursuing the even tenor of its way; whereas in reality it may be waging a desperate battle against increasing pride, prejudice, hardness of heart, and a whole battalion of the Fiend's picked legionaries. The Prosperous, consulting his bankbook, may easily be betrayed into saying "I shall not want," whilst the soul within him is choking. If our essential life is spiritual and consists in our love of the True, the Good, the Beautiful, riches are likely to prove a thin armour against the enemy. But three long and terrible years of war have transformed the situation, and there are few to-day who do not know that there is " a striving for the truth unto death." Little need now to emphasise the dark side of life; myriads are but too well acquainted with its tragedies.

The Jewish proverbs offer no philosophy of Suffering; for that one must go to the Christian religion, which has faced the worst of the problem and is unique in having found a reassuring answer. When, however, we turn to the immediate question, how best to meet and deal with hardship, physical or mental, behold! Christianity is content to appropriate the language of a Jewish proverb and reiterate its counsel, though with a glorious new confidence: *Therefore let us also, seeing we are compassed about with so great a cloud of witnesses, lay aside every weight, and the sin that doth so easily beset us, and let us run with patience the race that is set before us, looking unto Jesus, the author and perfecter of our faith. . . . For consider Him who endured such gainsaying of sinners against himself, that ye wax not weary, fainting in your souls. Ye have not yet resisted unto blood, striving against sin, and ye have forgotten the exhortation which reasoneth with you as with sons,*

My son, regard not lightly the discipline of the Lord
Nor faint when thou art reproved of him;

Conduct

*For whom the Lord loveth He disciplines,
And chasteneth[1] every son whom He receiveth* (Pr. 3 11, 12).

It is for discipline that ye endure; God dealeth with you as with sons; for what son is there whom his father doth not discipline? (*Hebrews* 12 1-7). To use or to refuse this idea of the educative opportunity in suffering makes an amazing difference to life. Says a commentator of the older school writing upon this passage in *Proverbs*: "First, *Despise not* the discipline. . . . Do not meet sorrow by a mere hardihood of nature. Let your heart flow down under trouble, for this is human: let it rise up also to God, for this is divine. And secondly, *Faint not*. . . . This is the opposite extreme. Do not be dissolved, as it were—taken down and taken to pieces by the stroke. You should retain presence of mind and exercise your faculties. If the bold would see God in his afflictions, he would not despise; if the timid would see God in them, he would not faint. . . . The same stroke may fall on two men and be in the one case judgement, in the other love. You may prune branches lying withered on the ground, and also branches living in the vine. In the two cases the operation and instrument are precisely alike; but the operation on this branch has no result, and the operation on that branch produces fruitfulness."[2]

*My son, if thou comest to serve the Lord,
Prepare thy soul for trial.
Set thy heart aright and with constancy endure,
And be not terrified in time of calamity* . . .

---

[1] The quotation in *Hebrews* is taken from the Greek (LXX) text of *Proverbs*: the Hebrew text of *Proverbs* now reads "Even as a father the son in whom he delighteth," but the original text probably had "and paineth" instead of the words "Even as a father"—the difference in Hebrew is very slight (cp. p. 192).

[2] Arnot, *Laws from Heaven*, p. 130f.

Studies in Life from Jewish Proverbs

For gold is tried in the fire,
And acceptable men in the furnace of humiliation,
Put thy trust in God and He will help thee;
Order thy ways aright and set thy hope on Him (E. 2$^{1\text{-}6}$).

Never in living memory has there been greater need for wise and persuasive advice how to conduct oneself in time of anxiety and affliction. In the gales of life many a ship is flung on the rocks for lack of a little good seamanship on board. But ships need care even when they are sailing summer seas; and so, because one hopes that brighter days are coming to the world and coming soon, there is room for one more counsel in conclusion. Religion, and particularly Christianity, has been robbed of half of its power over men's souls, by reason of the absurd and tragical notion that it bears chiefly on the woes of man and very little on his joys. On this score also the Jewish proverbs preach a useful and pleasant sermon, with their natural honest desire for the good things of life and their strong and salutary conviction that in Wisdom—being that fear of the Lord which is to depart from evil—will be found a never-failing source of refreshing happiness:

The fear of the Lord is glory and exultation
And gladness and a crown of rejoicing.
The fear of the Lord shall delight the heart,
And shall give gladness and joy and length of days

(E. 1$^{11,\,12}$; cp. Pr. 2^{10}, 3^{16}).

CHAPTER XIX

Faith

BEN SIRACH has a wise passage in recognition of the transcendent majesty of God. He has been seeking to describe the marvels of the universe, and words have failed him; how much more then if he should strive to declare the glory of the Creator! Wonderful as the visible world may be, *Many things are hidden greater than these, and we have seen but a few of His works. . . . The Lord is terrible and exceeding great, and marvellous is His power. When ye glorify the Lord praise him as much as ye can, for even then will He surpass. When ye exalt him, put forth your full strength; be not weary; for ye will never attain* (E. 43$^{29\text{-}32}$). These words give the reason why expressions of belief in God so often appear to the unbelieving mere platitudes. Before the thought of the living God, men of intense and sensitive faith are either silent, or at the most will speak in simple language, being conscious that *we may say many things, yet shall we not attain; and the sum of our words is " He is all "* (E. 49^{27}).

The Jewish proverbs recognise that God makes one fundamental demand from men, namely Honesty of purpose—the very quality or attitude of soul which, as we have just seen, is so essential to the growth of moral character:

All the ways of a man are right in his own eyes,
But God weigheth the heart (Pr. 21^{2}).

Studies in Life from Jewish Proverbs

He that sacrificeth of a thing wrongfully gotten, his offering is made in mockery; and the mockeries of wicked men are not well-pleasing (E. 34^18).

Ben Sirach says of a sinner, confident in his wrong-doing because no man seeth him—*But he knoweth not that the eyes of the Lord are ten thousand times brighter than the sun, beholding all the ways of men, and looking into secret places* (E. 23^19).

And again he writes of the hypocritically pious:

The Most High hath no pleasure in the offerings of the ungodly, neither is He pacified for sins by the multitude of sacrifices (E. 34^19; cp. Pr. 21^27).

It does not seem probable that the Almighty will be any the better impressed, should the wicked offer up hymns instead of sacrifices. Motive is still the criterion of worship: take heed how ye praise or pray, lest your words be no more than the sound of a voice; take heed how ye hear, lest, judging a sermon, you fail to hear God's judgment of you; and above all remember that the chief act of worship, without which all else is in vain, must be rendered at home and in the city's streets, for—said a Wise-man on whom the spirit of the prophets had descended—*to do justice and equity is more acceptable to the Lord than sacrifice* (Pr. 21^3). A plain commandment, but there is none greater: "Thou shalt love thy neighbour as thyself."

And to them that are fain to keep the commandment God giveth gifts. "But" says one, "how know you that they are *God's* gifts? Is there a God to give? Faith is very difficult to attain." Certainly faith is difficult to the sophisticated in this and every age; but to the Wise it has always seemed natural, and never impossible. Said a young Russian modernist, "I find it difficult not to believe in God." So much in passing; we shall return to the question a little later. Meantime, however, let us turn to what cannot

Faith

be denied, the reality of the gifts and the axiomatic truth of the assertion that they are from God in the sense that they are the consequence of believing God is and is good.

To believe in the true God, the high and holy and merciful God of Israel's noblest thinkers, the God and Father of the Lord Jesus Christ, certainly gives men confidence and courage, not because the dangers and difficulties of life are removed, but because our strength being increased, it becomes possible to overcome them: *The name of the Lord is a strong tower; the righteous runneth into it and is safe* (Pr. 18^{10}). Through the new spirit that is ours, life is lifted to a higher plane where we feel that, when sorrow and pain and sin have had their say, still the Lord reigneth; God is greater than His foes: *Whoso feareth the Lord shall not be afraid and shall not play the coward; for God is his hope* (E. 34^{14}).

To them that seek Him God gives illumination. *Evil men understand not justice, but they that seek the Lord understand it altogether* (Pr. 28^5)—which does not mean that the pious are omniscient, but does mean that to follow after truth and goodness enlightens, whereas to seek evil and pursue it makes men blind. Accordingly it is said, *There is no wisdom nor understanding nor counsel against the Lord* (Pr. 21^{30}), and the truth of that great saying has been repeatedly displayed in the rise and fall of mighty nations and empires, as well as in the lives of individuals. Selfishness is always short-sighted, snatching greedily at shadows and missing the best there is in life. Again, *The curse of the Lord is in the house of the wicked, but He blesseth the habitation of the righteous* (Pr. 3^{33}); and that is true because it is seldom that such things as passion, hatred, cruelty and haunting moral fears are absent from the former, and, whatever the good man's house may lack, it will generally have love, joy, peace and all the fruits of the Spirit.

Studies in Life from Jewish Proverbs

One remarkable proverb claims that *When a man's ways please the Lord, he maketh even his enemies to be at peace with him* (Pr. 16⁷); and the value of the saying is perhaps increased in that, regarded pedantically, the claim breaks down, whereas on a wider consideration it seems to be subtly and profoundly true. Thus, our truthfulness may not prevent some particular individual (our enemy) from deceiving us by a lie, but it helps many, who might become false and some day deceive us, to persevere in truthfulness; and if all men really were liars, heaven help our race! Our honesty may not prevent *a* thief from breaking through and stealing, but it does make it easier for other men to be honest and so helps to reduce dishonesty in the world; and if all men were deceivers, peaceful trade would cease. Mercy begets mercy; the kindness of all true men who love God and follow Christ is making the world more kind. In a word, the effect of righteous example is magnificently great. What matter then if the truth be superlatively phrased? Let us affirm it boldly: "When a man's ways please the Lord, he maketh even his enemies to be at peace with him."

Here is a verse that sums up the whole topic:—

The eyes of the Lord are upon them that love Him,
A mighty protection and strong stay,
A cover from the hot blast and a shelter from the noonday,
A guard from stumbling, and a succour from falling.
He raiseth up the soul, and enlighteneth the eyes;
He giveth healing, life, and blessing (E. 34¹⁶,¹⁷).

The gifts are good. But is there a Giver, a God who cares? Why not so believe? It is neither impossible nor incredible. In the last chapter we shall touch further upon the great question. For the moment our concern is only with the answer to it that we find in the Jewish proverbs. That answer is boldly affirmative. Let us begin, however,

Faith

with a rather hesitant saying; *A man's goings are of the Lord, how then can he understand his ways?* (Pr. 20²⁴). Possibly the author intended not to assert God's guidance but only to complain of the baffling character of our fortunes. If so, we will have none of it. If there be no God at all, at least let us struggle to determine our path with such intelligence as we can muster. In the following, however, there is no dubiety about the affirmation of faith: *A man's heart deviseth his way, but the Lord directeth his steps* (Pr. 16⁹). Hard doctrine! theoretically possible perhaps, but is it probable? Certainly it is hard to believe, almost incredible, so long as it is considered merely from the critic's chair. But the sublime hope that God careth for men displays an astonishing vitality; and the altogether amazing and significant fact is this, that just where it ought most surely to die down and be extinguished, there it always rises up and burns again—as now in the trenches.

Here is the witness of an educated man, who had long ceased to be a Christian in the conventional usage of the term. He is writing freely to one who had been more than a friend for Christ's sake, and it is fair to give his words, because death is no longer a mystery to him. "Half-unconsciously I hummed the tune rather than the words of the famous hymn [*When I survey the wondrous Cross*]; As I did so there appeared before me, not a vision of Christ's person, but of the meaning of the glorious crown of thorns He wore. The King of Heaven, the Prince of Peace, is a man—He took not upon Him the nature of angels. That would have been easy but futile. It would not have linked Him with us closely enough. So my vision told me. He must needs suffer for us. . . . And if suffering, and forgiveness, and love of our fellows, and general self-forgetfulness be what is required of every one of us, how greatly we all stand in need of His atonement. That was the lasting impression of my vision: but, subsidiary, there was

Studies in Life from Jewish Proverbs

another. I felt, for a moment, a sense of divine spectatorship, as if there was but God in the world besides me; and God, all-seeing, all-understanding, with whom no words were necessary[1]."

But also those whose training in the school of life has brought them no such command of words as had the writer of the above, have their own way of voicing the instinct, saying that "if a fellow's name is written on a bullet he'll get it, and if it isn't he won't." Press the naïve metaphor. Who writes the name on the bullet? Not Krupps; they are too busy for that. Then is the writing the writing of God, graven upon the bullet? Probably the man himself would say, Fate is the writer. "Fate" on the lips of men who have nineteen centuries of Christian tradition behind them is only another name, and imperfect, for God the Father. There is fatalism and fatalism. The fatalism of men who, being conscious (however dimly) that duty has drawn them into a war which is at bottom an immense conflict of ideas and ideals regarding the use and abuse of national power, feel somehow that they will not die except they were appointed to lay down their life for others; *that* fatalism is separated by a hair's breadth from explicit trust in the overshadowing love of God. Belief in God's providence may seem difficult to the student at his ease, but it is high human doctrine. It was the doctrine of Jesus; and keen and earnest thinkers, and simple men and women innumerable, facing the sternest facts of life, have found it possible to place their trust in it, and, trusting, have found themselves at peace.

Be not afraid of sudden fear, nor of the desolation of the
  wicked when it cometh ;
For the Lord shall be thy confidence, and shall keep thy foot
  from being taken (Pr. 3^{25f}).

[1] From a letter quoted in Holmes, *Walter Greenway, Spy; and Others, Sometime Criminal.*

Faith

In conclusion, here is a proverb which needs a few words of introduction. The graces and benefits of religion are frequently associated in the Bible with "meekness" or "humility." Now those English words carry unfortunate associations which are absent from the Hebrew they represent. The "humility" commended by the Prophets and Psalmists is a certain frank simplicity of soul—a quality from which not a few of the most effective and virile personalities in the world's history have derived their power. It has little or nothing to do with softness or timidity of character; indeed courage is its hall-mark. Those who first rallied round the Maccabean leaders in the struggle against an unclean Hellenism were of "the meek ones of the earth." The Russian peasant has this Biblical "humility," but the proudest military empire in the modern world has tasted the fortitude of his soul. Wherefore we may claim that this exquisite saying is not merely beautiful, but is also profound:

The prayer of the humble pierceth the clouds (E. 35^{17}).

CHAPTER XX

The Gift of God

THE sayings we have been quoting in this volume for the most part belong to the life of ordered and peaceful society. There is no tramp of armies, no sense of imminent death, no outrage of gigantic suffering and injustice, in the pages of *Proverbs* or *Ecclesiasticus*. To-day, however, the ordinary problems and interests of peace-time seem altogether irrelevant. Twenty million fighting men in Europe, asked what a maxim is, would talk to you of machine-guns; the maxims otherwise called proverbs belong to a different and forgotten world. For trifling moralisms we have to-day neither taste nor time.

But the Jewish proverbs range wide enough to have a word for everyone, for the grave or the gay, for pious or profane, for those in haste just as much as for those at leisure ; and many of their comments on life are very far removed from being trifling. In our enquiry we have met not a few winged words worth capturing and holding fast even in war-time ; great thoughts such as this assertion, *He that followeth after righteousness shall attain unto life, but he that pursueth evil doeth it to his own death* (Pr. 11^{19}), or this reassuring hint of the fundamental goodness of human nature, *When the righteous triumph there is great glorying, but when the wicked come to power men hide themselves* (Pr. 28^{12}; cp. 11^{10}), or this grand medicine for a tempted people, *Righteousness exalteth a nation, but sin is a disgrace to any folk* (Pr. 14^{34}).

The Gift of God

Moreover it ought to be recognised that, properly regarded, morality is never unimportant; moralisms being trifling only so long as they remain mere words, not when they are translated into deeds. Act upon the good that is found in these proverbs, and immense results would follow. But just there is the crux: "It is a small matter to get right principles recognised, the whole difficulty lies in getting them practised. We need a power which can successfully, contend against the storm of our passion and self-will."[1]

Now there is one deeply significant fact which we have seen in our study of the Jewish proverbs, but on which we have not yet laid sufficient stress—the fact that they seemed to their authors to point beyond themselves to a Divine Source. They were not fortuitous atoms gathered no man knew whence or why, but part of a marvellous system inspired and originated by God, sustained by His inexhaustible power, and governed by His holy purposes. Whatever may be thought regarding particular proverbs, no sensible person can imagine that Wisdom itself is idle or unimportant talk. Wisdom remains wise even in such a war as this, though the nations rage and the kingdoms are moved.

But is there a Divine Wisdom? Or is the aspiring faith of men only an unsubstantial dream? From first to last the Jews believed that Wisdom is a reality, and, far from weakening as the years went on, their confidence even increased, and their thoughts of the wonder and glory of the Heavenly Wisdom became, if possible, more sublime and yet no less intimate. And high as they exalted Wisdom, her chiefest glory remained this, that she was willing to dwell with men. Let us take as a last quotation some beautiful and loving words from that late work, the *Wisdom of Solomon*, to which reference was made in Chapter IX:

[1] Horton, *Proverbs* (*Expositor's Bible*), p. 318.

Studies in Life from Jewish Proverbs

Wisdom is an effulgence from everlasting light,
A stainless mirror of God's working, and an image of His
 goodness.
And it, being one, hath power to do all things ;
And remaining in itself, reneweth all things :
And from generation to generation passing into holy souls
It maketh men friends of God and prophets . . .
Wisdom is fairer than the sun, and above all the constellations
 of the stars.
Being compared with light, it is found to be before it ;
For to the light of day succeedeth night,
But against Wisdom evil doth not prevail (W.S. 7^{26-30}).

Is there this Heavenly Wisdom ? Century by century, Life is accumulating its patient answer to the question, building up its vast evidence that the word of God endures, generation by generation confirming the intuition that the visible is for man the least real and that it is the unseen things that are eternal. But out of the midst of history there has also come one finished and marvellous reply—the personality of Jesus Christ.

Wisdom, whence cometh it? And where is the place of understanding? cried one who had despaired to find an answer. But the day came when certain of the Jews declared that Wisdom was *found*, that the infinite Divine Wisdom in its full glory had dwelt amongst us. All, and more than all, that had been said or thought or hoped of the Heavenly Wisdom, they had discovered in Christ Jesus. For one who had been man among men to be thus *by Jews* identified as the Perfect Wisdom, which was but an aspect of God Himself, is clearly wonderful ; but just how utterly amazing it is, perhaps only those can realise who are conscious of the innate and magnificent monotheism of the Jews, and who have listened with sympathy and understanding to these reverent and rapturous praises of Wisdom. That a

The Gift of God

human being could possibly be felt to be the incarnation of Wisdom's Self is a miracle. But the miracle is precisely that which has happened, and it is explicable only by a cause as great as the effect ; that is, by the miracle of what Jesus was and is.

Recognition of Christ as the Divine Wisdom, and of Wisdom as incarnate in Christ, permeates the tradition and theology of the New Testament. It is visible in almost every passage where His disciples have sought to express the mystery and majesty of Him whose human love they had known on earth, whose divine power they now felt from heaven. The idea of Wisdom is the basis of St. Paul's great utterances regarding Christ in the *Epistle to the Colossians;* of the affirmations in *Hebrews* that by Christ were the worlds made and that He is the Radiance of the Divine Glory and the Reflection of the Divine Being ; and behind the wonderful opening chapter of *St. John's Gospel* there is a hymn to the Eternal Wisdom, which was in the beginning, and was with God, and was God.[1]

Who hath ascended into heaven and descended ?—asked a sceptical questioner in the *Book of Proverbs* (Pr. 30:4). *No man ascended into heaven, but He that descended out of heaven, even the Son of Man*, rings out the answer of the Gospel (*John* 3:13).

If any man lack Wisdom let him ask of God, who giveth to all liberally, and upbraideth not ; and it shall be given him, writes St. James. Surely God's gift is Christ ? There are now nineteen centuries to show that nothing that has set itself against His wisdom has endured and been accepted as the truth.

" We need a power which can successfully contend against the storm of our passion and self-will "—St. Paul

---

[1] See the articles by Dr. Rendel Harris on *The Origin of the Prologue to St. John's Gospel* in the *Expositor*, Aug. 1916-Jan. 1917. Note also the acknowledgment of Christ as Wisdom, implied in the story of the homage of the Wise Men at His birth, *Matt.* 2:12.

Studies in Life from Jewish Proverbs

affirms that the need has been met and answered in Christ crucified, *the Power of God and the Wisdom of God*, and the Gospel holds out the same promise: *as many as received Him to them gave He power to become the children of God*.

But are they many who throughout these centuries have sought to find Wisdom in Christ, and in His redeeming compassion, His perfect knowledge of human weakness and human need, His calm unfailing strength, His infinite holiness, His glorious ideal, His faith, His sacrifice, have declared that they have found that which they sought? They are very many. Already they are a multitude which no man can number—out of every nation and of all tribes and peoples—of whom some have sealed the confession with their life-blood, and some have given equal testimony in the unfaltering purity and patience of a quiet and unselfish life. Some of them have been learned and some unlearned in this world's knowledge, but it is abundantly evident that all who have been faithful to His word have possessed in its fulness the deeper Wisdom which is from above.

The sum of it all is this. Christ has come. There are those who do not trouble to seek for Wisdom with their whole heart, but that is a foolish attitude which should be shunned. The miracle has happened, and we ought to face its challenge. What think ye of Christ? Whose son is He?

Index

A BRIEF BIBLIOGRAPHY

Articles on *Proverbs, Ecclesiasticus, Wisdom Literature, Hellenism*, etc., in the Encyclopædia Brittanica (11th edition), Hastings's Dictionary of the Bible and the Encyclopædia Biblica.
C. H. TOY, *Proverbs* (International Critical Commentary).
G. CURRIE MARTIN, *Proverbs*, etc. (The Century Bible).
C. F. KENT, *Wise Men of Ancient Israel*.
W. O. E. OESTERLEY, *Ecclesiasticus* (Cambridge Bible for Schools and Colleges).
S. R. DRIVER, *Literature of the Old Testament*, s.v., Proverbs, etc.
G. A. SMITH, *Modern Criticism and the Preaching of the Old Testament*, ch. viii.
A. R. GORDON, *The Poets of the Old Testament*, chs. XV.-XVIII.
C. TAYLOR, *Sayings of the Fathers (Pirke Aboth)*.
A. COHEN, *Ancient Jewish Proverbs* (Wisdom of the East Series).
E. L. BEVAN, *The House of Seleucus* (2 vols.)
E. L. BEVAN, *Jerusalem under the High Priests*.
H. P. SMITH, *Old Testament History*, chs. XVIII., XIX.

I.—INDEX OF REFERENCES

PROVERBS

CHAPTER I.
ver.	page
4	130
7-9	157, 276
10ff	153, 181, 184, 200
17	231
22	130, 180, 181
24	180

CHAPTER II.
ver.	page
3, 4, 9,	267
10	217, 272
16-19	186

CHAPTER III.
ver.	page
3, 4	145, 269
5, 6	158
7	246
11, 12	192, 271
13-15	170
16	272
17, 18	217, 231
19f	172
25f	278
27, 28	155, 211
29	154
31, 32	153
33	275
34	267

CHAPTER IV.
ver.	page
7	177
10-19	77
13	142
18	236
19	51
23	264

CHAPTER V.
ver.	page
1-14	153
22	188

CHAPTER VI.
ver.	page
6-11	128, 233
12-15	123
16-19	48
20-vii. 27	153

CHAPTER VII.
ver.	page
1-27	153
14	108
20	234

CHAPTER VIII.
ver.	page
1-3	182, 200
10	171
15, 16	172
19	222
21	167
22-36	173
23	222

CHAPTER IX.
ver.	page
1-5	171, 212
7	135, 180
10	157
17, 18	171

CHAPTER X.
ver.	page
2	154
3	188
11	143
12	145
15	119
20, 21	143
22	25
23	134
26	140
27	189

CHAPTER XI.
ver.	page
1	253
2	143
4	211, 257
5	143
10	259, 280
11	258
12	140
18	188
19	280
22	241
24, 25	122, 253
26	254
28	211
30	143

CHAPTER XII.
ver.	page
1	142
5	143
7	211
9	243
15	123, 134
16	123
18	145
19	143
21	188
26	144

CHAPTER XIII.
ver.	page
1	180
2	211
3	140
5	143
7	122
8	257
11	257
12	246
19	134
22	252
24	149

CHAPTER XIV.
ver.	page
1	133
3	134
13	192
15, 16	133
17	139
20	120
32	190
34	259, 280

CHAPTER XV.
ver.	page
1	145, 246
2	123
4	145, 211
5	134
8	108
17	120
18	139
20	134
23	140
24	190
25	155
28	143
29	188

CHAPTER XVI.
ver.	page
1	211
3	264
4	189
6	269
7	276
8	154, 211, 254

Index

ver.	page
9	277
16	171
18	140, 246
19	210
24	51
26	116
27	123, 181
28	122
32	139, 206, 246

Chapter XVII.

ver.	page
1	108
2	151
5	144
7	129
9	253
10	135
12	232, 241, 242
13	140
16	134
17	142
21	130
23	153
24	133, 242
28	140

Chapter XVIII.

ver.	page
2	134
7	123
8	125
9	242
10	275
11	183, 257
13	262
17	243
20, 21	140, 211
22	148

Chapter XIX.

ver.	page
4	120
12	232
14	238
17	211
26	150
27	183
29	135

Chapter XX.

ver.	page
1	138, 185
3	141
6	192
10	222, 253
14	113
17	266
20	150
22	140, 188
23	153, 253
24	277
28	152

Chapter XXI.

ver.	page
2	273
3	108, 153, 274
6	253
9	242
13	253
14	152
17	138
20	133
22	233

ver.	page
23	211
24	135
27	108, 274
30, 31	247, 275

Chapter XXII.

ver.	page
1	51, 257
2	252
3	58
4	167
6	15
7	113
8	188
10	180
11	143
13	128; cp. 242
22, 23	153, 181
27	113
28	58

Chapter XXIII.

ver.	page
1-3	124
4, 5	256
9	134
10, 11	59, 153
13, 14	149
17, 18	190, 263
21	253
29-31	153, 185
29-35	138, 233

Chapter XXIV.

ver.	page
1	263
3, 4	234
11, 12	144
16	246
17, 18	141, 207
24	256
27	262
28	153
29	145
30-34	128, 242

Chapter XXV.

ver.	page
2, 3	152
6	211
11	231
13	234
14	123, 235
16	17
17	30, 262
19	243
20	125
21	145
24	242
25	236
27	222, 243
28	246

Chapter XXVI.

ver.	page
2	51, 236
3	134, 232
4	135, 262
7	134, 242
11	135
12	123, 246
13	242, cp. 128
14, 15	128, 242
16	128, 181
17	141, 238

ver.	page
18, 19	124
20	122
21	141
23-26	141
27	154
28	125

Chapter XXVII.

ver.	page
1	211, 262
3	134
4	141
6	245
8	231
14	125
15	242
17	245
18	231
19	236
20	58
22	135, 242
23-27	232

Chapter XXVIII.

ver.	page
1	246
5	275
6	154, 245, 254
7	138
8	155
12	280
13, 14	268
15	152, 232
17	245
22	122
23	125
24	150
26	134
27	155

Chapter XXIX.

ver.	page
1	142
4	152
5	125
11	139
12	259
13	252
14	152, 259
15	149
19	151
20	124
22	139

Chapter XXX.

ver.	page
1-6	192
4	283
7-9	155
8, 9	121, 211
12, 14	256
15, 16	46, 52
17	150, 232
18, 19	51, 233
21-23	47, 129
24-28	47, 233
26f	232
29-31	47, 232
33	141

Chapter XXXI.

ver.	page
4, 5	152
6, 7	185
10-29	147f
14	255

Index

ECCLESIASTICUS.

Prologue 198

Chapter I.
1	..	158
11, 12	..	272
26	..	267

Chapter II.
1-6	..	271f
12-14	..	246

Chapter III.
6-9	..	150
12-15	..	150
30	..	252

Chapter IV.
1	..	120
8, 9	..	252
11, 12	..	245
17	..	171
28	..	266, 269

Chapter VI.
7ff	..	142
19-25	..	171
26-29	..	171
35, 36	..	262

Chapter VII.
1-3	..	263
9, 11	..	263
10	..	264
15	..	118
18	..	263
20, 21	..	152

Chapter VIII.
5-7	..	263
17	..	133

Chapter IX.
3-9	..	186

Chapter X.
8	..	259
11	..	190

Chapter XI.
2	..	262
11	..	238
26-28	..	189

Chapter XIV.
3, 4	..	122

Chapter XV.
1	..	198
11, 12	..	263

Chapter XVII.
ver		page
28	..	190

Chapter XVIII.
19	..	262

Chapter XIX.
1	..	246
2	..	186
10	..	244
20	..	198

Chapter XX.
5, 6	..	243
12	..	243
14f	..	40
15, 16	..	133
29	..	163

Chapter XXI.
6	..	272
10	..	266
14	..	134
26	..	133

Chapter XXII.
7	..	134, 162
8	..	134, 242
12	..	162
18	..	134
19	..	274

Chapter XXIV.
3-11	..	174
23	..	198

Chapter XXV.
1, 2	..	48
7-11	..	48
16	..	232
20	..	242

Chapter XXVI.
5	..	48
29ff	..	113, 254

Chapter XXVII.
1, 2	..	113
9	..	231
11	..	133
25	..	233

Chapter XXVIII.
1, 2	..	269

Chapter XXIX.
4, 5	..	113

Chapter XXX.
8	..	232
9-12	..	149
14	..	121
15	..	257

Chapter XXXI.
ver		page
3	..	120
12ff	..	124
19, 20	..	139
27f	..	184
29, 30, 31	..	185

Chapter XXXII.
5	..	133
6	..	232
24-28	..	151
30, 31	..	151

Chapter XXXIV.
1	..	236
10	..	161
12	..	160, 161
14	..	275
16, 17	..	276
18, 19	..	274
20-22	..	256

Chapter XXXV.
17	..	279

Chapter XXXVIII.
1-15	..	115
5	..	114
16ff	..	191
24-34	..	117

Chapter XXXIX.
1-3	..	198

Chapter XL
11	..	190
28f	..	114

Chapter XLI.
1	..	163
1-4	..	191
17-19	..	163
20	..	186

Chapter XLII.
9-11	..	146

Chapter XLIII.
1-5	..	234
8-12	..	234
15-19	..	235
24-25	..	233
27-32	..	273

Chapter XLIV.
1ff	..	20

Chapter L.
6, 7	..	234
8-10	..	231

Chapter LI.
3ff	..	160

Genesis **10** 9 (50); **23** 10-19 (49).
Exodus **15** 25 (114); **20** 5 (67).
Numbers **21** 27 (69).
Deuteronomy **27** 17 (59); **30** 11-14 (215).
Joshua **7** 24, 25 (66).
Ruth **2** 7-14 (235).
1 Samuel **10** 11 (62); **24** 9-13 (63); **24** 16 (64).
2 Samuel **1** 23 (64); **14** 1ff (68); **20** 16-22 (68).
1 Kings **4** 29-34 (69, 231).
2 Kings **4** 18, 19 (235).
2 Chronicles **16** 12 (144)
Job **5** 4 (189); **15** 18 (73); **24** 2 (59); **28** 20 27 (175); **28, 38** (235).
Psalms **1** (77); **1** 1 (180); **19** 1 (229); **90** 3 (43).
Ecclesiastes **7** 6 (133); **9** 4 (232).
Canticles **2** 11ff (235).
Isaiah **5** 8 (59); **28** 10 (109, 200); **29** 13, 14 (70); **40** 27 (44); **55** 8 (106).
Jeremiah **18** 18 (70); **31** 28-30 (65f).

Index

Ezekiel 12 21, 22 (67); 16 44 (65); 18 1f (65).
Hosea 5 10 (59).
Amos 5 21f (83).
Zechariah 4 6 (106).
St. Matthew 2 12 (283); 5 3f (210); 5 42, 10 14, 12 36, 22 1-14, 25 40 (211).
St. Mark 5 26 (115).
St. Luke 4 23 (115); 12 16-21 (211); 14 7-11 (211).
St. John 1 12 (284); 3 13 (283); 7 17 (267); 13 26ff (230).

Acts 18 1-3 (119).
Romans 5 20 (67); 12 20 (145).
1 Corinthians 1 24 (284).
2 Corinthians 11 9 (119).
Ephesians 6 12 (76).
Hebrews 12 1-7 (290f).
James 1 5 (283); 4 6 -(267).
1 Peter 5 5 (267).
1 Maccabees 2 29-38 (202).
Wisdom of Solomon 7 22ff (176, 282); 9 4 (176).
Sayings of the Fathers 49 206f.

II.—INDEX OF SUBJECTS

Abbreviations, 40, 205, 207.
Agnosticism, 176, 192, 218.
Almsgiving, 113f.
Anger, 139f.
Antiochus Epiphanes, 201f.
Aristotle, 45.
Athletics, 88, 93, 96, 183, 201.

Bacon, Francis, 22, 245, 256.
Beggar, 114.
Ben Sirach, 39, 160ff.
Bribery, 152, 163, 257.

Children, 145ff, 271.
Chronicler, 109, 114.
Church, 182, 195, 199n, 216, 220 225.
Commerce, 113, 254.
Craftsmen, 116f.
Cromer, Lord, 226.

Death, 163, 168, 190f.
Democracy, 86ff.
Desert, Arabian, 54f, 141.
Discipline, Self-, 139, 171, 191f.
Doctor, 114f.

Ecclesiasticus, 39f, 162, 205
Education, 149.
Epitaphs, Greek, 89f.

Farmer, 232.
Fatalism, 278.
Flattery, 125f.
Fools, 129ff, 242.
Forgiveness, 144, 268.
Friendship, 142.

Germany, 206, 217, 237.
Ghetto, 209.
Greek, City-State, 86ff.
——— philosophy, 95n, 159, 175f.

Hasidim, 201.
Hellenism, 84ff, 110, 196, 201f, 225.
Heredity 65f.
History, 21f, 43, 81, 194f, 214f.
Honesty, 141, 143f, 153, 253f, 265, 273.

Idealism, 213, 222.
Individualism, 218f, 252.

Jealousy, 141.
Josephus, 98.
Justice, 152, 258, 269.

King, 152, 258.

Labour, 116ff.
Law of Moses, 38n, 104, 108, 110f, 198, 209.

Mercy, 144f, 276.
Miserliness, 122.
Morality, 90, 94f, 153, 181, 183ff.

Nationalism, 89, 94, 164, 174n.

Oesterley, 151, 162, 168, 267.
Old Testament, 249.

Pindar, 229.
Poseidonius, 96, 121.
Pride, 123, 140, 143.
Proverbs: Arabic, 23f; Chinese, 34; Egyptian, 166; English, 14-25, 179, 246; Greek, 25, 166; humanism of, 19f, 22, 162, 227 280; Indian 51f; Italian and Spanish, 23f, 141; New Testament, 194, 212; numerical, 46ff; Scotch, 25; Rabbinic, 41, 49, 55, 206f, 218, 243, 247 253, 259, 262; wandering of, 51f.
Providence, 276ff.
Ptolemy, 91, 97, 101, 103.

Rabbis, 119.
Receptivity, 142, 171, 266.
Religion, 157f, 220f, 272.
Ruskin, 30.
Rutherford, Mark, 35.

Scribe(s), 116f, 160, 198n.
Seleucus, 91, 97.
Sheol, (see Death).
Slander, 122f, 154.
Slaves, 86, 150f.
Sluggard, 127ff, 140, 242.
Solomon, 37, 71f, 231, 243.
Solon, 99, 189.
Suffering, 187ff, 270, 275.
Synagogues, 197f.

Temperance (see Wine).
Theophrastus, 126.

Universalism, 108f, 111.
Utilitarianism, 29, 167ff.

Wealth, 119f, 154, 256f.
Wine, 138, 153, 161, 184.
Wisdom, Greek, 99, 106.
——— personified, 174f, 282.
Wisdom of Solomon, 39, 175, 281.
Woman, 146, 154, 186, 241f.

www.ingramcontent.com/pod-product-compliance
Lightning Source LLC
Chambersburg PA
CBHW070238230426
43664CB00014B/2345